Stories of Faith

Carmichael Presbyterian Church at 100

Compiled and Written by Susan H. Herman

A follow-up to
Heritage of Faith:
A 75-Year History of Carmichael Presbyterian Church,
published in 1998

Carmichael Presbyterian Church
Carmichael, California
2023

Stories of Faith
Carmichael Presbyterian Church at 100
CPC Centennial Committee
Compiled and Written by Susan H. Herman

Published by
Carmichael Presbyterian Church
5645 Marconi Avenue
Carmichael, California 95608

Cover and interior design: Kate Zarrella, Calling Card Books

On the cover: (Top photo) Carmichael Community Church and
Scout lodge, built 1927 and 1928. (Background design) Illustration
on the cover of *Heritage of Faith*, by Mary Kay Exstrom and
Phil Mishler. (Bottom photo) Carmichael Presbyterian Church's
current sanctuary, built 1951. Photo by Bruce MacLean. Back cover:
The three domes of Carmichael Presbyterian Church, photos by
Bruce and Sharon MacLean.

Copyeditor: Thomas Burchfield

Proofreader: Donna Lane

*To all the members and friends of CPC
—past, present, and future.*

Mission Statement of Carmichael Presbyterian Church, adopted by the Session in 2018

Responding to God's love through Jesus Christ, we:

- *Welcome all*

- *Nurture relationships*

- *Grow in faith together*

- *Connect with and serve our community and the world*

Table of Contents

Who Are the Members and Friends of Carmichael Presbyterian Church?
Leading the Flock: Pastors and Ministry Staff
The Session

Spaces for Welcoming All: The Legacy of Faith Building Projects
Sunday Worship and Music
Monday Through Saturday at CPC
Membership Process
Commitment to Continual Welcome

Mission and Social Organizations
Congregational Care
Staying Connected
Commitment to Nurturing Relationships

Sunday School for Children
Youth Ministries
Adult Christian Education
Intergenerational Ministry

Foreword

What I discovered very early in my tenure at Carmichael Presbyterian Church was that they, the members and friends of CPC, knew how to do and be church.

This became evident to me upon reading the minutes of one of the very first committee meetings I attended as the new co-pastor with Jim Clark. I noticed first of all how precise they were and how they were so "decently and in order." The Apostle Paul would be so proud! What struck me the most, though, was the reference to those in attendance and my designation as their guest. In the list of those in attendance, I was simply listed as a guest. Not their new pastor, but a guest, who had been given an invitation to join them in forging a co-pastor relationship and creating a new model of pastoral leadership and a new way of being church in this place called Carmichael Presbyterian Church.

This place that was formed by a group of moms searching for a place to hold Sunday school for their children, for God's children. This place that is the first church in Carmichael; this place that responds to those in need; this place that was built with your very own hands, forming the adobe bricks to construct buildings that serve and worship the living Lord. This place that has been blessed with amazing staff members and pastoral leadership over the last 100 years; this place that has been blessed with dedicated members and friends who would do almost anything in the name of Jesus Christ to make God's love tangible and concrete as adobe in Carmichael and throughout the world for the past 100 years.

Like all churches, CPC has had its grand moments, as well as its failings and missed opportunities; a vivid reminder that like every church everywhere, it is comprised of flawed human beings on the way to discovering that they are children of God. At our worst and at our best, we are simply God's children.

So I invite you, just as I was invited many years ago, as a guest in this endeavor brought into being 100 years ago. Read these pages and remember the faithful saints past and present who are the foundation of what CPC has become.

I am particularly grateful for all of the members and friends of CPC who have answered God's call to worship and service, the staff and pastoral colleagues who have blessed me and allowed me to call them my friends and my family, those who have worked tirelessly in putting together these centennial celebrations, and Jenny, my partner in life and ministry for the past forty-three years. And finally, my profound appreciation to Susan Herman, for saying "yes" when I asked, and for the countless hours she devoted to inviting all of us into these *Stories of Faith*.

May it be so!

Amen & Amen

    —Pastor Keith

Preface

Planning for the centennial of Carmichael Presbyterian Church (CPC) started long before 2023. The Rev. Keith DeVries, senior pastor of CPC, approached me in June of 2018 with some ideas, and it was clear that he'd been mulling them over for a while already. We had coffee at the sparkling new Milagro Centre on Fair Oaks Boulevard. There, he presented me with his vision for 2023. The church's 100th anniversary would be marked by a special activity or recognition every month. Guest preachers would be invited to the CPC pulpit. And (gulp) a new book would be written, commemorating the congregation's history as a community of faith and as a vital resource in the growth and flourishing of the Carmichael neighborhood. The book would be a follow-up to our existing 75th anniversary volume, titled *Heritage of Faith*. Would I be the writer of the new book? And would I assist in recruiting people to take charge of the special centennial events?

In keeping with my general tendencies towards overcommitment, perfectionism, and people-pleasing, I said yes, yes to all of it. But I needed a while to process the idea. That was my nice way of saying I needed to figure out how to make time for the project within the framework of my writing and editing business and my other volunteer gigs, while still being at least occasionally present for my two teenagers and spouse (who happens to be the Rev. Ivan Herman, a.k.a. Pastor Ivan, CPC's associate pastor).

Thankfully, Pastor Keith understood very well the realities of my family and economic situation, as his spouse Jenny also worked outside the home while managing family caregiving duties and church commitments. After some internal back and forth, and with the blessing of others on the nascent Centennial Committee plus the chair of our Session's Administration Division, I asked for and successfully negotiated a modest independent contractor agreement, funded mainly by monies from 1998 still in the Heritage Committee account. This helped me get over the mental hump of starting out, and it allowed me to hire a consultant to assist me through the technical parts of the book publishing process that I knew little about, despite twenty years' experience developing editorial content.

By the summer of 2019, I was ready to get down to business. I did my first couple of oral interviews, testing a transcription software called Otter.ai that no one knew was about to hit the big time. Along with COVID-19, widespread use of transcription apps as an add-on to videoconferencing was just on the horizon.

In October of 2019 Jimmi Mishler, who had chaired CPC's 75th Anniversary Committee, gave me an orientation to the church archives in the bell tower room and Room 202. Jimmi also passed along some helpful literature from the Presbyterian Historical Society on how to write a congregational history.

Gradually our Centennial Committee took on more members: interviewers, event planners, a fundraiser, helpers for media outreach, and a team to create and sell shirts with the CPC logo on them.

My practical concerns now settled, I found that I still needed to wrestle with something else. The truth was, for all my involvement at church—its music and education programs, plus a stint on the Nominating Committee, spending time with my Mariner ship, and daily "shop talk" with my spouse—I wasn't yet emotionally invested in the history project. I could block out time for writing and for meetings, and the interviews were proving to be stimulating and fun, but I was missing the motivational drive to move forward.

The COVID-19 pandemic may have had something to do with that. During those initial weeks at home in the spring of 2020, while trying to adjust to the changes the spreading virus had brought to my own world, not to mention the whole world, my long-term planning brain struggled. Day-to-day concerns took precedence.

After many months, I was able to articulate two key questions that I needed to answer if I were to find true motivation. They were:

- Why are we celebrating the church's centennial?
- And, frankly, who cares that our church is turning 100?

I knew that part of the answer to "why celebrate" was "to give credit where credit is due." The people of CPC are very good about recognizing the saints who make up our cloud of witnesses. We formally recognize our living saints on Heritage Sunday each May, and those who have passed on we celebrate on All Saint's Day each November. So, a centennial celebration would be a more structured, intentional way to recognize our history and to bring more names and stories actively to mind.

Also, I knew that we'd be celebrating because celebrating is fun, and CPC people are fun-loving. I had experienced many demonstrations of CPC members' fun-loving spirit almost weekly since my family's arrival in Carmichael in 2009. A year-long centennial celebration would surely allow the church family many opportunities to laugh and remember the good times together. We would need that more than ever after the pandemic.

But there was also a future element to "Why celebrate the centennial?" that I wanted to tease out in some way. If there's been one Big Conversation in the church in recent decades—and I mean among Christian churches nationwide, not just CPC—it's this one: where are all the churchgoers anymore? Church is simply not on the weekly agenda for many people. For a lot of folks, church is not on their radar at all. And that can be sad to think about, even a little scary. I'd been in many conversations with CPC folks that ended with some version of, "Gosh, back in the day these pews were full. What will happen if a vital congregation like ours shrinks away to nothing?" Another version of the conversation went like this: "What if the next generation doesn't step up and lead? Can our programs and mission survive?"

In the face of these fears, I decided, we must choose hope. Hope is why we celebrate.

Hope in the face of fear is what converted my *saying* yes to the Centennial project into a purposeful, *actual* yes. I do have hope—for Christianity, for the Presbyterian Church (USA) as a denomination, and for the congregation of Carmichael Presbyterian Church. This idea of hope, and challenging others to hope, became my drive to move forward with the writing and event planning.

In that spirit, I'd like to challenge all CPC members and friends, plus any other readers who are struggling with questions of what's next for the church, for their congregation, to choose hope. Sometime while you're reading this book, I challenge you to reach within yourself and look for the hope. Get a little introspective. Maybe through reading these stories you'll discover a new spark—of joy, of gratitude, of holy anger, of discomfort, of curiosity, of desire to connect. Whatever you discover, think about how you can put that into action in some way in your church, in your life. Taking small but purposeful actions: that is what hope looks like. Hope is why I am celebrating CPC's centennial.

This brings me to the "who cares" question.

Well...I care.

Given the amount of time I spend at church you might think it's obvious that I care about my church, but honestly, I've been a church person for so long (yes, even before meeting my husband) that spending time there isn't always that meaningful. Some days it's more like brushing my teeth. Just another routine. I had to affirm that I care, for myself, before I could really dig into this project. Specifically, I care about CPC. And I care about all other communities like ours that are walking in faith together. I care about us continuing to be creative. I care about us continuing to ask questions: What is God calling us to do right now, as the body of Christ? What is God saying to each of us personally? As long as we're still asking those questions it doesn't matter if we are a congregation of 3000 or of 30. If we stop asking what God is calling us to do, or if we don't care to listen, then we're dead no matter our congregation size.

The Centennial Committee decided together on a slogan for this special year: "100 Years of Praising God and Serving the Carmichael Community." That is the collective answer to why we are celebrating and why we care about this milestone anniversary; however, I hope each reader can identify personal reasons too. Why do *you* care about your church? How have *you* praised God or felt God's presence, inside your church's walls or outside of them? How has God called *you* into service to your community? What do *you* want to celebrate about your church's history? What can *you* do to manifest your hopes for its future?

Here's to 100 years of praising God and serving the Carmichael Community. Happy 100, CPC!

—Susan H. Herman

Acknowledgments

This book would not have been possible without the members of the CPC Heritage Committee who created our church archives and wrote our seventy-five-year history, *Heritage of Faith*. Along with the archives and book they provided oral histories, which I dipped into often, and they preserved many details about the process of curating all these valuable resources. Thank you, Marie Segur, Faye White, Margaret Herman, and Jimmi Mishler. Bill Davis guided the collection and indexing of the archives. A team led by Wayne MacRostie conducted and transcribed the oral histories. These, along with the photos and other memorabilia, are treasures that I hope more CPC members will have a chance to enjoy.

The work of another CPC committee—Communications Network, ComNet for short—also informed this book. ComNet operated from 1991 until about 2002. They pitched dozens of stories about the church to local media and kept an excellent collection of news clippings. I drew liberally from the binders of articles for this book. ComNet's original members were Wilma Boland, Bobbi Jones, Faye White, Marie Segur, Dick Piper, and Barbara Sebastian; others are memorialized in annual reports from the years the committee was active.

To everyone who has ever served on CPC's staff, or as a division chair on CPC's Session, or in another leadership role that required you to contribute an annual report—an immense thank you! Annual reports from about 1995 up to 2022 helped me assemble the "skeleton" of this book, and the names listed in the annual reports helped me figure out who to consult for fact checking.

Karen Orlando was the first person I turned to when Pastor Keith asked me to be part of the centennial project and write this book. Because of her deep connections in our church family, I knew Karen would be able to pull in collaborators to execute all the practical aspects of putting on the year-long party that Pastor Keith envisioned. And because Karen makes wonderful art across multiple media, I was also confident she'd be a good sounding board for my creative quandaries with the book. All of this turned out to be true; plus, Karen wrote a series of *Mission Bell* articles that bring to life many of the people and episodes mentioned in this book and in *Heritage of Faith*. Thank you, Karen.

Kathy Lewin stepped up early on as well. As she and I sipped hot coffee after church one day, she casually commented, "I'm a history nerd. What can I help with for the centennial?" And just like that, she was conducting interviews, organizing a vintage cookbook swap and luncheon, and rotating display items in the Heritage cabinet. Sharon MacLean and Allison Cagley also played central roles: Sharon with interviewing, taking photos, and marshalling event volunteers, Allison in heading up the fundraising and offering inspiration for events and how to promote them. Lisa Benadom conducted interviews and provided valuable guidance in the early stages. Monica Dahlberg masterminded the centennial gala; Kathy Phillips also guided many planning sessions and was involved behind the scenes. Dozens of others pitched in for special events—they are recognized in the *Mission Bell* newsletters and event programs from 2023.

Interviewees for the early phases of book conceptualization, which occurred during the height of the COVID-19 outbreak, met safely with interviewers outdoors or over the phone, and some graciously submitted written responses via email. These exploratory interviews with long-standing members helped me develop some of the book's core themes about building leaders and living into our identity as a connectional church.

Several individuals provided written reports on different topics, not unlike the mini-histories used to compile *Heritage of Faith*. These writers included John Wallace, Garrett Torgerson, Brenda Mock, Pat Chaney, Trina Spivack, Karen Orlando, and Randy Benfield. Marie Segur provided a three-inch binder full of material including Food Closet history, changes to the church bylaws, and lists of CPC pastors and staff kept current from the moment the 75th anniversary wrapped, up through 2019. Marie was thinking of "next steps" all along. She is, for this and so much else, my inspiration.

Centennial Campaign Donors

Emily Moulton

John & Mary Simpson

David & Judy Antonson

Rob & Claudia Hollingsworth

Kathy Shay

Kathryn & Peter Davalos

Keith & Jenny DeVries

Liliane Morin

Kathy Lewis

Mary MacDonald

Pat Warren

Laura Janik

Margo Scandella

Allison Cagley

Jennifer Carroll

Bonnie Hard

Colleen Dottarar

Paul Kinsella

Terry Sakuda

Janann Poteet

Una Edwards

Ron & Cindy Morris

Michael & Carol Honnold

Richard & Sandra Ficenec

Harvey & Jane Swenson

Barbara Sebastian

Bud & Karen Banker

Don & Nancy Marcheschi

Naomi French-Parker

Sharlene St. Clair

Bill & Misty Dunn

Daniel & Hazel Smith

Gail Ball

Darlene Little

Duane Johnson

Marti Wallace

Beth Lindley

Hal & Sharleen Millering

Thomas Dobbins

Patricia Grimm

Jeannie Graham

Ele Crispell

Charleen Lee

Lora Cammack

Gordon & Carolyn McGregor

Lawrence (Ray) Collison

Cindy Magness

Linda Sweetman

Mary Jane Bryan

Marcia Law

Steve & Karen Orlando

Ed & Bonnie Pearson

Judith Stewart

David & Mary Root

Howard & Donna Ross

Wayne & Barbara Reimers

Tony & Glenda Perrou

Joan Oakley

Chad Muilenburg

Michael Miller

David & Barbara McVey

Sheila Mun Jacobs

Carol Hayes

Gayle DeVries

Don Cox

Ernie & Olene Chard

David & Phyllis Brewer

William Boland

R. Scott Seekins

Paul & Mary Camozzi

Kathy Phillips

K. Robert Taylor

George Burbank

Terryl Summers

Lisa Benadom

Christa Brewer

Erin Forest

Paul & Lynn Shultz

Kenneth & Katharine DeYoung

Timothy & Barbara Farley

Leonard Tozier

Carolee Roach

Linda Hatch

Philip & Jimmi Mishler

Bob & Doris Beckert

Howard & Sally Willey

Thelma Wever

David & Chris Beeby

David & Marie Segur

Companionship

Timeline: 100 Years of Praising God and Serving the Carmichael Community

Summer 1918

Three mothers—Mrs. Cowan, Mrs. Champlin, and Mrs. Ellithorpe—start a Sunday school for children, which meets in the two-room Carmichael School on Sutter Avenue. The Sunday school runs for two summers and one winter season.

February 1923

Members of the Carmichael Community Club re-start the Sunday school. By summer, 113 children are attending. A retired Methodist minister, the Rev. J. W. Babcock, begins offering worship services after Sunday school.

December 2, 1923

Carmichael Community Church is officially founded. It has a pastor (Rev. Babcock), 54 charter members, elected officers, a constitution, pledged financial support, and a meeting place.

July 1925

The Rev. Samuel Holsinger begins serving the church and officially becomes its first called pastor later that year.

Summer 1925

The church offers a summer Vacation Bible School for the first time—a tradition that continues as of 2023.

September 1925

Carmichael Community Church begins its affiliation with the Presbyterian Church.

May 1927

H. A. Hobbs donates part of his acreage on Marconi Avenue for a new church building site. He is reported to have said, "I haven't been able to make a thing grow on this piece, but maybe a church will grow there."

October 23, 1927

The congregation erects its first building on Marconi Avenue, a simple wood structure painted white with a bell tower.

November 1929

Rev. Holsinger leaves Carmichael Community Church and forms a new, independent fundamentalist church called Wayside Chapel on Fair Oaks Boulevard.

1930–1943

During the Depression eight different pastors serve the church. Many are working their way through training at San Francisco Theological seminary.

1943–1954

The Rev. James Comfort Smith serves as senior pastor.

1946–1947

To accommodate growing membership, the Spanish Mission-style chapel is built. Members of the congregation mold some of the adobe bricks themselves.

December 1951

The new sanctuary, also built with white adobe in the Mission style, is completed.

1953

Carmichael Community Presbyterian Church women first served as elders in the 1930s, but from 1953 on they are nominated and elected with regularity to serve on the Session.

1954–1973

The Rev. Dr. Pyron McMillen serves as senior pastor. During this period the education wing and social hall are built. The social hall is named after Rev. Dr. McMillen following his retirement.

ca. 1957–1981

Weekday preschools operate on the church campus, led by Jessie Glasse, Jessie Burnett, and Marsha Cook.

March 1964

After two intermediate name changes in 1950 and 1959, the congregation adopts the church's present name: Carmichael Presbyterian Church.

March 21, 1965

Rev. McMillen participates in the third Selma-to-Montgomery civil rights march, in his role as moderator of the Synod of California. Synod and presbytery moderators from across the country participate alongside other clergy.

1966

Membership of the church peaks at 1707 members.

1973

The Carmichael Food Closet is established to serve its neighbors in need. Much expanded and integrated into the regional food bank system, the Food Closet continues operations in 2023.

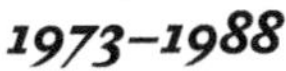

1973–1988

The Rev. Dr. William (Bill) Johnson serves as senior pastor.

1977

Carmichael Presbyterian Counseling Center opens on the church campus. Low-cost counseling is provided to community members until 2010.

1982

A CPC member co-founds the Sacramento chapter of Parents and Friends of Lesbians and Gays (PFLAG). The chapter's first meeting is held in the CPC chapel.

June 1983

Northern and Southern US branches of the Presbyterian Church, having been divided since the Civil War, reunite and the PC(USA) is formed.

1986–2008

CPC youth and adults go on mission travel yearly to colonias in northern Mexico, in partnership with Azusa Pacific University and Amor Ministries. Around 600 youth from the area participate over this time period.

September 1986

Carmichael Presbyterian Preschool welcomes its first students. The preschool continues until 2019.

1987

A Korean Presbyterian congregation begins meeting at CPC and stays for about ten years. Two other Korean congregations "nest" at the CPC campus between 2005 and 2021.

1989

A CPC member starts Mustard Seed School at Loaves & Fishes in downtown Sacramento. Service teams from the church help regularly at the school and soup kitchen for about thirty years.

1989

CPC members begin a recreational and tutoring outreach with children at the Woodland Towers apartment complex and at Deterding and Carmichael Elementary Schools.

1990–2002

The Rev. James (Jim) E. Clark serves as senior pastor.

November 1991

CPC holds its first Alternative Gift Market, supporting grassroots organizations and self-development groups around the world. The annual event continues in 2023.

1992

CPC begins to participate in Hunger Sundays in partnership with Bread for the World. Members of CPC write to their elected officials on hunger-related issues.

1994

A CPC member launches the Sacramento Microenterprise Assistance Program (MAP), providing business development assistance for low-income refugee and immigrant families. CPC joins eleven other churches in sponsoring MAP.

1997–2007

A major building campaign takes place to remodel the sanctuary, install sound and video systems and a new organ. The Food Closet gets a dedicated building and warehouse storage. McMillen Hall is rebuilt with a commercial-grade kitchen and shower facilities.

March 2001

The Rev. Keith DeVries begins serving CPC as co-pastor with the Rev. Jim Clark, then becomes senior pastor when Rev. Clark retires in 2002. Rev. DeVries continues serving as of 2023 and is the longest-serving pastor at CPC.

2005

The congregation begins its community Supper on Saturday ministry, a once-monthly plated meal served to all who hunger for food and fellowship.

2006

CPC becomes a sponsoring congregation with Family Promise of Sacramento.

2006–2016

The Presbyterian Church (USA) suffers a slow-rolling schism when it votes to allow ordination of LGBTQ+ people as pastors, elders, and deacons, and later approves same-sex marriage.

2014

CPC begins to open its shower and restroom facilities to neighbors living outside. This service continues in 2023 in partnership with Carmichael HART.

Winter months 2016–2019

CPC serves as part of Sacramento County's Winter Sanctuary program.

2018

CPC partners with World Relief to host English language classes for local Afghan women. The partnership continues in 2023 and includes use of McMillen Hall for children's soccer practices.

April 2019

CPC's high school youth build a community garden on the Robertson property behind the church.

March 15, 2020

Last in-person worship service before COVID-19 lockdown. The next Sunday, services are livestreamed and business continues online, along with coffee hour, education, and prayer groups. The Food Closet stays open.

2021

CPC donates Robertson House; Carmichael HART renovates it for use as transitional housing for men.

2020–2023

CPC signs on to two denomination-wide initiatives: Matthew 25 and Earth Care Congregations. CPC affiliates with Covenant Network of Presbyterians.

2023

CPC celebrates 100 years of praising God and serving the Carmichael community.

Introduction

This book is a follow-up to *Heritage of Faith: A 75-Year History of Carmichael Presbyterian Church*, which was published in 1998. As such, *Stories of Faith: Carmichael Presbyterian Church at 100* covers the most recent twenty-five years in the church's history (1998–2023). It also reaches back farther, when needed, to show how various features of the church we know today are connected to important threads of its longer history.

I chose to organize the content in *Stories of Faith* around the church's mission statement, which was adopted in 2018. I figured that, with only twenty-five years to cover and a whole book to do it in, I would use the space to tell stories about how different people in the congregation have experienced the church as a channel through which they've been able to respond to God's love through Jesus Christ, welcome all, nurture relationships, grow in faith together, and connect with and serve our community and the world.

Heritage of Faith was organized chronologically. Being as there were seventy-five years of history to contend with, this editorial choice makes a lot of sense to me. A major emphasis of the Heritage Committee's work during the mid- to late 1990s was pulling together documents about the church's history—from private collections, news clippings, denominational resources, and various storage locations on the church campus—to create the church archives. The Heritage Committee's meticulous work in setting up the church archives carried over to their creation of the book, which, while not exhaustive, is comprehensive in its coverage and well-indexed. That they were able to accomplish this largely without the use of the internet boggles my mind.

The chapter titles in *Heritage of Faith* distill the story of CPC's first seventy-five years into four phases: The Beginning Years (1918[1]-1942), The Growing Years (1943-1972), The Changing Years (1973-1990), and The Continuing Years (1990-1998). I mention the phases here because I believe there is much food for thought in these four simple, capsule stories of beginning, growing, changing, and continuing.

Carmichael Presbyterian Church at age seventy-five was indeed in the process of continuing its journey. With the ten-year Legacy of Faith building campaign well underway, the vision was clear: new buildings will help us better serve our evolving community. We will keep our Sunday Bible lessons coming; we will continue to wield "hammers and paint brushes, trowels and pruning shears, pans and ladles...to keep the facilities functioning and carry out the ministry of this faith community."[2]

At age 100, the dust from construction has settled, but I'm not sure the vision is as clear. In some areas of ministry, CPC is continuing its legacy of faith with all the vigor described above. In other areas, it seems the congregation is searching for—while simultaneously walking and charting—a new path. Each step on the path is still made in faith, but the map, instead of a foldable paper bearing reliable markings, is now a modern smart device full of data but somehow also devoid of answers. How do we stay culturally relevant while remaining Christ-centered in years to come? How do we keep developing our leadership pipeline? How can we best serve our children and youth?

As the age of the congregation approaches and surpasses the limits of a human life, it makes perfect sense to feel a little unsure of what's next. That is why we have stories to keep us grounded. Stories may describe quirks of life in decades past that will never come around again, but the best stories contain truths that endure.

---

1 The worshipping community had its roots in a Sunday school begun in 1918 but formally incorporated as a church congregation in 1923.
2 Faye White, Margaret Herman, and Marie Segur, *Heritage of Faith: A 75-Year History of Carmichael Presbyterian Church* (Carmichael Presbyterian Church, 1998), ii.

In the next section, I'll do my best to add another capsule story of CPC history onto the four already laid out in *Heritage of Faith*. Then, I'll provide an overview of this book and a few notes about my storytelling approach and style choices. Lastly, I will invite you to keep sharing your stories, as I believe the practice of sharing stories will be vital to CPC's next 100 years.

A Capsule Story About the Years 1998–2023

From 1998 until about 2009 CPC went full throttle on its mission and outreach. During that period, it ran three essentially independent centers on its campus, serving different needs in the community: the Food Closet, the Counseling Center, and Carmichael Presbyterian Preschool. Large youth groups ventured yearly to northern Mexico, carrying on a mission relationship begun in 1986. A whole new worship service had just started up, featuring contemporary music and more spontaneous expressions of prayer and preaching. The new Food Closet warehouse was built, along with a new McMillen Hall, increasing the church's capacity to host events and meet new regulations for its food-related operations. Multiple new ministries began.

In 1999 and again in 2008 CPC leaders carried out extensive self-studies of the congregation and produced visioning documents that would help them discern how best to tailor the activities of the church to meet the needs of its changing community. These self-studies also shaped the Church Information Forms (CIFs, now called Ministry Information Forms or MIFs) used in the Presbyterian system to call new pastors. The Rev. Keith DeVries joined the pastoral staff in 2001 and is, at the time of this writing, the longest-serving senior pastor in CPC's history. The Rev. Ivan Herman was called in 2009 and is the church's longest-serving associate pastor. If we were to give the period from 1998 to 2009 a name designation as in *Heritage of Faith*, it might be The Energetic Years, or The Optimistic Years. Or, perhaps that decade could be grouped with The Continuing Years era begun in 1990.

The period from 2010 to 2023 was colored somewhat by aftereffects from the 2008-2009 US and global financial meltdown and later, the COVID-19 pandemic. CPC saw the closure of both its preschool and Counseling Center during those years. The Food Closet served increasing numbers of its Carmichael neighbors.

New members joined the church during this period, but not in numbers high enough to replace those who had died. Memorial services far outnumbered weddings, which in CPC's heyday were as many as four in a single Saturday, year-round. Smoke from wildfires in the nearby foothills and mountains descended with greater frequency. Missions to Mexico ended. The denomination faced a reckoning as well. The Presbyterian Church (USA)'s General Assembly in 2011 made a policy allowing ordination of non-celibate LGBTQ+ deacons, elders, and pastors, and this was ratified by the required majority of presbyteries by mid-2012. Nationwide, the PC(USA) lost a large number of congregations, including several in the Presbytery of Sacramento.

Leaders at CPC conducted another visioning and discernment process in 2017-2019, called PneuMatrix. Its intent, as the word *pneuma* in its name implies, was to breathe new life and new ideas into CPC's leadership, and indeed, the adoption of a new mission statement was one of its outcomes. However, the ink on the PneuMatrix Committee's reports was barely dry when the COVID-19 pandemic hit. Any fresh thoughts that had arisen during that process had to be shelved while energy shifted towards moving worship and other operations online and figuring out how to re-launch in person when that time came. For some, this period was a time of disengagement from church. The so-called Great Resignation was in the news nationally, and affected CPC in no small measure. Volunteering dropped off; leadership of CPC's music and children's ministries transitioned as well.

In the face of all this, however, an argument can be made that CPC's congregation became more committed. Many who joined the church after 2010 did so not because CPC was their family's church, and not because it was conveniently located in their neighborhood. Rather, they learned about the church's mission and values and wanted specifically to be a part of that. Data in the annual reports from recent years show that indeed, raw numbers of "giving units" went down as membership waned. However, the average amount pledged per giving unit went up, even after adjusting for inflation. The programs of the church are fewer in number today versus twenty-five years ago, but a perusal of recent years' annual reports also reveals that CPC's programs are becoming more focused and more integrated with other community partners. So, if we were to label the years 2010–2023, á la *Heritage of Faith*, we could perhaps call this period The Focusing Years, or The Discernment Years. Or, how about…The Committed Years?

It may be too early to assign a label or a lifecycle phase to the past twenty-five years or the most recent thirteen; at least, I think the jury is still out. But maybe some thoughts will arise for you as you read. What is your faith community in the process of *doing* right now, beneath the surface of its activities or programs? In what ways is your faith community *being* the church?

Overview of the Book

Responding to God's love in Jesus Christ, a body of believers in Carmichael Colony built a community, and became a congregation. Chapter 1 reviews a few details from the earliest years, but mainly describes how Carmichael Presbyterian Church continued to take shape as an organization from 1998–2023. Here we pick up with a few more details about the denomination, which by design is ever-reforming. The chapter also describes the pastoral team that was in place in the late 1990s and discusses pastorates and Session leadership since then.

Chapter 2 is on the theme of welcoming, and as such it begins with information about the Legacy of Faith building campaign, whose purpose was to update and create new spaces for welcoming worshipers and campus guests to CPC. Other topics include worship and music, the membership process, and the varied ways Carmichael-area people have found to spend time at the church on other days of the week besides Sundays.

Chapter 3 is all about nurturing relationships. It covers Presbyterian Women and Mariners, the activities of CPC's Board of Deacons and congregational care ministries, and communications.

Chapter 4 focuses on growing in faith together. It covers Christian Education for children, teens, and adults; intergenerational ministries; and stories of several children of the church who grew up to become faith leaders outside of Carmichael.

Chapters 5 and 6 describe various ways the church has lived out its mission to connect with and serve our community. Chapter 5 focuses on education and social support outreach to children and families. Main topics include Carmichael Presbyterian Preschool (CPP), church members working with organizations like Mustard Seed School to help children and teens facing homelessness, Carmichael Presbyterian Counseling Center (CPCC), and work with refugees. Chapter 6 focuses on food and hospitality ministries and describes the history of the Carmichael Food Closet; church members' advocacy on hunger issues; Supper on Saturday; the church's participation with Family Promise of Sacramento, Winter Shelter, and Carmichael HART; and the Deacons' Christmas Gift Ministry and benevolence fund.

Chapters 7 and 8 illustrate different aspects of CPC's mission to connect with and serve our world. Chapter 7 covers youth mission trips to Mexico, Honduras, and Belize. Chapter 8 describes the church's peacemaking and mission activities in India, Colombia, and Eastern Europe as well as the networking, education, and giving that makes these activities possible.

In addition to energy, optimism, continuation of CPC's legacy, questioning, re-evaluation, and commitment, I've chosen to emphasize a few other themes in this book that cut across topics. These include building leaders, developing partnerships, and working toward justice and inclusion. The church, by signing on to the denomination's Matthew 25 movement in 2021, is taking steps to shape its current and future programs around three main goals: building congregational vitality, dismantling structural racism, and eradicating systemic poverty.[3] My hope is to show that the seeds for all of this were well and duly planted at CPC from the beginning.

A Few Style Notes

With this book I've chosen to take a storytelling approach, rather than trying to create an authoritative or comprehensive historical record. In not attempting to create something comprehensive, I hereby set myself free from the expectation to include everything, every name, every program, and the kitchen sink.

---

3 "Matthew 25 in the PC(USA): Join the Movement," https://www.presbyterianmission.org/ministries/matthew-25/poverty/.

I also wanted to go the storytelling route because I thought that would make the book fun to read, and readable books get people talking and thinking. As noted above, I believe CPC and perhaps all Christians are in a very special moment in history in 2023. We can't take our faith or our institutions for granted. We need to pause and discern. We need to pray together. Our old assumptions and old roadmaps for growing the church may not be helpful anymore. In the face of uncertainty, it seems wise to share some stories and stay grounded. Let's share some stories and dream together about what is true and what comes next.

Because I am telling stories in this book, the style I've adopted is somewhat informal. For example, when naming people on the church staff and others who were or are deeply involved at CPC, I will call them initially by their first and last names, then switch to first name only, as this parallels the way most of us tend to speak in 2023 when talking about people we know.

Similarly, when a CPC pastor is or was commonly known as "Pastor First Name" or "Pastor Last Name" I will use that formula, following their initial introduction in each chapter as "the Rev. First Name Last Name." For pastors from more distant years in our history, and for those who did not work at CPC, I will use the "Rev. First Last" formula on first use and "Rev. Last Name" on subsequent use.

You may notice inconsistencies in the way I, and the people quoted in the book, talk about different leadership bodies of the church. This is because committees tend to change names and scope of responsibility, and because functions of different groups get added, or subtracted, or divided up differently as needs evolve and as new cohorts of leaders rotate in. One change I'll highlight here is that CPC's Session—that is, its body of elected elders—changed in 1993 from working in committees to working in divisions, allowing for some types of decision-making to be streamlined. Thus, for example, the Mission Action Committee, after being called just Mission Committee for a time, later became the Mission Division of Session.

I have tried to minimize church jargon or provide a definition when I must use a technical term. It is my hope that matters of style and word choice do not interrupt the reading experience too much.

An Invitation to Keep Sharing

The church's centennial celebration throughout 2023 was multi-platform by design. In addition to this book, by the end of 2023 there will have been a handful of local media columns, over a dozen *Mission Bell* articles, scores of Facebook posts and Instagram shares, and hundreds of photos documenting CPC history, people, and stories. Guest speakers took to the pulpit, and readers shared letters aloud from former pastors. Concerts, potlucks, art shows, and other events gave church members the opportunity to mingle with each other and with the wider Carmichael community, sharing memories of CPC's first 100 years.

If you feel that your story has been overlooked in any of these venues, please tell it anyway! Even in a non-milestone year, there are lots of opportunities to share about your faith and church family. For example, you can share your faith story on a Sunday morning in worship. You can write a letter to a new confirmand or a child receiving their first Bible. You can offer a devotional at choir rehearsal or a Mariner ship meeting. The possibilities are endless, so keep telling your story of faith.

Chapter 1
Responding to God's Love Through Jesus Christ

> *Responding to God's love through Jesus Christ, we:*
> - *Welcome all*
> - *Nurture relationships*
> - *Grow in faith together*
> - *Connect with and serve our community and the world*

Carmichael Presbyterian Church (CPC) was founded as a response to God's love through Jesus Christ, and for 100 years its congregation has kept responding, with joy and thanksgiving. This book explores the many ways CPC has responded to God's love throughout its 100-year history. But who is the "we" that responds to God's love with acts of welcome, nurture, growth, and connection? We are the people of CPC, both members and friends. We are also the faithful shepherds: pastors, ministry staff, and elders. Faith shapes our decisions and actions, which in turn inform and enrich our faith.

As a congregation on a faith journey together, CPC's people look for signs and listen for God's Word. They allow new input to change their focus. They share leadership and get things done, embracing community partnerships and denominational connections. And they adapt to change, never innovating for the sake of innovation, but continually seeking scriptural guidance and human witnesses to God's love. The people of CPC live out the motto of the Reformed Christian tradition, of which Presbyterians are a branch: "The church reformed, always reforming, according to the Word of God and the call of the Spirit."

This chapter describes the people of CPC and its leaders, starting with information about the church's congregational size and makeup, and its history of affiliation with the Presbyterian Church (USA). Next, we name and remember CPC's pastors, directors of Christian Education, and administrative staff members over the last twenty-five years, recognizing the special gifts each one brought to the life of the church. Some notes on the Session of CPC—that is, the congregation's council of elders—finish out the chapter. In that section I have chosen to focus on the role of the Session in stewardship and articulating the church's vision and identity.

Who Are the Members and Friends of Carmichael Presbyterian Church?

The fifty-four charter members of Carmichael Community Church, as it was first known, came from multiple Christian denominations. They viewed having a church as being on par in importance with having a water district and a school district. The first church to be organized in the rural farming community of Carmichael was not merely an amenity, but rather a vital resource that would make living in the newly-established Carmichael Colony possible. The church would help newcomers integrate socially and build trust in one another.[1]

The church's mission to help newcomers integrate continued after the founding of Carmichael Colony and well into its period of growth as a suburb of Sacramento. *Heritage of Faith* notes that "[t]he expansion of the military bases...during World War II brought increases in population

---

1 Faye White, Margaret Herman, and Marie Segur. *Heritage of Faith: A 75-Year History of Carmichael Presbyterian Church* (Carmichael Presbyterian Church, 1998), 5, 28, Appendix A.

and industry to Sacramento County. In the immediate post-World War II years, the population of California increased enormously as discharged service personnel flocked to the state to participate in the active economy generated as part of the war effort."

Illustrating this, CPC member Jan Olson in 2018 shared with the congregation her faith story, noting how her family came to the area in 1950. Their home was on a dirt road near the brand-new El Camino High School, which was welcoming its very first class of students that fall. The school would not give Jan a bus assignment because "[m]y street did not show up on their map!" Jan started high school feeling somewhat abandoned and alone, but soon made a new friend.

> As I stood in front of the school fighting back tears, a girl whom I had met in my algebra class that morning asked if I wanted to walk the few blocks with her to her house and see if her mother could help me get home. This small act of kindness became the life changing step in my faith journey. As we walked to my new friend's house, she told me that she was a "military brat" and that her family had just moved to Sacramento when her father was assigned to Mather Air Force Base. We were in the same boat! Newbies in town!... Priscilla and I became friends and a few weeks later, she asked if I would like to go to church with her family. They offered to pick me up on their way. Her mother told my mother that the first thing she did when they were transferred to a new base was to find a church with a strong youth program to call their church home. Carmichael Community Church, as it was then known, fit the criteria! Thus began my association with CPC.[2]

Congregational Makeup

From the initial fifty-four on the charter roll, membership numbers at Carmichael Community Church increased, seeing the most rapid growth during the 1950s and 1960s. Membership peaked in 1966 at 1,707. Just five years later the number had fallen thirty-five percent, due in part to layoffs

---

2 Jan Olson, Faith Story presented to the CPC congregation during worship, November 17, 2018.

at Aerojet Corporation, a major employer in the area. Membership held more or less stable at around 1,000 throughout the 1970s and 1980s, but by 1998 the number had dipped to 833. As of 2022 membership was 497, though when that number was reported the rolls had not been updated since before COVID-19.[3]

Similar patterns of church membership gains and losses have played out across mainline Protestant denominations and the Catholic Church in the US over the last half century. Various reasons for this have been cited, including a generational trend of loss of trust in authority (e.g., over the Vietnam War), frustration with increasing enmeshment of Christianity with nationalism, legal fallout and personal suffering caused by clergy sexual abuse, and shifts within Christian religious traditions themselves (e.g., differences over progressivism and fundamentalism). Rising membership in Christian evangelical groups during this time did not, for the most part, reflect rising numbers of people converting to Christianity from other faiths or adopting Christianity after having no religion, so much as they represented people switching over from traditional denominations.[4] In 2020, the COVID-19 pandemic forced church shutdowns that lasted months, accelerating the drop-off in attendance and active membership.[5]

Research organizations such as Barna Research Group and the Pew Research Center have tracked these trends and highlight the nationwide increase in the percentage of people who claim no religious affiliation, Christian or otherwise. "Nones," as they are called, accounted for eleven percent of the US population in 2000 and twenty-nine percent in 2021.[6, 7] Children growing up with no espoused religious tradition and no directive from

---

3 Numbers taken from *Heritage of Faith* and annual reports.
4 Cynthia Woolever and Deborah Bruce, *A Field Guide to U.S. Congregations: Who's Going Where and Why, Second edition* (Westminster John Knox Press, 2010).
5 Wendy Wang, "The Decline in Church Attendance in COVID America," January 20, 2022, https://ifstudies.org/blog/the-decline-in-church-attendance-in-covid-america.
6 Barna Group, *Signs of Decline & Hope Among Key Metrics of Faith* (2020), https://www.barna.com/research/changing-state-of-the-church/.
7 Gregory A. Smith, *About Three-in-Ten U.S. Adults Are Now Religiously Unaffiliated*, Pew Research Center (December 15, 2021), https://www.pewresearch.org/religion/2021/12/14/about-three-in-ten-u-s-adults-are-now-religiously-unaffiliated/.

their family to find a faith community is a reality for many churches, and CPC is no exception.

Focusing solely on membership numbers and nationwide trends may obscure some important congregational dynamics at CPC, however. One observation I have made is that because the church has historically been oriented towards community service and being a hub of community activity, distinctions between members and participating nonmembers have always been somewhat blurred. Nonmembers, for example, may remember being married at CPC, attending Christmas services and Eagle Scout ceremonies there, and they may even subscribe to the monthly newsletter. Some say that Carmichael Presbyterian is "my church" or "my family's church," not realizing (or perhaps not caring) that they are not on the official membership roll.

Likewise, non-CPC members and "nones" sometimes find that their child likes the youth group at CPC, or that CPC offers volunteering opportunities not available elsewhere. In 2021, for example, over one quarter of the youth group's regular attendees were children of nonmembers. Before Jan Olson's time in the 1950s, and ever since, CPC's youth group warmly welcomed friends invited by children of the church regardless of their religious affiliation or lack thereof. As another example, in 2022 over half of CPC Food Closet volunteers were not CPC members but came from the broader community. (The Food Closet began as a cooperative effort of multiple congregations; see Chapter 6.)[8]

Another segment of participating nonmembers that may be on the rise— again, informally observed—includes people who have been hurt in other churches. Their generosity was exploited, for example; their need for a season of rest and renewal was not recognized. Or, because of health challenges, neurodiversity, social status, or family structure, they felt excluded elsewhere. They appreciate being seen and heard at CPC but hesitate to go through the formalities of membership, out of a desire to test the waters for an extended time or simply preserve boundaries.

For all of the above reasons, this book, like most other CPC-related media, refers inclusively to people who are connected to the faith community as "the members and friends of CPC."

---

8 Carmichael Presbyterian Church, *Annual Report 2022.*

The congregation still counts several multi-generation families among its members and friends, including a few with ties to the founders. However, as former CPC member Christa Brewer observed,

> Diversity around the church continues to expand. Welcoming in neighbors is important. When I was a child [in the 1980s and 1990s], we had over 1000 members. Numbers are smaller now, as in many churches. One thing that makes me excited now, though, is scanning the pews while [watching services] online. I don't know a lot of people in the pews. And that's a good thing. That tells me that CPC is still vital and is bringing new people in.[9]

Christa is now the Rev. Christa Brewer, having been ordained to ministry in 2007 in a service at CPC. As of 2023, she serves a church in Myrtle Beach, South Carolina. The diversity she mentioned includes a mix of Carmichael-area natives and transplants. Among new attendees who have lived in the area for a long time, some came to CPC because the churches they were attending left the denomination (see next section). In addition, families of various configurations attend today, including single-parent families, adoptive families, same-sex parented families, and children attending with grandparents—a significant change since the 1960s when numbers were at their peak. The ethnic makeup of the church is still mostly white, though its younger generations include more adults and children of color.

Member Congregation in the Presbyterian Church (USA)

Carmichael Community Church affiliated with the Presbyterian Church in 1925. The denomination is a branch of Reformed Protestant Christianity with roots in sixteenth-century Scotland and Geneva, Switzerland. Its name comes from its form of government, which is led by elders—*presby* being the root world for old or elder. In Presbyterian churches, rather than having a bishop-led system as in the Catholic Church and the Anglican and Episcopal communion, elders nominated and elected from within each congregation's membership, together with ministers of Word and Sacrament (pastors), lead individual congregations and govern the denomination as a whole.

---

9 Rev. Christa Brewer, interview by Susan Herman, June 7, 2022.

A Connected Church with a Democratic Leadership Model

Elders in active service, known collectively as the session of a given congregation, form not only the visioning and governing body of the individual worshipping community, but they also may be commissioned to serve in larger councils known as presbyteries, synods, and the General Assembly. In these councils both ministers of Word and Sacrament and elders work together on matters of discernment and discipleship.[10] In practical terms, this usually takes the form of policymaking and determining how to use money and other resources.

Some US Presbyterian churches today celebrate their democratic form of government with a nod to the denomination's Scottish heritage. For example, they may hold a special worship service called the Kirkin' o' the Tartans, which is a blessing of the traditional Scottish plaid woolen banners and garments representing their clans. Its purpose is to demonstrate rededication of the congregation's families to God's service, independent of any loyalty to national authorities.

"King Charles I, who was crowned in 1625, resented the democratic tendencies of Presbyterianism and feared that it fueled feelings of Scottish identity separate from the English Crown," notes an article on the Presbyterian Historical Society's blog.[11] Though celebrations marked with bagpipes and other Scottish pageantry have occurred at CPC, they are not a regular part of the church calendar. Still, one can certainly surmise that a heritage of "democratic tendencies" appealed to the founders of Carmichael Community Church.

By the 1920s Presbyterians were well-established in the United States and were known for their emphasis on education and their structure for sharing resources with new congregations starting up in rural areas like Carmichael. At that time Presbyterians were active in other parts of the world as well, notably in Korea, where they had started educational institutions as early as 1884.[12]

---

10 Joseph D. Small, "What in the Church is a Council?" (Association of Executive Presbyters, Pittsburgh, PA, October 20, 2011).

11 David K, "The 1637 Book of Common Prayer," November 12, 2018, https://www.history.pcusa.org/blog/2018/11/1637-book-common-prayer.

12 William Yoo, "A History of Wrestling With Racial Prejudice and Colo-

The earliest members of Carmichael Community Church represented multiple denominations, a trend that has persisted over time. In her interview with Dick and Carol Piper, who joined CPC in 1973, Lisa Benadom asked why they had chosen to come to a Presbyterian church when they moved to Sacramento. "Their journey is an interesting one," she wrote:

> Carol had been confirmed Episcopalian, but attended a Congregational Sunday school. Dick was baptized in a Congregational church but raised in a Presbyterian church. Later Dick discovered that in the Methodist church he could take correspondence classes in place of attending seminary. After starting this program he decided to attend the Candler School of Theology at Emory University near Atlanta. After serving three years in the Holston Conference (East Tennessee) of the Methodist Church, Dick left the active ministry and moved his family to Sacramento. When reflecting on their many denominational affiliations, Dick commented, "Well, I've never been a Baptist."[13]

Unity and Schism Within the Denomination

At the time of its affiliation with the denomination, Carmichael Community Church was part of the so-called Northern branch of the Presbyterian Church. The Southern branch had split off in 1861 as the Civil War began.[14] On Friday, June 10, 1983, the two branches became one again, in a ceremony held in Atlanta, Georgia. "Known as the Presbyterian Church (USA), the reunited church has 3.2 million members," the *Sacramento Bee* reported, and is "the fourth largest body in U.S. Protestantism, after Southern Baptists, United Methodists and the mainly black National Baptists."[15]

Recent history shows that reunification of North and South, unfortunately, did not heal another major rift that still existed among Presbyterians.

---

nial Politics in the U.S. Presbyterian Mission in Korea," (Presbyterian Historical Society, December 4, 2020), Webinar. https://www.youtube.com/watch?v=2DEELntMgw8.

13 Dick Piper and Carol Piper, interview by Lisa Benadom, July 13,2020.

14 This is a much-simplified description, as in reality there were, and continue to be, numerous splinters of Presbyterianism in the USA.

15 George W. Cornell, "US Presbyterians Mend Split Dating to Civil War," *The Sacramento Bee*, June 11, 1983.

This one was over which type of unity Presbyterians valued more highly: unity in doctrine (which traditionalists, earlier called Fundamentalists, prioritized) or unity in mission (championed by progressives, earlier known as Modernists). The rift has persisted since the 1920s, and in various forms even before that.[16]

During the period from 2006 to 2013, the Presbyterian Church (USA) reported losing over 300 traditionalist congregations representing around 120,000 members. Some went to other existing denominations, while others became independent congregations; many joined with two new denominations called the Evangelical Presbyterian Church (EPC) and the Covenant Order of Evangelical Presbyterians (ECO). At the 2014 annual meeting of the Religious Research Association, Joelle Kopacz of the Presbyterian Mission Agency and two other scholars presented a report concerning this era of departures from the PC(USA):

> [It] began slowly and cannot be traced with certainty to any particular event, but rather appears to have started in a few of the 1000+ member, more conservative PC(USA) congregations that were tired of battling the more moderate majority over various issues, pre-eminent among them the question of ordination of sexually active gays and lesbians to the ministry.... The exodus grew slowly at first, then especially since 2012 following the removal of the ban on such ordinations (July 2011).

The Presbytery of Sacramento was hit especially hard, losing nine congregations for a total of 5,581 members. This was the highest number of departing members of all the US presbyteries experiencing attrition.[17] The exodus continued following a constitutional change at the 2015 General Assembly, ratified by presbyteries in 2016, to change the definition of marriage from "between a man and a woman" to "between two people."

---

16 Frederick J. Heuser, Jr., "Do Presbyterians Really Learn Anything From Their History?," *Journal of Presbyterian History* 78, no. 1 (2000).

17 Joelle Kopacz, Jack Marcum, and Ida Smith, *Congregations Leaving the Presbyterian Church (USA)*, Paper presented at the annual meeting of the Religious Research Association (Indianapolis, Indiana, October 31, 2014), https://www.presbyterianmission.org/resource/congregations-leaving-presbyterian-church-us/.

Consolidation of the Sacramento and Stockton Presbyteries

Over this period CPC in many ways retained its identity as a big-tent church; however, the Rev. Keith DeVries acknowledged the turmoil following publication of the report of the Theological Task Force on Peace, Unity, and Purity of the Church (informally known as the PUP Report) and its approval at the summer 2006 General Assembly of the PC(USA).[18] The report, in essence, said that faithful readings of scripture can lead to many possible courses of faithful action in response, including the ordination of non-celibate gay and lesbian people to serve as pastors, elders, and deacons. Pastor Keith noted that this was a "stormy event in the life of the larger church," as it created "much discussion and some confusion over our ordination standards" and "an uproar in some circles as many faithful Presbyterians have reevaluated their commitment to the PC(USA)." His conclusion did not articulate a specific position, but it did reveal his embrace of faithful questioning and comfort with moving forward while allowing tensions to exist:

> What I have witnessed in the midst of this conflict and differing interpretations is a greater intentionality in how we examine candidates for the office of Minister of Word and Sacrament and the offices of elder and deacon. In some ways the PUP report has sharpened our focus and challenged us to be more faithful in our witness. God is good![19]

The congregation of CPC both gained and lost members during this period. Several who joined CPC came from Fremont Presbyterian in East Sacramento, which had split into two congregations, one EPC and one PC(USA). Others came from neighboring Fair Oaks Presbyterian, which had affiliated with the EPC. In a 2013 article covering the denominational schism, *Sacramento Bee* reporter Stephen Magagnini interviewed the executive minister at Fremont, Mark Eshoff.

---

18 Presbyterian Church (USA), *A Season of Discernment: The Final Report of the Theological Task Force on Peace, Unity, and Purity of the Church*, 217th General Assembly of the Presbyterian Church (USA) (Louisville, KY, 2006), https://www.pcusa.org/site_media/media/uploads/oga/pdf/peace-unity-purity-final-report-revised-english.pdf.
19 Carmichael Presbyterian Church, *Annual Report 2007*.

> Eshoff said that the [PC(USA)] had been drifting away from orthodox interpretations of the Bible over the last 25 years. "Love and tolerance are becoming more important than holiness and righteousness," he said. "When they supplant what we believe is God's plan for our lives, that becomes a problem."[20]

Along with the exodus of over 5,000 members from churches formerly in the Presbytery of Sacramento came a loss of resources to support presbytery-level staff and activities. As a result, the Sacramento and Stockton presbyteries merged to become the Presbytery of North Central California, effective July 1, 2021.[21] Several CPC members helped facilitate the multi-year merger process, including elder Barbara Farley, who served on the presbytery's personnel committee. The Rev. Jerilyn (Jeri) Viera Dahlke, who became stated clerk of the new consolidated presbytery, recognized Barbara for her "wisdom, her ability to have hard, holy conversations as well as joyous ones, and her deep faith."[22] In 2021 the Rancho Cordova offices that had housed the Presbytery of Sacramento were sold, and the new Presbytery of North Central California and its Resource Center took up residence on the CPC campus, in the upstairs space next to the library.

Presbyterian Global Mission: One Example

Presbyterian global missions have encompassed a range of activities and ways of engaging. Preaching God's salvation, in the sense of saving heathen souls from damnation, was a central driver of many Christian missions in earlier centuries, including those of the Presbyterians. Their evangelism often went hand in hand with colonization, particularly in the Americas and

---

20 Stephen Magagnini, "Presbyterian Church Schism Over Gay Ordination Splits Congregations," *Scripps Howard News Service*, May 11, 2013, https://rapidcityjournal.com/lifestyles/faith-and-values/presbyterian-church-schism-over-gay-ordination-splits-congregations/article_14a55cc0-6062-5adc-a4b2-90eee7a1b562.html.

21 Rick Jones, "Two presbyteries officially become one," July 1, 2021, https://www.pcusa.org/news/2021/7/1/two-presbyteries-officially-become-one/.

22 Letter from North Central California Presbytery by the Rev. Jerilyn Viera Dahlke to CPC Session, December 14, 2020

Africa. In later years Presbyterians began more frequently to enact God's salvation in the form of healing and wholeness, in response to God's healing work through Jesus Christ. Presbyterian missions in Korea, mentioned earlier, offer an interesting example of this.

According to historian William Yoo, upon entering Korea in 1884, the Presbyterians set up schools and medical centers. During the Japanese occupation of Korea beginning in the early 1900s, the missionaries sought to offer, through their educational and healing outreach, a humanizing presence.

Among the missionaries, debates arose over how to respond to oppression of the Korean people under the Japanese occupation. Should they act through Christ in His role as deliverer, to help liberate the people? Or should they focus on supporting Koreans by continuing to teach and heal, while keeping on the right side of the Japanese authorities, whose approval they needed to stay in the country? For the most part the missionaries adopted the latter approach. Meanwhile Christian schools, many of them now headed by Koreans, became hotbeds of the uprising. When the 1919 Declaration of Independence was signed, only one percent of the country was Christian; however, among those who signed the Declaration, fifty percent were Christians.[23]

One upshot of this missionary activity is that about half of all Christians in South Korea today are Presbyterians. Many Korean immigrants to the US in recent decades have brought their faith with them and have formed congregations that affiliated with the PC(USA). To do this they enlist the help of sponsoring presbyteries, and sometimes they receive additional support from host congregations.

CPC Hosts Korean Congregations

Carmichael Presbyterian hosted a Korean Presbyterian congregation on its campus from late 1987 until 1997, a relationship that spawned moments of joyous collaboration along with considerable confusion. According to *Heritage of Faith*, much of the confusion was around whether the Korean

---

23 Yoo, "A History of Wrestling With Racial Prejudice and Colonial Politics in the U.S. Presbyterian Mission in Korea."

congregation would be able to "launch" in its own space. Various types of agreements for sharing facilities were drawn up over the years, and attempts made at mutual understanding of goals and the boundaries of CPC's hospitality. Ultimately the relationship ended with the Korean congregation departing to another existing church facility in Rancho Cordova.[24]

Since that time CPC has hosted other Korean congregations, including Holy Mountain Korean Fellowship from 2005 until its dissolution in 2012, and New Wave Fellowship from 2018 until it too shut down in 2021. Holy Mountain had started when the Rev. Ok-Kee Kim and a contingent from the congregation he had been serving in El Dorado Hills broke off from that church and needed a new space. Through presbytery connections, they were invited to use CPC's chapel for Sunday services and early weekday prayers. During CPC's relationship with Holy Mountain, annual reports of the Session's Mission Division consistently noted that "the church makes good use of the CPC Chapel and Parlor room for a nominal monthly fee that covers utilities and custodial costs. We have been blessed with the opportunity to assist the Korean congregation."

The church's leadership was stable under the Rev. Ok-Kee Kim and, later, the Rev. Jong Choon Kim. Holy Mountain Fellowship's numbers dwindled over time, however, and eventually the congregation closed. From that group, four children joined CPC through confirmation, as they had already been active in CPC's children's programs for some time.

New Wave was an English-language fellowship for second-generation Korean Americans, and had started as part of the denomination's 1001 New Worshipping Communities initiative.[25] New Wave had a collaborative leadership structure closely mirroring CPC's, whereas Holy Mountain had been more pastor-centric. New Wave's pastor, the Rev. Jason Ku, was a guest preacher for CPC's livestream-only service on October 4, 2021.

New Wave declined in numbers. Rev. Ku joined elder Wun Lee in CPC's sanctuary on December 26, 2021, to announce New Wave's closure and their intent to leave a legacy gift for CPC. Elder Wun Lee said:

---

24 White, Herman, and Segur, *Heritage of Faith*.
25 "1001 New Worshipping Communities," accessed April 17, 2023, https://www.presbyterianmission.org/ministries/1001-2/.

> I am very saddened by the closure of our fellowship, and as I always have done when my heart is heavy with sadness, I tend to look back. After our decision to close our fellowship, I look back at our relationship among the fellowship members, as well as our relationship with our sponsoring church—you folks....What little we had saved up to spread the Word through our fellowship, we hoped would be able to add to Carmichael Presbyterian's efforts to do God's work. Hope swells up in me. We hope the spirit that drove us to start the fellowship would continue. We know that the gospel will never die. And we hope that whatever we were trying to do through our fellowship would continue through Carmichael Church's people.

Though members of CPC's Session and pastoral staff were active stewards of the church's relationships with Korean congregations, it is likely that these congregations' struggles in the 2000s, in contrast to the 1980s and 1990s, had little to do with their sponsors and more to do with what the Rev. Sanghyun James Lee described as an underestimation by some Korean-American church leaders of "the unique social and cultural role engraved in their existence." Rev. Lee described the situation in an article for the *Presbyterian Outlook*:

> There are about 4,000 Korean-American churches in the United States. In the PC(USA), we have over 400 [Korean-American] churches with 50,000 members. A few of them have even grown into megachurches.... The outside appearance of Korean-American churches can be deceptive for two reasons. First, many Korean-American churches have the resemblance of their counterpart churches in the community but, in reality, their ministry concerns and priorities are very different from other churches because they continue to minister to immigrants.[26]

With improved communication technology and the ability to travel back and forth between the US and their homelands more easily, Rev. Lee noted that "[i]nstead of assimilating to the mainstream American culture,

---

26 Sanghyun James Lee, "Understanding Korean-American Churches," *Presbyterian Outlook*, July 25, 2017/Updated September 9, 2022, https://pres-outlook.org/2017/07/understanding-korean-american-churches/.

Korean-American churches have become more Korean than ever." They often serve as safe havens and a base for mobilization of the community to solve problems. Presbyterians would do well, said Rev. Lee, to stay open to understanding the needs of Korean-American churches, which add to the "diversity and inclusiveness that our denomination values" while making a "unique contribution to the mission of the church as a whole."[27] Perhaps a similar opportunity for CPC will come again.

Leading the Flock: Pastors and Ministry Staff

Early pastors of the Carmichael Community Church were "young student pastors who came from the seminary on Sundays to give us a message," recalled CPC member Anne Morse.[28] She was likely referring to the succession of young men who served the church during the 1930s after the departures of the Rev. J. W. Babcock, a retired Methodist minister who had helped start the church in 1923, and the Rev. Samuel Holsinger, who was pastor from 1925 until 1929.

Rev. Holsinger, who also served as scoutmaster for church-sponsored Boy Scout Troop 55, was known for his seemingly boundless energy and his close ties to the members of the congregation. Of particular note, records *Heritage of Faith*, he "was an immensely understanding and helpful counselor to bereaved families." Rev. Holsinger also held a narrow, literal view of Scripture that some would describe as fundamentalist. This alienated some church members, despite his great personal appeal. Ultimately, he and about half the families of Carmichael Community Church left and started a new church on Fair Oaks Boulevard and Grant Avenue called Wayside Chapel, later known as Carmichael Bible Church and now as Crossroads Church.[29]

The congregation's schism in 1929 mirrored a larger controversy and schism in the denomination going on at that time between Fundamentalists and Modernists, as mentioned above. Fundamentalists "argued that if the church was to survive in the midst of a secular culture it had to be grounded in

---

27 Lee, "Understanding Korean-American Churches."
28 Anne Morse, interview by Elsie Cosans, October 27, 1994.
29 White, Herman, and Segur, *Heritage of Faith*, 12-18.

precise doctrine," whereas the Modernists "placed less stress on doctrine and more on the united work of the church." It was mainly the Modernist streams of thought that fed into what we now know as the Presbyterian Church (USA), thanks to those who "embraced theological diversity" in the 1920s and 1930s.[30]

After several trying and uncertain years, the Carmichael congregation called another young pastor fresh from San Francisco Theological Seminary, the Rev. James Comfort Smith. His time at the church, from 1943–1954, initiated a period of spectacular growth in membership. He was also the first of many long-serving senior pastors. During Rev. Smith's time of service, the chapel and sanctuary were built, replacing the 1927 white clapboard church and the rough-hewn log cabin known as Stoner Lodge, which was used for Scout meetings as well as Sunday school. The new construction used adobe bricks in the Spanish Mission style. This was a cost-saving measure at the time, though today it forms an iconic part of the neighborhood landscape. With expanded capacity for worship and with Sacramento County's postwar building boom in full swing, membership at the church rose seventy-five percent between 1951 and 1954.

The Rev. Dr. Pyron McMillen served Carmichael Community Church from 1954 until his retirement in 1973. Several people interviewed for this book said that Dr. McMillen was the reason they joined the church—his preaching was both theologically rigorous and relevant to the times, and his personal commitment to the congregation was apparent through gestures large and small. In 1964, during his pastorate, the church officially changed its name to Carmichael Presbyterian Church. Dr. McMillen's time, as well as Rev. Smith's, is well documented in *Heritage of Faith*. Still, some features of his nineteen-year service seemed worth repeating here:

- The congregation purchased additional land and completed several more building projects, to include the education building, paved parking areas, and the social hall, which was named after Dr. McMillen on his retirement.

- The congregation continued to grow rapidly, so much that they began to hold three Sunday worship services and two separate Christian Education hours.

---

30 Heuser, "Do Presbyterians Really Learn Anything From Their History?."

- Women began to serve as elected elders on the church's Session.[31] Marge Beeby was the first woman to serve as Clerk of Session in the 1960s.[32]

- Dr. McMillen participated in the third Selma-to-Montgomery civil rights march on March 21, 1965, in his role as moderator of the Synod of California.

Dr. McMillen's service to the larger denomination as synod moderator reflected his exceptional leadership skills. It also illustrates the tradition of commitment to engagement in the broader community of Presbyterians that CPC's pastors have carried on since.

Following Dr. McMillen's retirement and a nine-month interim period, the congregation called the Rev. William (Bill) Noel Johnson, who served from 1973 to 1988. His time saw the launch of the Food Closet, Counseling Center, and Carmichael Presbyterian Preschool (see Chapters 5 and 6).

Pastors and Education Ministry Staff from the 1990s to 2023

Pastors and directors of Christian Education from the 1990s until today are listed in this chapter. Children's and youth ministry programs are described in more depth in Chapter 4; hence, youth ministry staff are listed by name there.

Rev. James (Jim) Clark, Senior Pastor 1990–2001 and Co-Pastor 2001–2002

The Rev. Jim Clark came to CPC during the Advent season of 1989 and was installed as senior pastor on January 14, 1990. He brought twenty-six years of pastoral experience in prior called positions. Pastor Clark was acutely aware of the need for churches to change in order to meet new kinds of spiritual needs that were previously unrecognized in the US culture of organized religion. Pastor Clark noted in an interview that when

31 In the broader denomination this shift was taking place as well. In 1956 Margaret Towner became the first woman to serve as an ordained minister in the Presbyterian Church.
32 White, Herman, and Segur, *Heritage of Faith*, 94.

he first arrived at CPC, "the church had gone through an unfortunate time." Immediately prior to his arrival, "There was a sexual misconduct issue on the part of one of the pastors [youth pastor Mike Spezia], which was very public in the community—front page news in the newspaper in Sacramento." He continued:

> Church analysis experts are around today and a number of them say that when something like that occurs it de-evangelizes the church no matter what you do. There will be losses that you can't even measure initially. [That incident was] not solely responsible for but feeds into the cultural change that we have undergone.... I don't know if it's because of Watergate or whatever attendant kinds of things, but people really want leadership. [However,] they are rather suspicious of their leaders. Whereas when I began in the ministry I might come into a church and I have immediate credibility because I am the pastor, today if I come into the church, particularly where there has been a history, I must earn piece by piece my credibility.[33]

One component of the task of earning credibility that Pastor Clark cited was building on member-led initiatives in the church that had begun shortly before his arrival—specifically, Wednesday Works (described in Chapter 3) and the Mexico mission trips (described in Chapter 7). Pastor Clark threw his support behind these ministries. He also supported the rollout of the contemporary worship service in the fall of 1997.

Pastor Clark served on the presbytery level, working with other churches that were in the process of pastoral change and helping other churches manage conflict. He was also active in stewardship matters such as new church development. "I have always had some activity beyond the local church," he noted, including what might be called "para-church movements, small group faith-at-work kind of things."[34]

Indeed, during his first pastorate in the 1960s at a church in Santa Ana, Pastor Clark had been active in the community. He consulted with African American pastors in a Baptist church and assisted them as they launched

---

33 Rev. James C. Clark, interview by Wayne MacRostie, June 12, 2002.
34 Rev. James C. Clark, interview by Wayne MacRostie, July 3, 1997.

a new chapter of the Southern Christian Leadership Conference. Pastor Clark's Santa Ana church was also involved in a countywide literacy tutoring effort with Spanish-speaking populations. That church counted several real estate professionals and developers among its congregation; Pastor Clark noted that with their assistance, the church hosted a series of meetings on fair housing issues, with the goal of making it easier for people of color to purchase homes in predominantly white areas.[35]

Pastor Clark's deep experience in change management, stewardship, and community relations helped CPC transform itself over the ten years from 1997 through 2007. It was Pastor Clark who challenged CPC's congregation to look at ways the church's physical plant could be improved to better serve its members, friends, and community. This challenge resulted in the Legacy of Faith building campaign, described in Chapter 2.

On the occasion of CPC's seventy-fifth anniversary in December of 1998, Pastor Clark's sermon reflected his forward thinking and big-picture orientation:

> The church really is an Advent institution. And it's appropriate that the official founding date of this congregation falls during Advent. The church gathers people to live in expectation of the future in Christ, who has come and is coming again. The church is a provisional institution. It is yearning for the fulfillment of the kingdom of God when the church will be needed no longer....
>
> The future always holds surprises. In fact, one way an event is defined as significant is because it was unpredictable. But our faith is this: whatever the future holds, Christ will go before us and because we believe that, we know that the future will be filled with light. Light to enable us to see and understand what is happening around us, light which will provide life-sustaining warmth, light showing us the next step we ought to take, enabling us to take the step safely as we journey with Christ. We journey into the light. My faith as well as my prayer is that this congregation will continue to be a luminous presence for Jesus Christ, faithfully following the light until the saints in this place

---

35 Rev. James C. Clark, interview by Wayne MacRostie, June 12, 2002.

celebrate their 100th anniversary, and then their 150th and then their 200th and even more. It will happen if we live in the light.

As the Legacy of Faith building campaign got underway, the Session created a task force to assess congregational and community needs, and to describe programmatic changes to best meet those identified needs. It was called the ReVision Task Force. As the ReVision Task Force began its work, Pastor Clark announced that he would retire in the next few years. Thus, the ReVision Task Force added to its charge an assessment of leadership needs.

Pastor Clark suggested that the congregation search for a co-pastor to join him on the church staff for his final years of ministry. To ensure continuation of the momentum built over the last ten years, the Session agreed that it made sense to seek a co-pastor to serve alongside Pastor Clark until his retirement, who would then simply continue as senior pastor after that. The two co-pastors would share administrative leadership for a period of time, and there would be no need to have an interim. Following a bit of "shuttle diplomacy" with the presbytery's Committee on Ministry, CPC's Session secured presbytery approval of the plan.[36] In this way, Pastor Clark became a co-pastor in 2001 and retired in 2002.

Rev. Dr. Gary Califf, Associate Pastor, 1990–1997

The Rev. Dr. Gary Califf came to CPC from his first ordained call at a church in Asheville, North Carolina. In August of 1990, he and his wife Kathy and their four children set off from Asheville "to drive coast-to-coast with great anticipation of Western adventures."[37] Pastor Califf wrote that on the day of their departure, while driving on Interstate 40 into Tennessee, news broke of the Iraqi invasion of Kuwait. Pastor Califf was an Air Force Reserve chaplain, and during his time serving CPC, he also carried out his military responsibilities at McClellan AFB and Beale AFB.

The Califf family bought a home in Elk Grove. "Interestingly, our children remember their rich involvement in many CPC ministries," Pastor Califf

36 David Studer, interview by Susan Herman, August 25, 2019.
37 Rev. Dr. Gary Califf, Letter to the CPC Centennial Committee, January 8, 2020.

wrote, "but not the forty-five-minute one-way drive in the wood-sided Plymouth minivan from Elk Grove to Carmichael.... I enjoyed the commute with the little ones beside me, as I drove them up and back from home." His letter continues:

> California in general, and Sacramento in particular, served to enlarge my view of the nation and the diversity of the Presbyterian Church. Ministry under Jim Clark's leadership taught me collegial teamwork, with Sherry Sauer and the deacons and elders of the congregation. My own leadership style evolved during these years, taking on an empowering model demonstrated by Jim.... Sherry taught me a lot of fundamental convictions about the Gospel message of Jesus: justice, equality, love, acceptance, principled commitment to ideals in the face of criticisms. Although [we were] not always on the same side of issues theologically, I found it helpful to meander toward the hopeful middle way that focused on Jesus over cultural-societal contexts. This lesson served me well in the ecumenical and inter-faith Air Force chaplain ministries in years to come.

Pastor Califf's leadership at CPC was focused on pastoral care, youth and young adult ministries, and fellowship. He traveled with the high school youth group on seven mission trips to Mexico, and to Navajo reservation lands in Arizona as well as agricultural sites in California's Central Valley. He worked with the deacons to help focus their ministry on hospitality and caring for the church family. Out of this work came CPC's health ministry, as well as its Stephen Ministry program (see Chapter 3).

As the pastoral resource for fellowship, Pastor Califf was part of the Lightship Mariners, a social group for younger couples (Mariners are described in Chapter 3). With their families, the Lightship would go camping at Westminster Woods over Labor Day weekend, and they also formed two softball teams that played weekly at Capital Christian School.[38]

Some members of the Lightship were interested in hearing contemporary Christian music in worship services rather than the traditional hymns

---

38 Rev. Dr. Gary Califf, interview by Wayne MacRostie, May 27, 1997.

favored by older members at the time. They suggested to Pastor Califf that he launch a new weekly service that would accommodate this. To obtain the required approval, according to CPC member Garrett Torgerson, Pastor Califf turned over to Garrett and to Mark Studer the task of proposing contemporary worship to the Session. Mark already played in a band with his brother Chris and was eager to lead music at a new service, to be offered on Sunday evenings. "Gary [Califf] understood that the church needs to foster leaders by giving them leadership roles for which they aren't yet prepared and letting them run," commented Garrett, continuing:

> Gary preached every Sunday at this service, and ever the adventurer, he let me pick the sermon topics. It was great. Each week I would propose a new topic about something I wanted to know more about and Gary would walk out among the congregants without notes and preach on it.... I don't believe Gary ever got much credit for lifting that service off the ground, but he was the force behind it. I am reminded of a saying attributed to Harry Truman that there is no limit to what you can accomplish if you don't care who gets the credit. Wonderful words to live by. I thank Gary for helping me to understand them in practice.[39]

After leaving Carmichael in November 1997 for a new position at a church in Ohio, Pastor Califf served combat duty with the U. S. Air Force in Ramadi, Iraq, and later served at Robins Air Force Base in Georgia as Chaplain for the Air Force Reserve Command.[40]

Rev. Sharon (Sherry) Sauer, Director of Christian Education 1990–1991; Associate Pastor, 1991–1999

The Rev. Sharon (Sherry) Sauer was hired at CPC in October of 1990 to be the director of Christian Education. She had completed seminary training in stages over the prior ten years and had recently passed her ordination exams. *Heritage of Faith* explains that she was not initially called as an ordained staff person because the Associate Pastor Nominating Committee had not completed the required steps for the call process, and a direct hire "was the most expeditious way of getting the urgently needed staff person."

---

39 Garrett Torgerson, CPC History Notes, December 11, 2020.
40 Califf, Letter to the CPC Centennial Committee.

The presbytery did approve her ordination once the APNC completed its steps and called her to be Associate Pastor for Christian Education. She was officially installed in that position in June 1991.[41]

In her letter to the congregation remembering her time in Carmichael, Pastor Sherry said: "Carmichael Presbyterian Church was my first call to ordained ministry. For me that meant a call to listen deeply to God's lead and follow." She continued:

> Thus, my ten years were filled with firsts as a Minister of Word and Sacrament:
>
> - First baptism and the joy of it
>
> - First time administering communion as we shared this holy meal in the sanctuary, and for the homebound
>
> - First wedding and counseling with couples
>
> - First funeral/memorial service including one for a homeless gentleman and circles of loved ones sharing stories of their loss as they grieved
>
> - First time preaching in Sunday morning worship, in the sanctuary that was faithfully filled with inspiring music and the congregation
>
> This faith community seasoned me for more faithful service, and I'm deeply grateful.[42]

Pastor Clark had known Pastor Sherry and her husband, Les (the Rev. Leslie Sauer) for nearly twenty years by the time she joined the staff at CPC. She had been an elder at Park Boulevard Presbyterian Church in Oakland, California, when Pastor Clark served there. He made no secret of their association but stayed out of the personnel discussions. Pastor Clark said the committee "interviewed about four or five candidates, I think, and [Sherry] was, in their minds, head and shoulders above the rest. That's how she came to join the staff here, and neither one of us has been sorry."[43]

---

41 White, Herman, and Segur, *Heritage of Faith*, 186.
42 Rev. Sharon Sauer, Letter to the CPC Centennial Committee, December 19, 2019.
43 Rev. James C. Clark, interview by Wayne MacRostie, July 3, 1997.

As part of the pastoral leadership team, Pastor Sherry's focus was on education for all ages. She was also the pastoral resource for the Session's Mission Division and a strong supporter of the Hunger Sundays advocacy letter-writing campaigns (described in Chapter 6). Her ministry vision for families included children being rooted in faith and adults who continued pursuing their faith, too. She launched the Godly Play curriculum at CPC (described briefly below and in Chapter 4) and created Godly Play learning centers in all the Sunday school classrooms for children up through age twelve.

To encourage adults to stay curious and keep studying the Word, she led the Session's Education Division in planning adult education on a year-round basis, rather than quarter to quarter. The hope was that this would increase interest in upcoming topics and thus boost attendance. Pastor Sherry's vision also included teaching adults how to build strong relationship skills so they could talk openly with their children about faith, or about any topic of concern.

Rather than treating family ministries and mission outreach as separate categories of her pastoral work, Pastor Sherry treated them as two sides of the same coin. Introducing the play-based Sunday school experience, she said, was something that "honors every child's spirituality; it lets them have access to the biblical stories in a way that the previous ways we had been teaching church school to children didn't really allow them to do."[44] Removing barriers for children to learn about God; training families about "what it is like to have weekly family meetings and talk about things that come up in the family"—these were building blocks of a peaceful and just society.

From healthier relationships, said Pastor Sherry, would spring a willingness for CPC families to "listen to the Spirit and be led in a deeper kind of spirituality with themselves and a deeper kind of spirituality with one another, with the community, with the world...to honor in a very serious way what it means to walk on holy ground with Jesus."[45] Not everyone at CPC appreciated Pastor Sherry's justice-oriented views. However, for some, having a leader who held these convictions greatly bolstered their faith.

---

44 Rev. Sharon Sauer, interview by Wayne MacRostie, May 29, 1997.
45 Rev. Sharon Sauer, interview.

Pastor Sherry left CPC in 1999 to begin mission service as the chaplain of the Woodstock School in Mussoorie, India, where her husband Les would serve as the PC(USA)'s denominational representative to the Church of North India and the Church of South India. More about their story can be found in Chapter 8.

Lynn Shultz, Interim Director of Christian Education, 1999–2000

After Pastor Sherry left CPC, Lynn Shultz took over coordination of the Sunday school hour for children and adults. Lynn, a CPC member, had re-launched the weekday community preschool on the church campus (see Chapter 5), and was also a strong advocate for the Godly Play program. Godly Play is a child-centric method for teaching the Bible. Its stated goal "is for children to enter adolescence with an inner-working model of the Christian language system that will continue to be of use as a means of maturing spiritually all one's life." It began to be adopted in churches in the late 1980s and early 1990s and was an outgrowth of Jerome Berryman's work in both secular and religious education for children.[46]

In Godly Play, children are allowed an extended period of free play with sets of wooden figures representing Bible stories. Under gentle supervision they may also play with the "desert box," a box full of sand representing the wilderness and the dusty roads of ancient Palestine where God's people traveled. The teacher tells a story using one of the sets—which also may have colored felt pieces to represent water or special clothing—and encourages children to ask questions, often beginning with the phrase, "I wonder...?" Class time ends with a "feast," which consists of a simple snack such as crackers and juice that introduces children to the concept of sharing communion, or the Lord's Supper.[47] In September 2000, Lynn and the whole congregation of CPC hosted Jerome Berryman at the church, where he preached and shared the philosophy and origin story of Godly Play.[48]

---

46 "Mission & Vision," Godly Play Foundation, https://www.godlyplayfoundation.org/the-foundation/mission-vision.
47 Todd Van Campen, "Godly Play lets children go their own way in developing faith," *Sacramento Bee*, April 22, 2000.
48 Carmichael Presbyterian Church, *Annual Report 2000*.

Rev. Pamela Jacobi Starbuck,
Interim Associate Pastor, 1999–2001

The Rev. Pamela Jacobi Starbuck was a child of Carmichael Presbyterian; her parents joined in 1974 when she was three years old. As an older child and teen, Pamela attended summer camp at Westminster Woods and Calvin Crest. She was also in the first group of high schoolers making the Holy Week mission trip to Chorizo, Mexico in 1986 (see Chapter 7 for more about the Mexico missions). As of 2023 she serves at Manito Presbyterian Church in Spokane, Washington, where her husband, the Rev. Dr. Scott Starbuck, also serves. She shared her faith story in a May 2022 phone interview with the author.

"I felt the call to ministry at age seventeen, during one of CPC's hardest moments." This was in 1988. Pamela was in the church youth group when the youth pastor and one of the teens became involved in a romantic relationship. Pamela had to testify in some of the court proceedings that followed, and even had to delay her departure for college because of it. She took a job at CPC that summer.

> I was a junior high youth intern right out of high school. Pastor Bill Johnson and the associate pastor for youth, Mike Spezia, had left, and we had an awesome interim associate, Aart van Beek. Aart was the one who told my parents, "I think your daughter is going to be a pastor. Be prepared." For that moment, the secretaries and I were the only staff members who knew everyone in the church—there were a lot of interims.

That same summer a teen who was associated with a CPC family died by suicide. "He had been MVP of his football team," Pamela said. "I learned then that kids can be happy on the surface but not be happy. That showed me that we had to look deeper." This lesson informed Pamela's call to ministry and her focus on young people's spiritual wellness.

The Rev. Aart van Beek "was very vested," she said. He was "on the ground," meeting people, acting as a connector, bringing a fresh kind of humor to his interactions. "He connected Carmichael to a more global perspective; his children were learning four languages." (More of the Rev. Dr. Aart van Beek's story can be found in Heritage of Faith. After CPC, he went on to teach pastoral care and counseling at the Jakarta Theological Seminary in Indonesia, then returned to serve at Parkview Presbyterian in Sacramento. As of 2023 he remains active in the presbytery as a consultant for congregations that want to become more intercultural.[49])

Pamela enrolled at Whitworth College in Spokane, Washington, and in January of 1990 traveled with a group from college to Central America. That summer she and a few other young adults from CPC worked at Calvin Crest summer camp. "I felt a stirring" to be a Christian leader, she said. She reflected on her formative youth leaders at CPC: Ken and Katharine DeYoung, and Scott and Willie Wilson. They had supported her consistently and taught her that "it was OK to ask hard questions," such as why God would allow intense poverty in Central America or damaged relationships in a faith community.

> In 1992, after my time in Latin America and graduation from Whitworth I got a bilingual teacher's aide job in Fresno and then became a part time bilingual substitute. I had learned about the civil wars in Latin America while there, and how it affected the people. This taught me a lot about what it means to be trauma-informed.

During the years 1992 to 1994 Pamela worked as a middle school youth intern at First Presbyterian in Fresno. Not long after, she attended seminary at Princeton and decided to become a candidate for ordained ministry. She completed a dual degree program: an MDiv and an MA in Youth, Church, and Culture.

Then Pastor Califf left CPC for his new call in Ohio, leaving an opening for an interim associate pastor in Carmichael.

> I learned about the job opening at CPC but didn't call my parents and talk to them at all. Instead, I asked Jim [Clark] if it was even appropriate for me to apply, as a former CPC kid. I told my parents the news when they came up to Princeton for my graduation.

While serving at Carmichael, Pastor Pamela married her beau, Scott Starbuck. During that time, Pastor Clark and several others at CPC mentored Pamela. She continued:

---

49 Mike Ferguson, "Is your church ready to embrace interculturalism?," April 14, 2021, https://www.presbyterianmission.org/story/april-14-2021/.

> Jim Clark had cancer during the remodel and not very many people knew. He finally told people when the funds came in for his sabbatical in 2000 that he had already been through about three years of cancer and on and off treatments. He came home [from his sabbatical] for me to get married, then left for a month again. A split sabbatical. His soul and his sacrificial service is part of the reason I felt comfortable coming home to my home church and starting my ministry there. His healing presence was a bridge over those painful times I'd had at church as a teen. I'm very grateful to have had the foundation of a mature leader like Jim, and faithful elders like Jimmi Mishler and Barbara Parshall, who had stayed committed to the church for so long, even during the hard times.

Pastor Pamela's last Sunday as interim associate was April 1, 2001, the same day that the senior high youth group was commissioned for their trip to Mexico. The scripture reading was Psalm 126. Pastor Pamela preached that day. In her sermon she shared several personal connections with the psalm, referencing for example the seed that was sown (verse 6) in her life, growing up as a child of CPC. She expressed her hopes that the congregation would flourish, "beyond making the budget or having satisfactory programs." She shared her vision of how the church might grow from the inside out.[50]

Rev. Keith DeVries, Co-Pastor 2001–2002, and Senior Pastor, 2002–present

The Rev. Keith DeVries came to CPC with eleven years of prior service at Community Presbyterian Church in Vallejo, California, and before that, seven years as the associate pastor of Opportunity Presbyterian Church in Spokane, Washington. He and his wife Jenny met at Whitworth College in Spokane and were married in 1980, "one month after Mount St. Helens blew its top!"[51] Pastor Keith brought a wealth of experience in leadership and pastoral care to CPC. He had served in various roles in the Presbytery of the Redwoods and on community boards. He was trained in the Stephen Ministry program and had worked with both of his earlier congregations

---

50 Rev. Pamela Jacobi Starbuck, *Waiting for God* (Sermon at Carmichael Presbyterian Church April 1, 2001), VHS Recording.
51 CPC Co-Pastor Nominating Committee, *The Reverend Keith DeVries, Candidate for Co-Pastor.*

to shape their deacons' ministries to be more intentional in their care and visitation with shut-in members and more responsive to those in crisis.

The Co-Pastor Nominating Committee had seen through their interactions with Pastor Keith that his sense of humor was an integral part of his ministry and leadership style. In sermons and in casual conversation, Pastor Keith had a habit of poking fun at himself and the many repairs needed to his aging car, a red convertible MGB. He adopted buzzwords like "plethora" when teaching children about the many saints of the church, for example, or the Bible story of the miraculous catch of fish. Satirizing the intense schedule of weekday and evening committee meetings characteristic of churches like CPC with strong lay leadership, he quipped, "Meetings are the life blood of the Presbyterian Church and the blood certainly flows freely and frequently here."[52]

While Carmichael Presbyterian Preschool operated on the church campus, Pastor Keith's skills as both an administrator and a pastor shone. Rachel Carter, who served as director of the preschool in its final years, commented on how much she learned from Pastor Keith. Rachel said,

> He really wore a pastor hat and a manager hat. Keith knows when to switch, and I have to give him a lot of credit for that because that's not the case for everyone. It's hard to do. You know, it's hard to manage a business on your campus and also be a pastor to your people and I think he did a really good job.[53]

Pastor Keith's sermons were memorable for many reasons, one being frequent references to relatable topics like forcing himself to exercise, getting the roadster repaired, or watching the San Francisco 49ers win or lose at football. He also incorporated biblical scholarship and poetry into his weekly message. To underline the idea that God works wonderous deeds through ordinary people, Pastor Keith quoted from Frederick Buechner's poetic prose, more than once returning to this section from the book *Wishful Thinking*:

> In His holy flirtation with the world, God occasionally drops a pocket handkerchief. These handkerchiefs are called saints.

---

52 Carmichael Presbyterian Church, *Annual Report 2008*.
53 Rachel Carter, interview by Susan Herman, January 27, 2023.

> Many people think of saints as plaster saints, men and women
> of such paralyzing virtue that they never thought a nasty
> thought or did an evil deed their whole lives long. As far as
> I know, real saints never even come close to characterizing
> themselves that way...[T]he feet of saints are as much of clay
> as everybody else's, and their sainthood consists less of what
> they have done than of what God has for some reason chosen
> to do through them.[54]

He also liked to quote the poet Ann Weems, particularly selections from her 1995 collection *Psalms of Lament.* While it was never Pastor Keith's style to focus extensively on current events or express opinions about public policy from the pulpit, he did not shy away from news of school shootings or other forms of violence and turmoil that grieved the nation, and Ann Weems's frank, often raw, verses helped bridge the scripture to the events of the day.

Ann Weems was invited to Carmichael and preached at CPC on Pentecost Sunday in May of 2005. She read from her poem, "The Church Year," a few stanzas describing Pentecost: "We are freed to free others/ We are affirmed to affirm others/ We are loved to love others," demonstrating in verse a response to God's love in Jesus Christ that CPC's people routinely seek to live out.

During Pastor Keith's first six years of service at CPC the Legacy of Faith building projects were completed and the new facilities—particularly the new Food Closet warehouse and McMillen Hall—were seeing heavy use. The community outreach components of the ReVision Task Force's work were being realized. Additionally, recommendations from the ReVision Plan to improve congregational care had largely been fulfilled. It was now time for a new round of visioning, and the 2008 Mission Study Task Force commenced its work. Findings from their report would inform the job description for the new associate pastor (or two) the congregation hoped to call and install. Two of the recommendations that came out of the 2008 report were:

---

54 Frederick Buechner, *Wishful Thinking: A Seeker's ABC* (Harper San Francisco, 1973).

- Use the campus to the fullest for the benefit of the congregation, the community, and God's glory.

- Expand our outreach into the community and improve community awareness.[55]

While some of the recommendations would be written into the new associate pastor's job description, Pastor Keith largely took ownership of the two noted above. He participated actively in the Carmichael Property and Business Improvement District (later called Carmichael Improvement District) and served on its board for three years. In those forums he made personal connections that helped raise the visibility of the church as a location for community care and as a meeting place for civic organizations and social groups.

In addition to forging these relationships in the community to make the church a welcoming presence, Pastor Keith sought to gently focus the congregation on the spiritual elements of welcome. In a sermon he delivered to an empty sanctuary in June of 2020, livestreamed during the COVID-19 lockdown, he read the instructions of Jesus to the disciples He was sending out (Matthew 10:40–42): "Anyone who welcomes you welcomes me...for whoever gives even a cup of cold water to one of these little ones in the name of a disciple—truly I tell you, none of these will lose their reward." Reflecting on the inability of the congregation to be together at that time and to welcome newcomers and regulars into the church building, Pastor Keith challenged congregants watching from home to re-frame their definition of welcome. It's easier to hunker down on the church campus and wait for people to come to us, he said, than to reclaim our identity as the "sent church." He continued:

> The reference to a cold cup of water is about more than just the kind act of providing someone something to drink. It is a sacrificial act to take Jesus seriously. To offer cold water to a stranger meant drawing water from a deep well where it's the coldest it can be, and often carrying it uphill in a heavy jar to the family home. This was much more than a simple act of convenience. It was a sacrificial act that might require an arduous trip downhill to the village well, and back again.

---

55 CPC Mission Study Task Force, *Report of the Mission Study Task Force* (April 22, 2008).

> … So what would happen if we practiced the act of welcoming and offered acceptance to all of God's children? What would happen if we lived with an open heart and open hands and practiced ordinary acts of kindness on a daily basis? What would happen if our practice of welcoming and accepting included everyone, regardless of race, gender, orientation, valuing everyone as precious children of God? What would happen if we were to simply be the church God has called us to be?

This message was powerful, timed as it was with the pandemic restrictions on gatherings. It would prove especially resonant as the congregation began its next phase of visioning, particularly their adoption of the PC(USA)'s Matthew 25 initiative and their decision to become a part of the Covenant Network of Presbyterians welcoming LGBTQ+ people into the full fellowship of the church. These decisions are described in more detail at the end of this chapter.

Rev. Carol Pagelsen, Interim Associate Pastor, 2002–2003; Stated Supply Associate Pastor for Congregational Care, 2003–2007

Having grown up in Texas and Alabama, the Rev. Carol Pagelsen was known for using a Southern storytelling style in her preaching. She had been raised in the Baptist church, but following a divorce, she attended Louisville Seminary and pursued ordination in the PC(USA).[56]

Early in her career she took part in a panel discussion at Eastern Illinois University alongside three other women professionals also serving in "men's jobs" (a lawyer, a probation officer, and a state police officer). An article advertising the talk, which was held in May of 1986, recognized Pagelsen as the first woman to serve the Presbyterian Church of Neoga, Illinois, and as the first woman minister in Coles County. It went on to make clear that she had been "voted into her position by the congregation," as opposed to being assigned there by another authority, and that this showed the congregation's "readiness to accept her as the first woman minister at the church."[57]

---

56 "We Welcome Carol Pagelsen," in *Mission Bell* (September 2002).
57 Carrie Fleszewski, "Panel discussion topic: Women in 'men's jobs'," *Daily Eastern News* (Eastern Illinois University, Charleston, IL), March 17, 1986.

After serving in installed pastor positions in Illinois and Indiana, Pastor Carol became a professional interim pastor. As an interim, she served congregations in Indiana, Washington, and Texas, usually in solo pastor or senior/head-of-staff positions. For a time she served as interim head of staff at Westminster Presbyterian Church in Sacramento and got to know a few CPC elders through her participation in the Presbytery of Sacramento.

She joined CPC's ministry staff as an interim associate under a special designation in the denomination called "supply pastor," which allows congregations to employ a minister member of a presbytery under a contract, which can be renewed annually, subject to approval from the presbytery.[58]

On first arriving at CPC, Pastor Carol said she wasn't sure she could be an associate pastor. However, "Keith's skills, experience, and easy-going way" quickly put her at ease. Her goal coming in was to interact with young people and "lay some organizational ground work for the new associate pastor."[59] She ended up staying almost five years. Her interim period ended when the Rev. K. C. Wahe was called as Associate Pastor in mid-2003, but she was able to stay on as Stated Supply Associate Pastor for Congregational Care and continued in this role after Pastor K. C. was dismissed.

Pastor Carol retired from full-time ministry in June of 2007. She and her husband, Dr. John Byer, moved to Myrtle Beach, South Carolina. In a letter to the congregation about her memories of CPC, Pastor Carol said:

> For years I had been telling God, "You owe me one!" because of all the messes I had cleaned up in interim ministry. After only a few short months [at CPC] I realized that God had delivered. I had served seven churches as an intentional interim and had seen the underbelly of the beast. At Carmichael I finally got to experience what I had only imagined previously. My husband John Byer and I were truly blessed to be part of the work and worship of this church. You are a gift from God.

Part of the gift package from God, Pastor Carol said, was that the church had a highly functional leadership in its office staff, Session, deacons, and

---

58 Church Leadership Connection and Office of the General Assembly, *On Calling a Pastor* (2015), 11.
59 Carmichael Presbyterian Church, *Annual Report 2002*.

other program volunteers. Pastor Keith had said on inviting her to CPC that the congregation didn't even need a pastor—"They do everything themselves!"—but she had to see it to believe it.

Pastor Carol got her chance to see CPC's lay leaders in action on her first day in the office, when Pastor Keith was out on vacation. Church member Sally Ann Walter had recently died and had willed her home on Verla Street near Carmichael Park to the church. Some commotion was reported at the house, which was in a run-down condition. Pastor Carol said,

> I received a call from the police asking what we intended to do with the "crack house" that belonged to us. Having never encountered such a situation, I called [elder] Harry Lindley and asked him to go with me to see the property which we had inherited from a deceased member. We met the policemen at the house and entered with fear and trembling. From that point on Harry took the situation to Session and the crisis was resolved. When Keith returned, Session had the matter well in hand. Shortly after that I was asked to stay on and continue to serve. What a Joy![60]

Excerpts from a sermon by Pastor Carol are included in Chapter 4.

Rev. K. C. Wahe, Pastoral Assistant, 2003–2004; Associate Pastor, 2004–2006

The Rev. K. C. Wahe was called to CPC's pastoral staff in 2003. He came from Southern California, having had twelve years of experience in youth and children's ministry. In his introductory sermon at CPC, he spoke of caring adults in his life who had freely "given the Gospel away" and "given up their lives" to help him along the Christian journey.[61] His goal was to model his ministry at CPC after them.

He had finished seminary and had one ordination exam still to pass, so his initial call was to be Pastoral Assistant for Youth and Families. After he

---

60 Rev. Carol Pagelsen, Letter to the CPC Centennial Committee, January 16, 2020.

61 Rev. K.C. Wahe, *Keep It Simple, Silly* (Sermon at Carmichael Presbyterian Church June 29, 2003), VHS Recording.

passed the last exam, his title changed to Associate Pastor for Youth and Families, and he was ordained and installed in January 2004. Pastor K. C. was the staff resource for the Education Division, and he enthusiastically attended the Mexico mission trips.

The congregation asked Pastor K. C. to leave in mid-2006, due to what was determined to be a poor fit between his goals and direction and those of the congregation. For one thing, he was more conservative in his approach to Biblical interpretation than many in the church.[62] Chris Studer, who led the youth group along with his wife, Aimee, also noted that a pattern of communication problems had caused profound disharmony in that area of ministry, and he said that Pastor K. C.'s way of interacting with the teens did not align with the empowering, inquiry-led faith mentorship style many of them had learned to expect from Sunday school teachers and youth leaders at CPC.[63] Soon after the dissolution of Pastor K. C.'s pastoral relationship with CPC, he was called to serve at another PC(USA) church in Littlerock, California, and as of 2023 he serves First Presbyterian Church of Burbank, California.

Lisa Torgerson,
Director of Christian Education, 2002–2004;
Director of Children's Ministries, 2006–2023

Lisa Torgerson first joined CPC's staff in 1999 as the child care coordinator, making sure the nursery had caring, trustworthy adults to look after babies and toddlers during worship and special events. She had grown up uninvolved in church, and had never been to a worship service until she began attending CPC in 1996 with her then-boyfriend Garrett Torgerson. Sunday service, Lisa said, was where Garrett chose to take her for their second date; a Labor Day weekend at Westminster Woods with the family camping group provided a more in-depth "date" some months later.[64] Lisa and Garrett were active in the Friendship Mariners.

Lisa's strong event planning and organizational skills soon became evident, and she was hired as Director of Christian Education in 2002. After a brief

---

62 David Studer, interview.
63 Chris Studer, interview by Susan Herman, November 3, 2022.
64 Lisa Torgerson, interview by Sharon MacLean, July 30, 2020.

stint working for Carmichael Presbyterian Preschool from 2004 until 2006, she returned to serve as the church's Director of Children's Ministries. On rejoining the church staff in that role shortly after Pastor K. C.'s departure, she also took over supervision of the junior high and senior high youth coordinators.

Multiple coordinators for junior and senior high youth came and went from 2007 to 2013, though a steady core of volunteers, including Alex Cavalari and John Wallace, faithfully supported the program. Starting in 2013 and through 2022, Lisa served as youth director for students in grades six through twelve, organizing and executing the program herself, with assistance from capable and committed interns, including Katherine Sawyer and Matthew Lillie.

While working in these ministry roles, much of Lisa's Sunday morning time was given over to preparation of Sunday school rooms and making sure volunteer teachers had the supplies and support they needed. For this reason, she noted, "I do not attend church service on a regular basis, so most of what I learn or study is preparing for Sunday school or youth group. This has benefitted me by allowing the time during my [weekday] work days to focus on God and to be present and not rushed." Lisa shared her joy of being present with God during several Advent seasons when she set up beautiful meditation stations in the chapel for worshippers of all ages to enjoy in quiet contemplation.

Youth group nights were boisterous and loud. Games of tag sometimes spilled from the upper-level rooms into the courtyard. While it may have seemed like chaos to some, it was part of a holistic learning package. Teenagers were learning to test relationships, to care for and repair them; they were learning that church was a safe place for them to be themselves. Lisa also made it a priority to integrate spiritual practices into the youth program. For example, she invited teens to wash worshippers' hands or feet during Maundy Thursday services. She encouraged them to build their music skills by playing in the worship band for Vacation Bible School and for Youth Sunday.

In addition to her work at CPC, Lisa took time to connect with other Christian educators by attending the annual conference of the Association of Presbyterian Christian Educators (APCE). For many years she also served on the APCE planning team.

Of her time at the church as a member, a member of the ministry staff, and as someone who had married into a family with decades-long involvement in the congregation, Lisa said:

> CPC is like family. We might not agree all the time, but it is a safe place to feel love, give love, and grow not only in faith but as a person. There are many people I cherish at CPC and have grown from, whether it was in faith or how to deal with different personalities and perspectives in a healthy way.

At the beginning of the COVID-19 pandemic, Lisa assisted Sunday school teachers in making the switch to teaching online. Once the school year ended and it was becoming clear that schools would continue for some time with online learning, Lisa conferred with the teachers and they agreed to discontinue Zoom Sunday school. This would offer some relief from "Zoom fatigue," a type of strain brought on by sustained online interaction.

While the church buildings were closed, Lisa put together activity and lesson bags for Sunday school and children's worship and delivered them monthly to all CPC families with children. She marshalled a small team of youth to help give out "VBS-to-go" materials in the summer of 2020, and, in July 2021, again brought in youth as leaders for an in-person Vacation Bible School with the theme "I Go Green." That year VBS was offered only to children of the church, rather than the broader community, as COVID-19 vaccinations were still rolling out for children and the public health department was still discouraging large gatherings.

Both "COVID-19 summers" (2020 and 2021) Lisa coordinated Youth Sunday services and recognition of high school graduates, then did so again once worship and schools were back in session beginning in the fall of 2021. By fall of 2022 Sunday school was back in session at CPC, with Mary MacDonald and student teachers leading Godly Play for children up to fifth grade, and Caron Treon leading sixth grade through high school using an animated Bible video series by SparkHouse.[65] Feeling the weight of the COVID-19 disruptions and the need for a career transition, Lisa resigned her position with CPC in April 2023 after twenty-four years of exemplary leadership.

---

65 "Re:form Ancestors [Curriulum for youth Sunday school]," SparkHouse, an Imprint of 1517 Media, Evangelical Lutheran Church in America, https://www.wearesparkhouse.org/store/category/286825/Re-form-Ancestors.

Rev. Jack McNary,
Interim Associate Pastor, 2007–2009

Before joining the pastoral team at CPC, the Rev. Jack McNary had served for eleven years as an associate pastor at Fremont Presbyterian Church in East Sacramento. As of 2006, he was an at-large member of the Presbytery of Sacramento. He was hired as CPC's interim associate pastor in May of 2007 following Pastor Carol's retirement.

"The congregation loved Jack. He was a lot of fun," commented CPC member Dave Studer.[66] Pastor Jack was a frequent guest at Mariner gatherings during his two years with CPC. He provided pastoral care to the congregation, serving as staff resource to leaders of the church's caring ministries: deacons, Stephen Ministers, Cancer and Faith Experience (CAFÉ), and Widows and Widowers group. He also met with the young adult fellowship group, as Pastor Carol had done. In addition, he met with the Mission Study Task Force whose findings and report would inform the job description for the church's next called associate pastor.[67]

Pastor Jack shared Pastor Keith's sense of humor. The pair served as grill masters for the church's Harvest Festival in 2007 and 2008, cooking hamburgers and hot dogs. On those occasions Pastor Jack sported a full-body mustard bottle costume, calling himself Colonel Mustard. Of their time working together, Pastor Jack wrote:

> I was thankful to work with Pastor Keith DeVries. He was (and still is) one of the most open and giving pastors with whom I have served over my 39 years of ordained ministry. Many pastors are controlling and jealous of others on their staff. Not Keith. It was fun to work with a friend and a colleague. (I did fail in helping him plan ahead farther on his sermons and newsletter articles but, I am not a miracle worker.)[68]

For a short time after leaving CPC, Pastor Jack served on the board of Family Promise of Sacramento (see Chapter 6). He also began serving in

---

66 David Studer, interview.
67 Carmichael Presbyterian Church, *Annual Report 2007.*
68 Rev. Jack McNary, Letter to the CPC Centennial Committee, November 15, 2022.

a called position at Northminster Presbyterian in Arden-Arcade, where he continued serving until his retirement in 2023.

Many CPC members remembered that Pastor Jack led summer tours to Scotland, not as one of his pastoral duties, but because he loved to travel and because Scotland was one of his favorite destinations. Pastor Jack's trips often included visits to spiritual sites, such as the island of Iona.

As noted above, Pastor Jack's time with CPC allowed the Mission Study Task Force to do its work, and, in fact, he served as part of the task force. They held fifteen small-group conversations involving over ninety church members; they surveyed members of the Carmichael Chamber of Commerce and parents with children at Carmichael Presbyterian Preschool, conducted a demographic study, and received detailed input from an interview with Pastor Keith. From the data they identified several goals for the church that a new associate pastor—or possibly two, once the economy improved—would help the congregation to realize. In addition to the community outreach mentioned earlier, the 2008 mission study identified several goals having to do with increasing levels of engagement, leadership, and social support among current members (rather than growing the congregation by a certain percentage). These included:

- Meet the needs of young adults—including singles, couples, and families with children—and involve them in service and leadership roles.

- Help small groups to form and meet for specific purposes, such as Bible study fellowship, support groups, and mission work, and provide the support and resources needed to help them thrive.

Pastor Jack was pleased to be part of the task force, and said in a pastoral letter that this group was determined to be "forward-looking...not complacent but seek[ing] to do more within the congregation and the community."

Rev. Ivan N. Herman,
Associate Pastor, 2009–present

The Rev. Ivan Herman came to CPC after serving two and a half years in his first ordained call as Associate Pastor at Balmoral Presbyterian Church in Memphis, Tennessee. That church had unfortunately suffered some effects of the global financial meltdown of 2008, which led it to eliminate its associate pastor position, so he was actively searching for a new call in the summer of 2009.

Pastor Ivan had grown up the child of Baptist missionaries, and attended first through ninth grade at a Christian Missionary Alliance school in Quito, Ecuador. He earned his Masters of Divinity at Wesley Theological Seminary in Washington, DC. His wife, Susan (the author), was a lifelong Presbyterian, and had introduced Ivan to that tradition during their high school years in Roanoke, Virginia when she invited him to her church's active youth group and choir.

After marriage the Hermans lived in San Antonio, Texas, for a few years, where Susan attended University Presbyterian Church (UPC) and served as a deacon. Ivan joined the church, and served on UPC's Session. He cited that time as formative in his decision to become a Presbyterian. By the late 1990s many Baptists had ceased recognizing women as leaders in the church (or never did to begin with), and UPC's pastor at that time was a woman. An influential leader both in her congregation and in the community, the Rev. Elizabeth (Lib) McGregor Simmons served on the boards of multiple secular organizations, including one dedicated to ending gun violence. Another thing Ivan appreciated was the connectional nature of the Presbyterian Church. Rather than making decisions solely as a congregation, Presbyterians have an interconnected structure that facilitates cooperation in mission and provides oversight on policy and personnel matters.

While studying in Washington, D.C., Ivan worked as an intern at the PC(USA) Office of Public Witness, the denomination's public policy ministry. Its staff help Presbyterians connect with their members of Congress and "advocate the social witness perspectives and policies of the Presbyterian General Assembly."[69] As an intern, Ivan prepared educational materials on topics such as the Campaign for Fair Food, which the denomination had launched in 2001 in partnership with the Coalition of Immokalee Workers, to improve wages and working conditions for farmworkers in Florida.[70]

---

69 "Office of Public Witness," accessed April 25, 2023, https://www.presbyterianmission.org/ministries/compassion-peace-justice/washington/.
70 Kathleen Wood and Kate Mitchell, *Farmworker Justice: Select Tools for Allies of the Coalition of Immokalee Workers*, Interfaith Action of Southwest Flor-

Pastor Ivan's role at CPC as Associate Pastor for Congregational Care meant that he would mainly carry out acts of public theology—attending rallies and the like in Sacramento—through informal roles as a member of interfaith communities, and through his connections with other members of the presbytery. He often brought an advocacy perspective to his preaching, but mainly formed bonds with CPC's members and friends through his presence at hospital bedsides and helping bereaved families plan memorial services. He also supported the church's caring ministries, the formation of new small groups, and led Presbyterian Women Bible studies (see Chapter 2 for more information on Presbyterian Women). Elder Dave Studer, who chaired many Pastor and Associate Pastor Nominating Committees, including Pastor Ivan's, commented:

> We knew that we already had one fairly progressive pastor of the church in Keith, so the question was, are we going to want somebody that's even maybe more progressive than Keith coming into a church that is balanced between conservative and progressive people?... I think Ivan has worked out because so much of his responsibility had to do with pastoral care in the congregation. And by embracing that job so well that even the more conservative people in the church have grown fond of him because of his personal interaction with people, even though there are times when his sermons kind of rub some people the wrong way. I remember having a conversation with Ivan early on, before he had accepted [the job], saying, you know, if you can figure out how to get along here, you can almost go anywhere if you want to, because this is an equally balanced church; there are going to be some progressive people that are going to embrace you and there are conservative people that you're gonna have to figure out a way to get along with. And he's done a good job, I think, with doing all that.[71]

---

ida (2007), https://www.hungercenter.org/wp-content/uploads/2011/07/Farmworker-Justice-Wood-Mitchell.pdf.
71 David Studer, interview.

Worship and Administrative Ministry Staff

As CPC's congregation grew in numbers over its first five decades, the job of ministry became more sophisticated and less pastor-centric. Formal music programs overtook simple congregational hymn-singing; Sunday school curricula became more doctrinal in nature (see Chapter 4); personal counseling became a more widely recognized need, as behavioral health entered the mainstream. In addition, the congregation began to emphasize a more outward-focused social mission. People began asking how the church might play a role in helping not only the upwardly mobile "newbies in town" but also those who had fallen on hard times. How might the church staff and its volunteer force be configured to support these social missions and other changes?

The makeup and skills of the church staff at CPC have responded to fluctuations in the size of the congregation. They have also responded to enormous changes in the culture of religious practice, and to changes in information and entertainment, even since the publication of *Heritage of Faith* in 1998. That book's final segment on church communications ends with these musings: "E mail, fax/modems, the internet—all relatively new tools for communication. How will CPC employ them in carrying out God's mission?"[72] Very few at that time could envision the existence of the hand-held, internet-enabled devices we call smartphones. The possibilities and pitfalls of social media, videoconferencing, mobile health, and livestreaming technologies were still in the future. Amplification in the CPC sanctuary was new in 1998, as was the recording of Sunday services on video tape for distribution to members at home who were unable to attend worship. It is probably an understatement to say that church staff who could adapt to rapidly changing technology were highly sought after, as were those who could imagine ways to keep people engaged and connected around spirituality in this new age.

One outcome of the above-mentioned trends is that over the years CPC hired a greater number of staff. New paid staff had formally defined roles and reporting structures, to keep in compliance with evolving labor laws and social norms around transparency in religious organizations. At the same time, those who staffed the CPC office broadened their skill sets, as

---

72 White, Herman, and Segur, *Heritage of Faith*, 207.

they began to support the congregation in different ways than before and supported more aspects of the church's mission.

Reports from staff members in church annual reports from the last twenty-five years reveal the extent to which they began to handle both member-facing and public-facing communications, including the website, newsletter, and social media channels, which either didn't exist or were handled solely by volunteers before. The reports also demonstrate how office staff and volunteers became frontline workers who interfaced with unhoused neighbors and others who came in for help with their daily needs. In 2010, for example, church secretaries Karen Gray and Sally Stephenson routinely fielded ten or more phone calls per day "requesting some sort of financial assistance ranging from help paying rent to receiving a bus pass."

> Processing, approving, and fulfilling these requests was a team effort as our pastors, financial administrator and secretaries all had a part in this ministry. Our stalwart office volunteers were probably most impacted by this increase as they fielded hundreds of phone calls, called scores of landlords, and graciously welcomed the more than 400 people who came to our church for help.... In 2010 we helped 418 people with $17,568 of assistance. This is a 93% increase over 2009!

The amount, taken from Deacons' Fund (explained further in Chapter 6), assisted people with rent and utility payments, car fuel, emergency shelter in hotels, and bus passes.

Members of CPC's staff and its volunteers also became ministers to each other, as former CPC preschool director Diana West noted:

> One of my bigger challenges [as preschool director] was to learn how to temper my tendency to act too quickly. Early on, if someone came to me with a problem, staff or parent, my first thought was how to fix it and then do whatever that was. I learned, over time, that listening and patience often was a better solution than my immediacy. I can thank the CPC staff for helping me to see the wisdom in this.

I was not raised with religion. My mother was Catholic and my 3 elder brothers were all schooled in the Catholic Church. By the time I was born, for whatever reason, this all stopped. It is safe to say that I was non-committal when I came to CPC and [the preschool].... Over time, through the friendship of staff and volunteers, I developed a new, deeper awareness of spirituality and became open to the possibility of God. I now state, when asked, that I am an agnostic—I just don't know. I have had too many experiences that have touched me on a very deep level to unequivocally state I am an atheist.[73]

Names of administrative staff members can be found in Table 1.1. Office volunteers, including telephone volunteers, offering counters, and *Mission Bell* newsletter staff, are listed in annual reports. Worship ministry is covered in detail in Chapter 2, and its staff members are listed there. Youth coordinators and directors are listed in Chapter 4. Directors of the preschool and counseling center are listed in Chapter 5; Food Closet directors (all volunteers) in Chapter 6.

---

73 Diana West, interview by Susan Herman, January 25, 2023.

Table 1.1: Administrative Staff of CPC, 1998–2023

Position	Name	Years Served
Pastors' Secretary	Elaine Rietz	1986–2000
	Pam Garcia	2000–2001
	Dorothy Sherrard	2001–2003
	Karen Gray	2003–present
Church Secretary	Ramona Stubblefield	1983–2001
	Jacqueline Blount	2001–2003
	Kate Erlich	2004–2006
	Sally Stephenson	2006–2011
	Julie Ueltzen	2011–present
Financial Secretary	Barbara Krefting	1980–2000
Financial Administrator	Joan Eisner	2000–2003
	Paul Shultz	2003–present
	Mary Menssen	2018–2019
Maintenance Manager	Jack Hatfield	1984–2005
	Jeff Eagen	2000–2004
	Ray Villarreal	2005–2012
	Ron Morris	2013–present
Custodians	Larry Williams, Greg Thaden, John Biggs, Tilico Paredes, Tyler Cann, Christian Bolen, Josh Hogge, Troy Bilaver, Aiden Logan	Overlapping from 2002–present
Child Care Coordinators	Jennifer Voorhees	1998–1999
	Lisa Torgerson	1999–2001
Child Care Providers	Hope Reyes	1999–2001
	Mary Camozzi	2001–present
	Paul and Mary Camozzi	2003–present

Wedding Coordinators	Victoria Bush, Viki Tozier, Lisa Levering, Gloria Williams, Tracie Hewitt (Reception Coordinator), Julie Ueltzen	Overlapping from pre-1998 to present
***Parish Nurse, later called Faith Community Nurse** (Part of Health Ministry under Fellowship and Nurture Division)	Deborah Young	1995–2000
	Sue Bowington	2000–2015
	Joan Hurlock	2014–2018
	Sharleen Millering	2019–2021
***Librarian** (Part of Education Ministry)	Doris Beckert	1994–present
***Engagement Coordinator**	Sharon MacLean	2021–present
****Treasurer**	Carol Jones	1993–2016
	Tim Farley	2016–present

* Volunteer roles

** The Treasurer is an officer of the church's Session and serves as the Treasurer of the corporation for purposes of California nonprofit law.

The Session

According to the *Book of Order*, which is Part II of the constitution of the Presbyterian Church (USA)—Part I being the *Book of Confessions*, or beliefs—it is the duty of elders, individually and jointly, to strengthen and nurture the faith and life of the congregation committed to their charge (G-6.0304).[74] Elders, who are nominated and elected by the congregation, are ordained for service on the Session and serve active terms of three years. Alongside ministers of Word and Sacrament (pastors) they represent the congregation in regional councils such as the presbytery and synod, and may serve as commissioners to the national council, called the General Assembly. CPC's Session had twenty-one elders from 1978–2020, with seven elected in each of three "class" years. As of 2021 the Session comprises fifteen elders, the pastors, and the Clerk of Session (an ordained elder not actively serving on any of Session's divisions).

A major function of any session is to connect churches in the geographic area (the presbytery) to one another. In the last twenty-five years CPC's Session has had as many as fourteen people serving on committees of the presbytery or other denominational bodies. Elder Margaret Herman, who served on every Session division except for Mission over the years, said that she enjoyed being assigned to serve as the presbytery's representative on member churches' search committees when they were seeking new pastors. She said "that was a lot of fun. When they found the right person, everyone was so happy and excited."[75]

At CPC, Session members and others from the congregation also served on the boards of the church's preschool and counseling center. At various times CPC elders have also connected the congregation to local interdenominational and interfaith groups and served on the boards of homeless services organizations such as Carmichael HART, Family Promise of Sacramento, and Loaves & Fishes (see Chapter 6).

---

74 Presbyterian Church USA, *Book of Order: The Constitution of the Presbyterian Church (USA), Part II* (2021-2023).
75 Margaret Herman, interview by Lisa Benadom, December 21, 2020.

Another duty of the session is to help members of the congregation who are considering entering ordained ministry as pastors to discern their calling and to proceed with their seminary studies and other preparations. "Inquirers" approach the session of the congregation where they are members to express their interest in exploring a call to ministry; they then come "under care" of their presbytery's Committee on Preparation for Ministry. As they proceed through their studies and confirm their desire to be ordained, the presbytery may approve them as "candidates" for ministry. Inquirers and candidates typically engage in some form of supervised service to the church, such as an internship in a congregation or one of the denominational offices. CPC's Session sponsored Pamela Jacobi and Christa Brewer in this way, as well as several other children of the church in the last twenty-five years: Mark Studer, Karl Schafer, Jennifer Boyd, and Ryan MacLean.

The Session also names members of the congregation to the Nominating Committee, which is approved by the congregation to nominate new deacons and elders for active service in upcoming class years.

As a governing body, CPC's Session is responsible for setting policies and for executing them, to maintain compliance with state law and other standards for organizational transparency. Elders serving on CPC's Session often have professional experience in human resources or funds administration, and they strive to keep personnel policies, salaries, and training up to date while also offering consultation to members who wish to leave bequests. Bylaw changes adopted by the Session in recent decades are mostly to align with updates in California nonprofit law and the denomination's *Book of Order*.

CPC's Session has functioned in a few different configurations. At first, it was separate from the Board of Trustees, then in 1955, this function was folded into the Session's responsibilities. Until 1991 two members of each incoming class of active elders would be elected as trustees; this changed so that all elders, while serving a term on Session, would be considered trustees of the corporation. In 1993, instead of committees, the Session began operating in divisions as a way to streamline decision-making.[76] Divisions and their names and functions have shifted several times; as of 2023 they are: Education, Mission, Membership and Outreach, Administration, Worship, and Fellowship and Nurture.

---

76 White, Herman, and Segur, *Heritage of Faith*, 98, 193-94.

Major decisions that CPC's Session has grappled with are explained in various places throughout this book because they touch every aspect of the church's mission and operations. In the past quarter century, and particularly in the face of falling membership, stewardship of resources has been an intense focus. More recently, and especially since the COVID-19 pandemic, the Session initiated a new series of visioning conversations. These might also be considered conversations about identity: who the congregation is and wants to be.

Clerks of Session

The clerk of any congregation's session is a communicator. Their role is to keep accurate minutes, maintain membership records, and serve as liaison to other councils of the Presbyterian Church. They also notify the congregation of upcoming meetings and what business will be transacted in those meetings, and they assist the session moderator (typically the pastor or senior pastor) in preparing meeting agendas and dockets of items to be voted on.

CPC's Session has had only four clerks in the last twenty-five years: Howard Crowley (1968–1971 and 1978–2003), Marie Segur (2003–2018), Linda Hatch (2018–2023), and Mary MacDonald. Mary began serving mid-way through 2023, after Sharon MacLean served briefly as interim clerk.

Research for this section turned up a program from a thank-you celebration for Howard Crowley held on February 23, 2003. In recognition of his long and skillful service, the celebration featured a musical salute, remembrances, and a parody of the song "We'd Like to Thank You, Herbert Hoover" re-fashioned as "We'd Like to Thank you, Howard Crowley." Since 1986, the large upstairs room in the education wing where Session meets has been called the Howard Crowley Room.[77] More information about his time can be found in *Heritage of Faith*.

By the time Marie Segur became clerk of CPC's Session, she had been a church member for forty years, having joined in 1963 with her husband, Dave, and their five children. (One more child came along a few years later). She had been on the ground floor of the church's anti-hunger and peacemaking efforts through the 1970s and 1980s, and in the early 1990s,

---

77 White, Herman, and Segur, *Heritage of Faith*, 147.

she had also initiated a robust program of media outreach.[78] In a 2020 interview, Marie said of her time serving as Clerk of Session:

> It keeps you involved. It's wonderful. You sit quietly as you can, that's not the easiest thing for the Clerk of Session during the meetings.... It helps you to see the broader picture of the church. It helps you to see where improvements need to be made.
>
> ...Being Clerk of Session was a humbling experience because I've always been asked to do things that I never thought I could do. And I guess, you know...why would it come to [me]? And yet, it was humbling knowing that I'm just a very small part of a large part of the continuity of the church.
>
> ...Working with the pastors is very special. They made it very easy. And there was a lot of continuity, that was good having the same person as clerk for a long time. We started keeping the records rather consistently in format as far as the minutes and everything. So, it was a delightful experience. It helped me grow. I certainly grew a lot.[79]

Marie spoke of her service as Clerk of Session as being a privilege and as one more "open door" in a lifelong faith story of God opening doors for her. Following the December 2018 meeting of Session, Marie narrowly avoided the doorway out of this life. "I did not make it to my car, but collapsed in the parking lot," she said in a testimony shared in worship a year later.

> Members of Session surrounded me, called 911, and went home to get Dave. The immediate and knowledgeable care and attention of Pastors Keith and Ivan and Elder Beth Lindley (and others) made a difference!... I am grateful for this door of opportunity a year later to be here and to bless you personally for the care you give in many, many ways to God's families.[80]

Marie resigned her position as clerk to care for her husband and for her own health. Assistant Clerk of Session Linda Hatch took over at that time.

---

78 Marie Segur, interview by Karen Orlando, October 14, 2020.
79 Segur, interview.
80 Marie Segur, Faith Story presented to the CPC congregation during worship, December 15, 2019.

Linda is the daughter of Dick and Carol Piper (Dick was quoted earlier in the chapter), and became active at CPC around 1990 when her son Jeremy was twelve. She had volunteered in the Food Closet and played in the church orchestra and handbell choir, and had previously served as an elder. History interviewer Lisa Benadom wrote that Linda also chaired the church directory project one year: "The task was so big, and had so many components, that at times she felt overwhelmed. With great appreciation she marvels at how people would just step in right when and where she needed them most." As Assistant Clerk of Session, Linda had "made it very clear that she was only willing to be the back-up." After Marie's resignation,

> Linda was called upon to temporarily serve. As she began this new role, she realized that she loved it and that God had brought her to a place that allowed her to be His Hands. Linda is very organized and detail oriented. A perfect skill set for Clerk of Session.[81]

Serving on the Session during COVID-19 was no small task, as the body met for over a year solely on the Zoom platform, carrying on discussions that covered wholly new territory—for example, how to hold together as a church during lockdown, when and how to come back together, and how best to care for members and friends who fell ill. Thankfully, Linda noted, Pastor Keith was just as good an online moderator of Session meetings as in person:

> He gets them started on time, keeps us to the agenda, and does his best to keep the meeting moving along while still allowing for discussion when appropriate. He makes sure that when people have something to say on an issue that he takes them in order and listens. If it becomes apparent that an issue brought forward is controversial and needs more work he refers it back to the division. For the challenging conversations he listens carefully and takes the time to fully explain what the issue is. He's respectful of people with different opinions. He does all of this with a sense of humor (when appropriate) and an appreciation for the work of the members of Session.[82]

---

81 Linda Hatch, interview by Lisa Benadom, November 13, 2020.
82 Linda Hatch, personal communication, April 23, 2023.

In her interview Linda acknowledged that the congregation's strong culture of service, in which many take on "worker bee" roles, can at times pose challenges. "You can't pour from an empty cup," she said. When setting priorities for how to use the limited resources of a smaller congregation, Linda said she would like to see the church offer more opportunities to "replenish our souls so that we may serve others."[83]

Stewardship

Over its 100-year history the members of CPC have pledged both time and money to support the capital and operating expenses of the church, benevolence programs directly sponsored by the church, and the denomination's domestic and international programs and missions. The Session's Stewardship Committee (part of the Administration Division) typically develops the next year's budget in September, and then conducts a fall giving campaign around specific identified needs in the budget. In addition to mailings, Sunday announcements, newsletter articles, and posters—and more recently, social media posts—the pledge drive has in some years also included creative elements such as drama team performances and videos.[84]

The budget is presented to the congregation every year at its annual meeting. Though it may seem a boring exercise, CPC members seem to enjoy a bit of pomp and circumstance to spice it up. An interviewee said, "Annual meetings at CPC are like a party!" Indeed, from the annual meeting minutes of February 24, 2002, we learn that "more than the required quorum of 80 members" attended a festive potluck lunch and the Celebration Singers, directed by Zorana Randjelovic-Flores, sang four songs ("The Greatest Love," "Soon I Will Be Done," "Be Thou My Vision," and "I'm Gonna Sing Till The Spirit Moves In My Heart") and received a standing ovation.

Budgeting has at times been challenging, and in recent decades these challenges have come in parallel with nationwide economic downturns. In early 2001 (following collapse of the "dotcom bubble") CPC's Session confronted a budget shortfall. They asked members to consider revising their pledges upward from the previous fall.

---

83 Hatch, interview.
84 Carmichael Presbyterian Church, *Annual Report 2003*.

While the Mission Study Task Force in 2008 had envisioned hiring a part-time associate pastor in addition to a full-time associate, the mortgage-backed securities meltdown and global financial crisis that had resulted in Pastor Ivan's job loss in Memphis affected CPC's budget as well. The part-time ordained position was not realized.

During COVID-19, the Session feared that giving levels would fall precipitously. The church thus applied for, and received, a Paycheck Protection Loan from the federal government. Contrary to fears, giving actually increased. Elder Tim Farley reported in the February 2021 *Mission Bell* that the total amount pledged toward CPC's 2021 budget slightly exceeded the amount pledged in 2020 ($709,632, up from $708,725) even though the number of giving units shrank from 184 to 169 over the same period.

Members and friends of CPC are encouraged to engage in "second-mile" giving on top of their annual pledge (or multi-year pledge, in the case of capital projects). Options for second-mile giving include the Presbyterian Women, the Deacons' Fund, Carmichael Food Closet, Alternative Gift Market, and the denomination's quarterly Special Offerings (these are described in Chapter 8). Members and friends are also invited to engage in legacy giving.

The Session's Gifts and Bequests Advisory Council began in 1998 when CPC's Session recognized a need to provide oversight and receive advice on the faithful administration of special gifts, bequests, and endowments that benefit CPC, specifically:

- Their receipt, investment, and accounting
- Respecting the donor's wishes provided they were in harmony with CPC's mission
- Informing the congregation of the opportunities for gifts and bequests
- Informing the Session of the availability of special gifts' principal and/or income for the church's needs
- Determining whether proposed expenditures are in harmony with donor's wishes
- Recognizing donors

- Reporting on gifts and bequests made on an annual basis[85]

In addition to several named funds that are invested and generate income for the church, the Gifts and Bequests Advisory Council in 2022 created the Adobe Funds Legacy Program "to provide a lasting financial foundation for the mission and work of Carmichael Presbyterian Church for generations to come."[86] The legacy program was introduced in May of 2023 at a lunch and information session as part of the church's centennial celebrations.

Building projects in the three-phase Legacy of Faith campaign are described in more detail in Chapter 2; however, here I've captured a few notes about the fundraising aspects, which members of CPC's Session led. Regarding the series of capital campaigns that begin in 1997, elder Bill Dunn remarked,

> One of the interesting facts in my mind is the percentage of pledges that were paid. The total pledges for these six campaigns were $8,539,286. The total campaign contributions received amounted to $8,011,147. This means that 93.8% of the pledges were received. If I remember correctly, our consultant, RSI, informed us that anything over 80% is outstanding.[87]

Bill provided a summary of the capital campaigns, with research help from church secretary Karen Gray (see Table 1.2 at the end of the chapter).

CPC elders Steve and Karen Orlando both worked on Phase III of the campaign, which built McMillen Hall during 2006–2007. In an email, Karen remembered,

> Part of the way into the campaign, a couple from the congregation had lunch with Keith and said that they would donate up to $1,000,000 in matching funds. That really kicked off the money raising....What Steve remembers as the most impressive moments of the campaign was [having] group congregation meetings, mostly during the education hour, and there was

85 Carmichael Presbyterian Church, *Annual Report 1998*.
86 Carmichael Presbyterian Church, *Annual Report 2022*.
87 Bill Dunn, personal communication, October 23, 2020.

excellent turnout and participation. It really sold the campaign. Of course, the meetings were held in the old McMillen Hall, which didn't hurt....We made a promotional video, which I did with Jeff Hanson and Jack Shearer. It wasn't very good, I will admit. Most people loved the outtake video more. It was a TV host named Guy Smiley (a name I got from *Sesame Street*) going around and interviewing people on campus on why we needed a new building.... We had a lot of fun though and it was wonderful working with Jack as we edited the video.[88]

Vision and Identity of the Congregation

After extensive internal studies in 1999 and 2008, CPC's Session determined in 2017 that the time had once again come for a process of visioning. The church had been in "maintenance ministry" mode for some time, and while no staff transitions were on the immediate horizon, nearly ten years had passed since the last survey and evaluation.

The Pneumatrix study was initiated at CPC shortly after the Pneumatrix framework itself was conceived. In an article for *Presbyterian Outlook*, Pneumatrix creators Jim Kitchens and Deborah Wright noted that for a number of years—decades, even—it had been the case that "Church wasn't working the way it had in the post-World War II boom. Technical fixes that worked 20 years ago no longer helped us solve increasingly complex and daunting problems."[89] The main problem Kitchens and Wright identified was that the church was moving farther from the center of US cultural life, toward the fringes, particularly on the West Coast. As a result, they said, "New forms of Christian community are arising that are better adapted to our current situation of being closer to the fringes of American culture than are our inherited models for being church, all of which assume a time we were at the heart of that culture." The goal of a Pneumatrix discernment process then, was to identify what is working

---

88 Karen Orlando, personal communication, November 17, 2020.
89 Jim Kitchens and Deborah Wright, "Revitalizing Church Leadership: PneuMatrix joins the Holy Spirit in identifying adaptive change and positive deviance," *Presbyterian Outlook*, February 7, 2018, https://pres-outlook. org/2018/02/revitalizing-church-leadership-pneumatrix-joins-holy-spirit-identifying-adaptive-change-positive-deviance/.

in a church and what changes will help it to adapt, instead of continuing to try "attractional models" that were no longer effective.

Pneumatrix was designed mainly for use by small churches with declining membership. Carmichael, with 575 members as of 2017, was the largest congregation in the Presbytery of Sacramento to undertake the study. Most had under 100 members. Pneumatrix, as envisioned, was a cohort model, whereby multiple congregations in the same presbytery would each work with their own facilitators, and then representatives from each congregation would participate in group discussions about what they were learning and what new ideas were surfacing. Taking on the Pneumatrix study would demonstrate CPC's leadership in the presbytery. However, the cohort never really materialized as envisioned.[90]

What did come out of the study were two helpful insights: first, that mission is the congregation's DNA, as is a relationship-driven ministry—that is, "supporting each other and building deep relationships with each other." The second insight was that any changes made at CPC should focus on its people *being* the church, not just *coming* to church. Using these findings as a guide, the Pneumatrix team updated the church's mission statement, which was approved by the Session in December 2018.[91] They then set to work on a series of reports that laid out each of the church's programs against the mission statement and recommended refinements to each program based on how well they aligned with the new statement.

The mission statement, which informed the chapter structure for this book, reads:

> Responding to God's Love through Jesus Christ, we:
> Welcome all
> Nurture relationships
> Grow in faith together
> Connect with and serve our community and the world

Narratives about other church's experiences with Pneumatrix shared in the *Presbyterian Outlook* article described big changes—for example, pastors

---

90 Rev. Ivan Herman, personal communication, March 27, 2022.
91 Carmichael Presbyterian Church, *Annual Report 2018*.

transitioning to bi-vocational roles where they would serve both as minister to a congregation and director of a community center. The CPC Pneumatrix reports, by contrast, mainly suggest small changes, such as how to get more people involved in an existing program area. Taken as a whole, one might say they are more "matrix" (micro-analyses) than "pneuma" (the rushing wind or breath of the Holy Spirit).

Still, it is clear that the Holy Spirit was present in the discernment process. One highlight of the Pneumatrix reports was the interest expressed in building volunteers' capacity to work with special populations within the congregation. For example, the deacons' report noted that many of the people on their Care and Share ministry list (explained in more detail in Chapter 3) had Alzheimer's and other forms of dementia. Deacons often expressed discomfort with making telephone calls and visits to these members and friends because they lacked training in the necessary communication skills. Similarly, those who were interested in serving in-home communion noted a need for training to understand what to do, what scriptures to read, songs to sing, and so forth.[92]

Ultimately it would take the COVID-19 pandemic starting in 2020, whose effects continue to ripple through the church in 2023, to bring about deeper conversations about how best to adapt to change at CPC.

The Pneumatrix reports were in no way pushed to the side. In response to the suggestions about getting more people involved in church activities, elder Sharon MacLean created and assumed the new volunteer role of Engagement Coordinator in 2021. Sharon regularly collected information on volunteer needs from program leaders throughout the church and disseminated social media posts with details about these specific needs, such as Food Closet shifts, being a lay reader for worship, or setting up for events. She also started a monthly column in the *Mission Bell* newsletter with featured opportunities, along with an email contact through which interested people could get in touch. Language about "getting plugged in" was added to the church website as well.

---

92 CPC PneuMatrix Task Force, *Matrix for Assessing Deacon Responsibilities Against Mission Statement* (July 3, 2019).

Becoming a Matthew 25 Congregation

When considering the vision work that occurred from 2020 through 2023 after the formal Pneumatrix process, one might imagine that the realities of being a dispersed church during COVID-19 played some role in causing a shift in focus among CPC's congregation and leadership. Forced to confront losses of loved ones to COVID-19 and other health conditions—and often deprived of the ability to sit alongside them and say good-bye due to public health restrictions—the CPC community suffered, along with the rest of the world. As mentioned above, financial giving remained solid, but many people who had once participated actively with the church simply fell away, or were hesitant to return because of health concerns.

Meanwhile, the death of George Floyd at the hands of Minneapolis police in May 2020 and the ensuing protests[93] struck a chord with CPC folks. In the July 2020 *Mission Bell*, elder Barbara Farley reported:

> At its May 26 meeting, your Session passed a motion from the Mission Division to become a Matthew 25 congregation. The Matthew 25 vision grew out of the work of the 222nd General Assembly (2016) and the 223rd General Assembly (2018) of the Presbyterian Church (USA). It represents a call to congregations, presbyteries, synods, and other entities of the denomination to strengthen the collective work and witness of the PC(USA) to the gospel of Jesus. Matthew 25 has much to guide us. Our denomination has developed resources with a focus on:
>
> - Building congregational vitality
> - Dismantling structural racism
> - Eradicating systemic poverty[94]

Barbara noted that the Session had committed to continue reaching out to "the least of these" by prioritizing the church's Food Closet, Supper on Saturday, shower ministry, and partnership with Carmichael Homeless Assistance Resource Team (HART). She continued:

---

93 "How George Floyd died, and what happened next," *New York Times*, July 29, 2022, https://www.nytimes.com/article/george-floyd.html.
94 "Matthew 25 in the PC(USA): Join the Movement," https://www.presbyterianmission.org/ministries/matthew-25/poverty/

Ironically, May 25 was the day the focus on dismantling structural racism became a national one. The death of George Floyd has sparked a response from people all over America. Many here at Carmichael began asking "what can we do"? The Mission Division feels this is a time for us to move beyond our comfort zone and look at structural racism and justice for all.... Most of us do not feel we are racist, but if we are white, we look at the world differently than our brothers and sisters of color.

Later that year, several CPC book groups formed to meet and discuss the book *How to Be an Anti-Racist* by Ibram X. Kendi. Around twenty-five adults participated, among four book groups that all met on Zoom with volunteer leaders. It should be noted that this was the largest turnout for a six-week adult Christian Education class in many years, perhaps because of the topic, and also probably because of the flexibility afforded by the online meeting platform to meet on dates and times that suited all the participants.

Takeaways from the conversations varied. At least one group concluded that taking care of people experiencing hunger and homelessness, no matter their color or ethnicity, and giving special care and attention to the children and youth in the congregation (not taking them for granted), could be considered anti-racist acts.

Becoming an Earth Care Congregation

At its January 2021 meeting CPC's Session committed to the PC(USA) Earth Care Pledge and launched an Earth Care Team.[95] Pastor Ivan noted in his March 2021 *Mission Bell* article, "It was a group of teen members who led us to this certification focus as they see our most pressing challenge is climate change." In the absence of youth group meetings during the pandemic, several teenage members of CPC gathered for creek cleanups on a small waterway between Santa Anita Park and Howe Park. They voiced a desire to make a meaningful contribution to their community by doing Earth-friendly activities. In his *Mission Bell* article Pastor Ivan took care to explain how Earth care was connected to CPC's most recent

---

95 "Earth Care Congregations," https://www.presbyterianmission.org/ministries/environment/earth-care-congregations/.

commitment to being a Matthew 25 congregation, pointing out that care for God's creation, in being led in large part by the youth, was a way to build congregational vitality.

Likewise, Pastor Ivan noted that it supported the Matthew 25 goal of dismantling systemic racism by helping orient our congregation toward environmental injustices such as the ongoing lack of safe water in Flint, Michigan, and how vehicular pollution affected more Black and Latinx than white residents in California. Pointing also to the fact that the Earth Care certification process is maintained by the Presbyterian Hunger Program, Pastor Ivan concluded by saying:

> At CPC we amplify green theology by incorporating creation care into our worship. We promote sustainable practices by increasing composting, recycling, and reusable materials. In practicing sustainable living, we contradict an ethic of disposability, and so encourage resilience.

Youth mission trips during 2022 were Earth-care focused. The middle school trip took place entirely at the church campus over a long weekend in February—participants slept at their homes and came to church in the morning. It included work in the community garden on the Robertson property; harvesting backyard oranges in Carmichael neighborhoods for donation to the Food Closet (a collaboration with Soil Born Farms in Rancho Cordova); outdoor worship; and a lesson on tortilla-making and cooking from scratch in the McMillen Hall kitchen followed by a taco dinner. The high school group traveled to Zephyr Point Conference Center at Lake Tahoe over their April spring break and completed several indoor and outdoor maintenance projects, punctuated by meditative worship and socializing by the lake.

Becoming a Covenant Network Church

Early in 2023, CPC's Session voted on a recommendation by the Inclusion Task Force to affiliate with the Covenant Network of Presbyterians, an independent group that shares resources on policy and best practices for providing a safe and welcoming place for sexually- and gender-diverse people.[96] Members of the task force, led by elders Rae-Nani Stokes and Kathy Lewis, and with Pastors Keith and Ivan as advisors, spent about seven months studying together before bringing the recommendation to the Session. They read *The Bible's Yes to Same-Sex Marriage: An Evangelical's Change of Heart* by Mark Achtemeier and *Unclobber: Rethinking our Misuse of the Bible on Homosexuality* by Colby Martin. As part of their information-gathering process the group also attended an all-day workshop in June of 2022 at Westminster Presbyterian in midtown Sacramento, which featured workshops presented by six elders from the presbytery and the Rev. Brian Ellison, executive director of the Covenant Network.

People on the task force represented the congregation at large and all divisions of the Session,[97] and included parents of queer and transgender children. The task force continued meeting after Session approved their motion to affiliate with the network affiliate with the network, to look at policies and other practical ways to proactively welcome LGBTQ+ people as tellers of the faith story.

As Presbyterians, everything we do at CPC is in response to God's love through Jesus Christ. Pastor Keith more than once asserted that God's work of salvation is the healing of the world and the healing presence of Jesus Christ in our lives (emphasizing the "salve" in salvation). God's loving salvation is thus not a one-time event, nor is it something God's people must "be good" at and work toward, risking failure and damnation if they fall short. Rather, it is a gift in which to take joy. God's love and salvation through Jesus Christ is the source of all acts of welcome, of nurturing relationships, growing in faith together, and connecting and serving our community and the world.

---

96 "Covenant Network of Presbyterians," https://covnetpres.org/.
97 "CPC Affiliates with Covenant Network of Presbyterians," *Mission Bell,* February 2023.

Table 1.2: A Summary of Capital Campaigns at Carmichael Presbyterian Church

Building on a Legacy of Faith (1997)		
Goal	$2,000,000	
Pledges	$1,023,002	
Contributions	$1,070,539	
Actual Cost	Construction: $1,459,136	Interest: $23,170	Total: $1,482,306
Accomplishments	<ul><li>New Gathering Place</li><li>New Administrative Offices</li><li>New Music Center</li><li>New Counseling Center & Library</li><li>New Elevator</li><li>New Organ, Piano, & Choir Seating</li><li>Chancel Renovations, including New Sound System and Closed Circuit TV</li><li>Upgraded Nursery and Classrooms, East Side</li></ul>	

Legacy of Faith II (2000) **"Building Our Faith, Building Our Future"**		
Goal	$1,500,000	
Pledges	$1,384,388	
Contributions	$1,251,227	
Actual Cost	Construction: $1,422,410	Interest: $325,880	Total: $1,748,290
Accomplishments	<ul><li>Mission Building: Food Closet + Garage and Storage</li><li>Redesign of Back Parking Lot near Buildings</li><li>Added Parking Lot Lighting</li><li>Improved Handicapped Access</li><li>Debt Reduction</li></ul>	

Legacy of Faith III (2005) "Building God's Kingdom"		
Goal	$1,800,000		
Pledges	$3,009,001		
Contributions	$2,643,2711		
Actual Cost	Construction: $3,640,534	Interest: $540,703	Total: $4,181,237
Accomplishments	• New McMillen Hall • New Commercial Kitchen (in McMillen Hall) • New Back Entry, Patio, and Tower • Columbarium • Upgraded Classrooms, North Side • Remodeled Restrooms and Added Showers • Added Courtyard Room		

Moving Faithfully Forward (2009)
Goal — $1,500,000
Pledges — $787,812
Contributions — $668,721
Actual Cost — Interest: $388,152
Suggested Improvements — • Renovate Back Parking Lot, Including Lighting and Landscaping • Repair or Replace Sanctuary Roof • Earthquake Retrofit Chapel Roof • Extend Covered Walkway to Sanctuary West Door • Upgrade West Wing • Renovate Sanctuary Heating/Air Conditioning Systems, Including Re-routing Existing Ducting to Facilitate Completion of Chancel Windows as Originally Designed in 1951 (With pledges falling well short of the goal, Session chose to direct all monies received to debt reduction rather than construction).

Love in Action – Set Free to Serve (2012)	
Goal	$2,300,000
Pledges	$1,220,000
Contributions	$1,190,682 (as of 10/31/15)
Actual Cost	**Interest: $204,121**
Accomplishments	• Paid off entirely two loans which had a balance of $625,218 at the beginning of the campaign • Reduced the third loan by $468,972 to $1,054,478 • Saved $47,000 in just over two years and avoided almost $300,000 in interest costs over the full life of the loans.

Finish Strong, Reach Beyond (2015)	
Goal	$1,700,000
Pledges	$1,115,084
Contributions	$1,186,707
Actual Cost	**Interest: $50,699**
Accomplishments	• Paid off the remaining loan balance of $1,054,478 on May 1, 2018. • Avoided $349,000 in interest costs over the full life of the loans. • Many congregation members continued to contribute after the campaign was over. • The parking lot fund balance as of November 30, 2020 is $218,081. Included in this amount is $42,380 received by the FSRB campaign subsequent to the loan payoff. The rest of the total represents Undesignated Bequests received during the campaign which were then rolled into the parking lot fund.

Chapter 2
Welcoming All

Carmichael Presbyterian Church rang in its seventy-fifth anniversary in December 1998 amid unpainted walls and incomplete construction. But by October of 1999, thanks to the "Olympian efforts" of Ken DeYoung and the rest of the Building Committee, the first phase of the Building on a Legacy of Faith capital projects was complete.[1,2] It included extensive upgrades to the church sanctuary and chancel, including a new organ, sound system, and closed-circuit television. The nursery and preschool classrooms received upgrades as well. Several entirely new spaces were also added to make gatherings, meetings, rehearsals, and weekday life at the church more accessible and enjoyable. New construction included the Gathering Place, music room, administrative offices downstairs, and the Bea Durley Library and Counseling Center upstairs, along with an elevator for compliance with the Americans with Disabilities Act.

In all, 10,000 square feet of new space was planned for construction. The changes were not meant for increasing capacity for worship and Sunday school, however, as with prior building campaigns in the 1940s and 1950s.

---

1 Bobbi Jones, "The Carmichael Kaleidoscope," *Carmichael Times*, October 26, 1999.

2 The whole capital campaign was called Building on a Legacy of Faith; for brevity, it will be referred to hereafter as Legacy of Faith.

Rather, they were meant to improve the experience of those already using the buildings, and of course, to conform to new accessibility standards. The construction was also an opportunity to reignite enthusiasm for worship and ministry among younger families in the church. It would open more channels for community members to enter the building, whether to formally join the church, or to participate in its mission in some way.

The next two phases of the Legacy of Faith building campaign would expand storage capacity for the Food Closet and remake McMillen Hall into a larger, high-ceilinged, multi-use space with bathrooms, showers, and a commercial-grade kitchen. The new hall would serve both as shelter for the needy as well as an activity space for sports teams and other groups. "To be effective in reaching people in our community, we must create opportunities for them to enter our facilities," read the 1999 *Re Vision Plan*.[3] Gone was the assumption that worshipers would simply stream in the doors as they had done in the 1950s and 1960s. There had to be specific attractions—and the target audience, so to speak, had to be broadened to explicitly include people who might never attend a Sunday service or put an offering in the plate.

In some ways this philosophy was not so distinct from that which guided CPC's founders in the 1920s. The founders saw the church as an essential pillar of support for the fledgling, rural community of Carmichael. While Carmichael had become decidedly less rural by the 1990s, the church had continually functioned both as a worship space and as a community center. It had also hosted other worshipping communities. In addition to the three Korean congregations mentioned in Chapter 1, CPC's chapel had previously served as a temporary home for the congregation of St. Mark's United Methodist Church as it was starting up in the early 1950s, and Holy Cross Orthodox Church in the early 1970s.[4] Building on this legacy, CPC's leaders in the 1990s were intent on making the church—both its facilities and its programs—a welcoming place for all.

As mentioned in Chapter 1, CPC pastors and Session members participating in the Pneumatrix study began efforts in the late 2010s to help the

---

3 CPC ReVision Task Force, *Re Vision Plan*, 11, 13.
4 Dick Piper, *70 Years of Worship and Ministry: James Comfort Smith Chapel 1946-2016*, (CPC Heritage Committee).

congregation broaden its definition of welcome beyond "attracting people through the doors of the church building." They affirmed that welcoming still included hospitality: coffee and cookies after worship, nursery care, name tags, and accessibility aids such as large print. But they also wanted to consider different ways of "being the church" both inside and outside of its walls.

CPC's pastors brought this message to the congregation. In a sermon in June of 2020 (excerpted in Chapter 1), the Rev. Keith DeVries challenged members and friends of CPC to practice a sacrificial type of welcome. Be like the host who goes out to the well to fetch the cup of cold water to bring to the stranger, he said. Rather than assume you know what will make others feel welcome, instead learn about their real needs; dip your bucket deeply into the well, and offer the coldest water—that is, offer the best of what you draw from the well. Following on this idea, the Rev. Ivan Herman, referencing Acts 8:26–40, advised the congregation to go out and invite strangers—that is, people on the margins—into conversations and into church leadership. In a sermon from 2021 he put it this way:

> To engage in feeding those who are hungry; to care for those who are unhoused; to love those who are lonely, hurting and ailing—we do that through Stephen Ministry and Deacons and long-term relationships that care for one another. We provide hospitality and education and community to our new neighbors, immigrants, and refugees. We engage those on the horizons...and we know that we are giving people a glimpse of what the kingdom of God looks like, what the reign of God looks like.
>
> But...can we see those who are on our horizons also reflected in the center, in the heart, of our community? Who is missing? Who is underrepresented in our church and in our community? ...How can we elevate the voices of those who are different? How can we magnify their experience and bring those voices into our spaces?
>
> Diversity in the church can't be just about telling people hey, you're welcome. Come and join us. Come be like us. That's what we would call assimilation, not hospitality. So I'm convinced that

in Acts, it is also the church that changes. It is the church that is converted; it is the apostles who become converted over and over again. We think of the story as the conversion of the Ethiopian eunuch, but I also see within it that Philip is converted to a new understanding of the depth and the breadth of God's love.

In the same way, we too, need to be welcoming change within ourselves. Change makes demands on our hearts, our minds, our lifestyles, our music, our liturgies, that sometimes we would rather avoid. But this is the work of conversion that is always going on within us. This is the ongoing work of growing in faith, and in love.[5]

Spaces for Welcoming All: The Legacy of Faith Building Projects

> *It is ours to labor faithfully preparing the soil and planting the seed, waiting upon Him for the harvest.*
>
> *—Rev. Dr. Pyron McMillen*[6]

As shown in the table at the end of Chapter 1, the Legacy of Faith building and remodeling campaign played out in phases over ten years. After the building was complete, the church's stewardship team continued to mount capital campaigns for retiring debt. In August 2018, the congregation gathered in the olive grove courtyard to burn the mortgage and give thanks to God with a special litany.[7] The following sections describe what they accomplished.

---

5 Rev. Ivan Herman, *Horizons and Mirrors* (Sermon at Carmichael Presbyterian Church May 2, 2021).
6 Quoted by Jones, "The Carmichael Kaleidoscope."
7 Carmichael Presbyterian Church, A Litany for the Burning of the Mortgage, August 12, 2018.

Renovations to the sanctuary included extending the platform of the chancel area outwards to make space for a new grand piano and for instrumentalists. Music director Randy Benfield had recently launched a church orchestra; a praise band would also play for the new contemporary worship service. The expanded space would be well-used. The choir pews, originally situated in rows facing each other, were re-oriented to face the congregation. High performance speakers were added, along with a new screen onto which lyrics for the contemporary songs could be projected.

Randy Benfield, who was also the organist, told of replacing the Rogers organ with a new Allen Renaissance 370:

> We had a three-manual Rogers that had been here for about twenty years. I remember looking at that when I first came, thinking it's a large church, but the organ—not so much. Session put together a search committee: Barb Sebastian and Darrell Torgerson and me.... We spent six months looking. We looked at both a Rogers and an Allen. Rogers even flew Darrell, myself, and Barb up to Portland to tour their organ factory. The best part was that both organ companies brought an actual organ that we were going to buy and put it in the sanctuary. I got to have a couple of weeks to play both during the week and you can bet I spent a lot of hours over here just trying to compare every detail of the two organs. Then I was able to play them in the worship service on Sunday and the congregation could give their input. They were very similar. But in the end, the one that we thought would be best for us, or at least I thought and the committee concurred, was the Allen that we have. The three of us put in a lot of hours researching and playing organs. Session said we could spend $100,000 on a new organ, which was remarkable.
>
> That allowed us to get the console that we have which was just the electronic part, the digital part. We had $25,000 left over that allowed us to buy a set of pipes, but we kind of pilfered different places that were selling used pipes, so could get them cheaper. We bought nine ranks of pipes. We put those together with the

organ that we have right now. And fortunately, the technician we had, Blaine Rickets, was the technician for the San Francisco Symphony organ. He made lots of trips from the Bay Area and connected everything for us.[8]

Randy also recounted that church member David Fair donated money for a wooden case to house the new organ pipes and speakers, as a memorial to his wife Marty. The case replaced a cloth that, according to Randy, was painted to look like the adobe bricks, or more accurately, "like a funny folk painting of adobe brick." Choir member and woodworker Dave Mauerman salvaged the oak leaf carvings that now adorn the communion table and large cross above the pulpit from the original 1951 sanctuary furnishings.[9] As part of the new chancel design, workers also moved the pulpit forward and to the left.

For updates to the exterior of the building to accommodate the new construction, the building committee had to find new materials that were similar to the original adobe.[10] Their main challenge, however, was dealing with unanticipated fees triggered by adding square footage. These included a $6,000 conditional use permit and a traffic impact fee of $11,184. The traffic impact fee was codified in a county ordinance; however, the church building committee thought it would be waived, because the environmental documents already filed as part of the conditional use permit said that traffic would not increase as a result of the additions.[11]

Torrential rains and floods in the winters of 1997–1998 and 1998–1999 caused construction delays. Despite these setbacks, the updates were completed. Church historian Bill Davis applied to the Presbyterian Historical Society for recognition of CPC as an American Presbyterian and Reformed Historic Site. In October 1998 it became site number 415 on the registry.[12]

---

8 Randy Benfield, interview by Karen Orlando, October 4, 2020.

9 "Our Communion Table and Cross," in *Mission Bell* (August 2000).

10 Ursula Hull, "A new vision for Carmichael Presbyterian Church," *Arden Carmichael News*, June 25, 1998.

11 David Richie, "County Fees Put Area Church On Guard," *Neighbors Arden-Carmichael*, June 17, 1999.

12 Faye G. White, "Carmichael Presbyterian Church Identified as Historic Site," *Carmichael Times*, December 1, 1998. The American Presbyterian and Reformed Historic Sites Registry closed in 2002.

To celebrate the newly renovated space, two young adults who'd grown up in the church, Mark and Chris Studer, invited their art-rock band Azure to play a concert in the sanctuary on May 20, 2000. Celebrated organist Roger Nyquist showcased the features of the new organ, first at the wedding of Randy Benfield and Marsha Birdsall on June 25, 2000, and then in a concert on July 9, 2000.

One piece of church music infrastructure left out of the renovation was the carillon system, a set of small tower bells played via a keyboard-like device, which was donated by the Loyal Students (an adult Sunday school class) in 1961.[13] In 1977 the carillon was upgraded to an electronic model, which played pre-recorded music through speakers in the tower. The CT 724 control unit by Maas-Rowe Carillons resided in the space now known as the Welcome Center, at the northwest entrance to the sanctuary. For a time, church custodian Jack Hatfield changed the tapes so that the carillon rang three times a day at 9 a.m., 12 noon, and 6 p.m. During the remodel the control unit was moved to the balcony for storage.[14] Maas-Rowe Carillon Company sent information in 2006 about further upgrades that would replace the tape cartridge with a programmable CD player, but this option was never pursued. At the time of this writing the carillon control unit still resides in the balcony but the system is no longer used.

The Welcome Center—a small room off the sanctuary designed as part of the renovation to serve as a Sunday morning reception office—had its formal debut in 2008. CPC member Carolyn Biggers said that she enjoyed volunteering there because it helped her be more aware of people's needs. Before, during, and after worship, she made herself available to answer questions when newcomers walked in. Sometimes people would drop off Food Closet donations in the Welcome Center, or come asking for food or other assistance. Carolyn said:

> I helped people in great need. I would ask them to wait until after the service was over, then introduce them to either Keith or Ivan and explain what urgent help was needed. If I knew someone was new to the church, I would take them around the

13 Faye White, Margaret Herman, and Marie Segur, *Heritage of Faith: A 75-Year History of Carmichael Presbyterian Church* (Carmichael Presbyterian Church, 1998), 112.
14 Marie Segur, Detailed History of the Carillons.

grounds—have a cup of coffee in the Gathering Place, introduce them to whoever was there, make them feel welcome; that we were glad they were there.[15]

Phase Two: 2000–2004

The next phase of construction gave the Food Closet its own dedicated building with space for bagging, staging, and distribution of food, along with a warehouse and garage. CPC member Jim Shullanberger, and his wife, Carolyn Biggers (quoted above), made a game-changing $100,000 donation that allowed construction to begin earlier than anticipated. Food Closet director Don Wever reported that in 2004 the number of guests served numbered 19,018, which represented an increase from 1998 of eighty-five percent.[16]

The large parking lot on the Robertson Avenue side of the property was redesigned to include lighting and additional accessible parking spaces for people with disabilities. In addition, the church purchased the lot adjacent to the back athletic field (known as the Robertson property), and the house on the property. (For more information about the Food Closet and Robertson House, see Chapter 6.)

Phase Three: 2005–2008

The third phase in the Legacy of Faith campaign comprised several projects, with a new McMillen Hall as the centerpiece. McMillen Hall was known simply as "the social hall" when it was built in 1957. It was renamed McMillen Hall in 1980 after the retirement of the Rev. Dr. Pyron McMillen, who had served the congregation from 1954–1973. Over its first fifty years "the room was dressed up, set up, messed up, and cleaned up" many times.[17] Like clockwork, the church's annual meeting took place there, along with and deacon elections and holiday celebrations. A photo book commemorating the old McMillen Hall, assembled and edited in 2007 by Jimmi and Phil Mishler, includes documentation of "Dr. McMillen's" Scottish-themed

---

15 Carolyn Biggers, interview by Kathy Lewin, February 8, 2021.
16 Carmichael Presbyterian Church, *Annual Report 2004*.
17 Jimmi Mishler and Phil Mishler, *McMillen Hall Memories* [photo book] (2006).

retirement party, with a caption noting that the acoustics in the old hall were "not friendly to bagpipes." The book also chronicles decades of activity in the hall: plays and skits, Easter services, Advent breakfasts, Wednesday Works dinners, blood drives, Vacation Bible School, and elaborate staging operations for the Deacons' Christmas Baskets and youth mission trips.

Demolition began in 2005 following a luncheon where the children created popsicle-stick models to represent what they thought the new building would look like, and painted tiles to decorate the new spaces. Adults and children alike enjoyed a game of shuffleboard at the final Wednesday Works dinner in the old hall. The jazz band—a swing combo including members of the church and local Kiwanis Club—played for a "last dance," and church members marked the occasion by signing their names on the wooden door to the hall, around the plaque recognizing the McMillens.

Groundbreaking for the new McMillen Hall took place in the spring of 2006. "Several of the members who worked on the earlier building campaign for McMillen Hall [in the 1950s] became the groundbreaking crew for the new McMillen," Jimmi Mishler noted. The Rev. Carol Pagelsen threw the first shovelful of dirt.[18] Pastors' Secretary Karen Gray noted in her annual report for 2006 that she had purchased of a "stash of earplugs" to help staff members continue their work during those noisy months.[19]

Construction was complete in 2007. The result was a large, multi-purpose meeting room with modern lighting and sound equipment, ample seating to host large gatherings, and a commercial-grade kitchen. The space was perfect for hosting indoor soccer and other youth sports and games. Its regulation-size basketball court had goals that could be lowered by remote control and hidden behind a retractable panel when not in use. CPC member Clair Daugherty photographed the progress of demolition and construction of the new hall.[20] Members and friends of the church celebrated its completion at a dedication service in August 2007, with songs of praise, a litany, and the first official free throw into

---

18 Mishler and Mishler, *McMillen Hall Memories.*
19 Carmichael Presbyterian Church, *Annual Report 2006.*
20 Lori Keeney, "Rebuilding McMillen Hall Art Show," in *Mission Bell* (February 2023).

the basketball hoop by architect Don Mariano.[21] With completion of the new McMillen Hall came new responsibilities for setup and cleanup, and most importantly, new Sacramento County Health Department requirements for inspection, permitting, and food safety certification,[22] since the assembly space and kitchen would see increased usage by community groups.

Along with the new McMillen Hall, the third phase of construction included upgrades to the preschool classrooms, the addition of a small meeting space called the Courtyard Room in the breezeway next to McMillen Hall, and remodeling of the restrooms in that breezeway to include showers. In addition, the entry area facing the parking lot was rebuilt to include a patio with light bollards, a columbarium courtyard, a tower and balcony off the new library, and a set of large windchimes. Regarding the windchimes, building committee chairperson Ken DeYoung shared this story:

> When the remodeling project was nearing completion, a strange thing happened. While visiting my brother, we were rummaging around in his workshop storage area. We came across eight brass pipes that had a very melodic tone. I asked my brother where he got the pipes and what they were used for. He said one day while he was in front of his business, the neighboring business was being dismantled. He observed the neighbor throwing the pipes into a dumpster and heard the tone they were making. With the neighbor's permission, he retrieved the pipes and took them home and stored them. An idea popped into my head that those melodic pipes could serve as a wind chime at the back of the church. My brother was excited about that idea also. I obtained permission from our committee to hang them in the tower. Bill Clark agreed to make all the necessary hardware to hang the pipes and Don Chamberlin artfully crafted the clapper. Out of a dumpster arose a wind chime that emits melodic music when the breeze blows.[23]

---

21 Carmichael Presbyterian Church, A Service of Dedication for McMillen Hall, August 26, 2007.
22 Carmichael Presbyterian Church, *Annual Report 2006.*
23 Ken DeYoung, Letter to the CPC Centennial Committee, July 8, 2020.

Saving the Adobe and Installing New Stained Glass Windows

A capital campaign begun in 2009 originally included paying down debt on completed work along with a bundle of new projects, such as renovating the back parking lot and re-roofing the sanctuary and chapel to protect the adobe bricks from water erosion. Due to economic uncertainty as the Great Recession unfolded, the Session chose instead to use all money raised toward debt reduction. Two years later they conducted a targeted mini-campaign to "save the adobe" and raised $96,000 for the purpose. The building committee made the money stretch farther, thanks to a Carmichael-area neighbor who donated two pallets of terra cotta tiles that matched the existing roof tiles, with enough left over for future repairs.

The campaign's call to action—Save the Adobe—lent itself nicely to CPC's Drama Team (see Chapter 4), which presented a skit for worship featuring a talking white brick played by Scott Rathburn, who explained in humorously specific detail what would happen if he and his fellows were allowed to keep deteriorating. The stewardship team made Save the Adobe buttons to advertise the campaign. The buttons featured an illustration of the brick, complete with arms and legs, and a face with glasses and red curly hair to look like Pastor Keith.

Following on the heels of Save the Adobe came another back-burner project: restoration of the small stained-glass windows in the chancel. "Plans for the restoration were developed years ago, but funding was always a problem," explained Buildings and Grounds Committee chair Dick Jacobi in his annual report for 2011. "However, with the roof work underway, now seemed to be the right time to do it." Memorial and honorary gifts raised an additional $22,000 for the update, and again the budget was stretched due to home-grown ingenuity. A team of church high schoolers put in a long weekend mixing mud and molding adobe bricks to replace those that would need to be moved for the window installation.

Jimmi Mishler led the effort for the new chancel windows, to be placed above the choir loft, having learned by happenstance that designs existed for them. She described her discovery this way:

> I was researching background on Cummings Studios, in preparation for the 75th anniversary of our founding, and found that they were no longer in San Francisco but had moved to Massachusetts. In talking to the son, who had taken over [the business] from his father, he asked if we had ever completed the chancel windows. I had no idea what he was talking about. He dug into the files then stored in his attic and sent me the rough designs drawn in 1951. It took several more years before we could get the chancel walls rebuilt to their original design, raise memorial gifts and get the windows installed.[24]

In 2013 the final eight windows were installed, completing the original Cummings Studios design from 1951. They depict:

- The Annunciation
- The Nativity
- The Epiphany
- The Baptism of Jesus in the Jordan
- The Transfiguration
- The Crucifixion
- The Resurrection
- The Ascension of Jesus into Heaven

The windows were dedicated on June 16, 2013. Former Pastor Jim Clark joined with Pastor Keith DeVries in leading a litany of dedication.[25] Describing the process that had taken place, Jimmi continued:

> The architect who reworked the window openings and oversaw the project is Joe Sanford, son-in-law of CPC member Ray Collison. He deserves much credit for the detail work, even to...getting the raw materials to make the bricks, and arranging for our youth to make the bricks that were needed to rebuild the openings.[26]

---

24 Jimmi Mishler, personal communication, May 21, 2023.
25 CPC Sunday Bulletin, June 16, 2013
26 Jimmi Mishler, personal communication, March 24, 2020.

Local historian Susan Maxwell Skinner recounted in *Carmichael Times* how, in 1946, teenagers from the church had made some of the adobe bricks for CPC's chapel. The church's current youth group had repeated history. "In one muddy weekend, young congregants...used 67-year-old templates to produce nearly 200 bricks for the chancel project."[27] Two of the youth, Drew and Doug Dickson, were grandchildren of Jim Dickson, who had helped build the chapel.

In 2017, subsequent to the work on the chancel windows, the sanctuary doors were replaced using funding from memorial gifts and gifts honoring loved ones. The new doors featured stained glass windows with words from Psalm 100: "Enter His gates with thanksgiving and His courts with praise." Jimmi Mishler said that the windows, given by the family of George Daugherty, had been moved from the chancel during the 2013 installation. Artist Gerry Ensminger re-worked them to fit the space in the new sanctuary doors.[28] During the dedication litany for the new doors, the congregation gave thanks for the opportunity to create both a welcoming entrance and "portal to the world in which we are called to serve and share the good news of God's love."[29]

HVAC and Parking Lot Upgrades

The heating, ventilation, and air conditioning system for the church sanctuary reached the end of its life span in 2021 after forty-plus years of service. Informed both by the COVID-19 pandemic and the church's recent Earth Care Congregations pledge, the Buildings and Grounds Committee elected to install a new, energy-efficient HVAC unit that included a UV-C filtration system to help keep viruses from circulating in the indoor air.[30]

As noted above, a campaign drive to renovate the back parking lot was started in 2009 but the monies received were ultimately re-directed toward debt reduction. Nevertheless, enthusiasm for repairing the parking lot

27 Susan Maxwell Skinner, "Windows of Faith," *Carmichael Times*, July 17, 2013, http://www.carmichaeltimes.com/back-issues/pdf_files/volume_33_pdfs/Times%2007-17-13.pdf.
28 Carmichael Presbyterian Church, *Annual Report 2017*.
29 Carmichael Presbyterian Church, Dedicating Our Sanctuary Doors, June 25, 2017.
30 Keith L. DeVries, "Happy New Year," in *Mission Bell* (February 2021).

inspired many gifts and bequests to the Parking Lot Fund. Among its defects was poor drainage, which during the rainy season resulted in a persistent puddle and mosquito vector known to CPC folk as Lake Carmichael. By 2021 when the Parking Lot Task Force began meeting, ample funds were available for paying design consultants. Shade structures with solar panels had been discussed as part of the Earth Care Congregations designation, and as a way of saving on the church's energy bill, but this was tabled until the main design was complete. First, the task force had to consider whether to:

- add fencing and gates for security, as had recently been done to restrict entry to the administrative offices and alleyway

- upgrade the bricked-in planter boxes, which were vulnerable to weedy overgrowth and sometimes used as garbage dumps and toilets by people camping overnight

- incorporate a drainage or stormwater treatment plan[31]

On consultation with a certified arborist, the parking lot team decided to adopt a "green" approach, which would include attractive landscaping, shade, and drainage to be provided via a central bioswale area containing low vegetation and trees, and a permeable pavement material. The upgrade would also include a ramp next to the stairs leading to the back entrance of the church, and new efficient LED lights.[32]

Parking lot upgrades had not yet begun at the time of writing. However, in conversation about the anticipated work, CPC member Ann Kerr shared this family story:

> My dad, Bill Levering, did the land surveying for all the property between the church building and back to Robertson Avenue. He also purchased that land and donated it to the church, and basically made sure all the jaggedy property lines were straight. When my granddaughter Gretchen did her architecture engineering internship with Mogavero Architects, she got to do some work on the parking lot, which is on that property. It came full circle back to her great-grandfather.[33]

31 Tim Farley, "It's Not Easy Being Green," in *Mission Bell* (May 2022).
32 Carmichael Presbyterian Church, *Annual Report 2022*.
33 Ann Kerr, personal communication, October 2022. Bill and Cathy Levering's 1978 land donation is documented in *Heritage of Faith*, 138.

Technological and Spiritual Infrastructure for Welcome

As part of the sanctuary upgrades made during the Legacy of Faith building campaign, a new sound system with microphones, amplification devices, and control board was added, as were capabilities for video recording. The "tech team," as the people responsible for these new systems came to be called, created VHS tapes, and later DVDs, of each Sunday's service, which office staff then mailed to church members who could not attend worship.

Those in the building on Sundays benefitted from the tech team's work as well. Thanks to the new microphones and a closed-circuit television system, parents rocking their babies in the "cry room" could follow along with the service, as could volunteers working in the Welcome Center and those preparing coffee in the Gathering Place. New monitors added in later years allowed choir members, seated in the loft pews behind the pastor, to see the pastor's face during the sermon, and to see the children when they came up for the Children's Time.

In addition, the tech team used computers and a projector to display words for the contemporary songs on the drop-down screen. They also published audio versions of sermons, and later video, to the church website. When the church buildings shut down after the March 15, 2020 service in compliance with public health orders to contain the spread of COVID-19, most of the needed technology infrastructure was already in place, as were several knowledgeable and reliable tech people (who also all happened to be CPC members). Despite this, pivoting to livestreamed services to allow worshippers to stay contagion-free at home, was no small feat.

Steve Parker, Jeremy Sparks, and others who led the church tech team had, over the previous eight years, begun posting sermon videos online to the church's YouTube channel. They now needed to arrange for livestreaming of full worship services on YouTube, which in addition to new technical procedures, involved a quick study of whether copyright laws would still apply to churches playing copyrighted music. They added text for all the prayers and readings to the videos to make online worship services as accessible and welcoming as possible.

Members of the Session's Worship Division printed out photos of church members and taped them to the pews in the nave and choir loft, as a reminder that the congregation could still be together even while dispersed. They reached out to families and individuals of all ages to solicit lay readers. Instead of coming to the sanctuary to read from the lectern microphone, readers would create videos at home on their personal devices and submit them via a link to the church's cloud internet service. Pastor Ivan emailed materials to readers during the week and assisted those who needed help with technology in recording the prayers and calls to worship. As the choir could not meet to rehearse, online worship sometimes featured videos of choir anthems recorded years before. On a few occasions Pastor Ivan assembled "virtual choir" collage videos, unifying six to ten singers' parts into one audio track. Of this time in the church's history, choir member Nancy Studer said that by offering livestreamed worship services each Sunday, CPC was acting on an opportunity to live out its mission of welcoming. She continued:

> I know it takes a lot of work to put those [videos] together! I think we are able to reach shut-ins in a new way that may help them to feel like they are at our services too. We enjoy being able to come together with our friends as well as participate in meetings through Zoom. Thank goodness for technology that makes that possible.[34]

In 2020, the traditional Palm Sunday parade down the center aisle of the sanctuary became a car parade in the church parking lot, with church members proceeding slowly through the route in their vehicles, waving palm branches out of their windows, to thank all the worship leaders as they stood outside after the service. In similar, though more subdued fashion, Ash Wednesday in 2021 was a drive-through experience, with each worshiper provided a small, sealed cup containing a communion wafer and grape juice, and a cardboard square pre-marked with ashes to mark their foreheads.

All meetings moved to the Zoom platform through the church's new institutional account. Sunday school students, Session division leaders, deacons, pastors, and all who wanted to participate in virtual coffee hour

---

34 Nancy Studer, interview by Lisa Benadom, August 15, 2020.

had to quickly learn to log in and use their device's microphone and camera controls. Worshipers watching the livestream learned to register their attendance using a Google form, and used the comment function in YouTube to greet one another. Considering the high median age of the congregation, online participation was surprisingly robust.

The 2021 church annual meeting on Zoom achieved a quorum, and new elders and deacons were duly voted in. They were ordained and installed online that spring as well. Prior to COVID-19, the protocol during ordination and installation of church officers was for currently serving deacons and elders to proceed to the front of the sanctuary for a laying on of hands during the prayer of blessing. With the ceremony happening on Zoom, newly elected leaders instead wore stoles with colorful hand shapes lovingly sewn on them by Mary MacDonald. Those attending the Zoom meeting raised the right hand of blessing on their device cameras to symbolize the laying on of hands.

Of the many COVID-related worship changes that provided a welcoming presence online, perhaps the most theologically significant was the Session's approval of "extending the communion table." This allowed worshipers to serve communion to themselves and their families at home while they watched the once-monthly celebration of the sacrament online.

According to the *Book of Order*, the sacrament of the Lord's Supper is normally observed in communion—that is, in the physical company of others. When pastors, deacons, or elders bring the bread and wine (or juice) to a person's home, their presence represents the whole congregation. But can that communal presence be replicated for worshippers using a television or computer screen to connect with others? The Office of the General Assembly and the Stated Clerk of the General Assembly of the PC(USA) issued a statement on March 24, 2020, offering guidance for congregations in this matter. It read, in part:

> In emergency circumstances there may be situations in which the pastoral needs of that moment require that the church take actions that run contrary to normal practice. During an emergency or a pandemic in which the church is unable to gather or advised not to gather in person for reasons of public

health, a congregation's session may determine that this includes observing communion online.[35]

Once home communion was instituted, one could scroll the Friends of Carmichael Presbyterian Church Facebook page on a communion Sunday and see a variety of devotional place setting photos shared by worshiping friends. As of 2023, CPC member Bep Van Der Mik would still regularly post photos of her dining table set with bread and wine, simple dishware, and wooden cross, laid with care alongside her worn Dutch-language Bible.

To continue its mission of welcome during the pandemic, CPC still needed a steady flow of income. Even though operating expenses were lower while most of the church buildings sat empty—the Food Closet kept going, as it was classified as an "essential service"—staff salaries and other bills still needed to be paid. The church thus applied for and received a Paycheck Protection Loan from the federal government.

On first shutting down in March 2020, church leaders worried that pledge receipts would drop off, as people either experienced financial difficulty due to job loss, or forgot to send their offering by mail. Various methods of online giving had been available for some time, but these were now more actively publicized in the newsletter and on slides shown at the beginning of the livestream worship service, to encourage more people to switch over. Pastor Ivan wrote a prayer on the spirituality of pledging for CPC's November 2020 stewardship campaign, which was also published in the national magazine *Presbyterians Today*:

> Dear God, I liked licking the bittersweet glue and sealing it tight. That was my unique number on those offering envelopes. I would place it upside down in the plate, and piled with others, it had some heft to it. Now I just tap "send," "submit" or even "checkout," and I worry my lonesome commitment is not a tangible-enough response to your generous grace. As I click to make this commitment, help me feel the heft of your yoke and

<hr>

35 "Advisory Opinion: Communion in an Emergency/Pandemic," updated March 24, 2020, https://oga.pcusa.org/site_media/media/uploads/oga/pdf/advisory_opinion_communion_in_an_emergency_or_pandemic.pdf.

submit to the bitter burden of discipleship made sweet by your gentle and humble heart. Don't let me check out, but instead go all in with your church so we can discern your way and be sent together. Amen.[36]

As it turned out, fewer people pledged for 2021 than had for 2020. However, the amount pledged per "giving unit" was higher, more than canceling out the difference. CPC would stay financially stable through the pandemic.

With the church expending so much energy on the effort to keep members engaged, one perhaps unanticipated advantage of livestreaming worship was that it allowed potential new members to learn about the congregation. The services were publicly accessible on YouTube, with links clearly noted on the church website. CPC members David Stoffel and Marianne Lowenthal, who joined in 2023, said CPC seemed so welcoming online that they felt encouraged to visit when the building opened for worship and meetings again. They enjoyed both pastors' sermons, and were glad to learn of the church's concern for Earth care and its commitment to ending systemic poverty and racism.[37] The saw the video calls to worship, Youth Sunday service, and Advent candle lightings featuring children, and felt confident about bringing their two young boys to church along with them.

Sunday Worship and Music

Let all things be done decently and in order.

—1 Corinthians 14:40

Presbyterians who have led worship planning, session meetings, or any other aspect of church business will likely agree that 1 Corinthians 14:40 is a touchstone in their theology of showing reverence before God and of getting things done. And many Presbyterians conveniently forget that

36 Robyn Davis Sekula, "The spirituality of pledging: Praying our way into 2021," *Presbyterians Today*, October 23, 2020, https://www.presbyterianmission.org/story/pt-1120-money/.
37 David Stoffel, personal communication, December 4, 2022.

the biblical writer Paul was counseling the Corinthians on the practice of speaking in tongues. They hear the phrase "Let all things be done decently and in order" as a call for disciplined action, such as sitting through training as a new deacon or elder, or learning about church governance from the *Book of Order*. For some it may evoke anxious memories of trying to follow correct protocol for communion serving. And for others, it provides comfort, as it describes the predictable unfolding of each Sunday's hour of prayer and praise.

The Rev. Matt Gaventa of University Presbyterian Church in Austin, Texas, pointed out in a sermon posted to his blog that the first letter of Paul to the Corinthians is not about suppressing those who speak in tongues during worship or who otherwise behave in ways considered disorderly. While the gift of tongues isn't commonly exercised in Presbyterian worship, Paul's instruction means that if someone does speak in tongues, there should also be someone there to interpret the meaning of the speech, so that all may experience the Holy Spirit moving.

> [W]hen Paul talks about "decency and order" he's not talking about suppressing any particular kind of aberrant speech or aberrant behavior. He's talking about creating worship that recognizes the fundamental and equal dignity of everyone who comes, that everyone who comes has an equal right to participation in the life of the Spirit.[38]

It is in this spirit of welcome and inclusion that order and predictability continue to characterize worship at CPC, as they have since its start as a worshipping community.

Though exact notation in worship bulletins has varied over the years, CPC services, like those in most Presbyterian churches, proceed through the same basic stages every Sunday:

- Gathering in God's Name

- Confession and Assurance of Pardon

---

38 Rev. Matt Gaventa, "Decently and in Order," August 24, 2014, https://mattgaventa.com/2014/08/24/decently-and-in-order/. The sermon is also a reflection on the public statement issued by PC(USA) following the shooting death of eighteen-year-old Michael Brown in Ferguson, Missouri.

- The Word Proclaimed
- Thanksgiving and Response to the Word
- Prayers of Intercession
- Charge and Benediction
- Closing Song or Postlude

On examination of bulletins from 1998 to 2023, the only substantive variation was the position of the sermon, which until about 2002 fell near the end of the service. Since that time, the scripture reading and sermon took more of a central role, falling closer to the halfway point of the hour-long service.

Worship as Welcome

> *As kids we were always welcome in worship participation. Seeing the example of my parents being liturgists and so on, taught me "this is how we live at church."*[39]
>
> **—Rev. Christa Brewer**

Interviewees for this book who grew up at CPC echoed the Rev. Christa Brewer's comment above. For example, Deborah Bush Sneed said,

> I remember watching my father ring the church bell, walk down the aisle to collect the offering, and serve communion. My mother, who was also a deacon...welcomed guests at the guest book in the narthex. I had the same opportunities as a deacon. I was involved with CPC because it was my church home.[40]

Part of the church's welcome is its inclusion of many people in active roles. Children are specifically welcome to watch and learn how to serve from adults, just as they would watch and learn how to do different tasks in their own homes.

---

39 Rev. Christa Brewer, interview by Susan Herman, June 7, 2022.
40 Deborah Bush Sneed, interview by Kathy Lewin, March 2021.

In the 1960s, CPC ushers—all men— "wore suits and ties and they would take the lady by the arm to their pew," said Carol Honnold.[41] However, by the 1990s, entry into the sanctuary on Sunday was markedly less formal and more practical. Dick Piper, church greeter extraordinaire, explained that in 1977 after he "graduated" from his first three-year term on the Session, he realized how bleak the rear entrance to the church was. Even though the space provided ample parking, "there was no sign on the back of the church at the time. There was no way strangers could find their way through without asking." Dick therefore assumed the duty of greeting and orienting visitors who entered from the Robertson Avenue side of the building. By 1985 Mariner groups began sharing the duty of greeting among themselves, covering both north and south entry points.[42]

In the late 1990s hospitality became a major focus for CPC leaders. The Rev. Dr. Gary Califf worked with the deacons and the newly formed Parish Nursing program (later Health Ministry; see Chapter 3) on hospitality.[43] These groups over time systematized practices like signing the pew registry pads, wearing name tags, offering hearing devices and large print hymnals. They also purchased first aid kits and an AED (automated external defibrillator), and created safety protocols. Duane Johnson, longtime usher captain and retired Air Force officer, spoke of putting his organizational and management skills to use serving as an usher, which he did on and off since joining CPC in 1984. He recalled numerous times when a parishioner fell ill and he had to call 911. He put together teams of ushers that were "well-oiled machines," helping worship services proceed seamlessly.[44]

Once safely into the sanctuary, one can see that worship at CPC features its pastors and music leaders, but also includes lay readers, children who come to the front of the church for the Children's Time (a short lesson with the pastor), and prayers of thanksgiving and intercession voiced aloud by individuals in the congregation. Starting in 2010, individual members' faith stories also became part of the worship experience, and were shared as a response to the Word.

---

41 Carol Honnold and Caron Treon, interview by Susan Herman, March 1, 2020.
42 Dick Piper, A History of Greeting, April 5, 1995.
43 Rev. Dr. Gary Califf, interview by Wayne MacRostie, May 27, 1997.
44 Duane Johnson, interview by Lisa Benadom, February 11, 2021.

As mentioned in Chapter 1, for a few decades the church had over 1,000 members. To manage the large classroom capacity that was needed, children's Christian Education time took place in multiple shifts, including during the worship services. But by the late 1990s Sunday school had its own dedicated time slot in between the two services. Children up to age ten or eleven still had the option to spend part of the worship hour in their own age-appropriate programs, but were not required to do so. In 2015 the deacons began placing special bookmarks in all the pew Bibles reminding adults in the congregation that the presence of children in worship—yes, even their restlessness, crying, or animated scribbling—was a gift to the church.

As part of the order of worship in Presbyterian churches, congregations actively respond with gratitude to hearing the Bible message. They give their offerings during this time. The "response to the Word" is also another opportunity to welcome. It can be a time to welcome all to the table for the Lord's Supper; it can be used for baptism, confirmation, reception of new members, or recognition of another milestone. Commissioning a group that is leaving on a mission trip can also be a response to the Word, as can the ordination and installation of new deacons and elders. The celebration of Christian marriage can also be a response to the Word. In recent CPC history, at least one couple chose to be married on a Sunday morning during worship (Leon Wartinger and Laura Garwood in April of 2017).

Music Groups

Carmichael Presbyterian Church has had many choirs over the years; *Heritage of Faith* mentions that at one point in the 1970s there were seven vocal groups—and that was not counting Living Water, an *a cappella* group that ran from 1979 until 1991. In addition to adult, children, and youth choirs, many other groups have shared in music leadership at CPC. These include handbell choirs, the church orchestra, and the contemporary worship band.

As a leader in multiple music groups over the years, Karen Gray said,

> I have most experienced God when I sing. There were moments singing with the Celebration Singers that we would sing a certain phrase or hit a certain harmony "just so," and I felt the Spirit of God in me and in that room. There have been moments singing with the Contemporary Worship Team that have moved me nearly to tears

because God is speaking to me so clearly through the music.... It's hard to explain the visceral reaction I have when those moments come—it's an overwhelming surge of emotion that brings a smile to my face, tears to my eyes, gratitude and joy to my heart. One Sunday, shortly after my mom [Viki Tozier] had begun treatment for cancer, we sang: "You walk on the water, You speak to the sea, You stand in the fire beside me. You roar like a lion, You bled as the lamb, You carry my healing in your hands, Jesus." Thinking about my mom and all she was enduring in light of those lyrics made me cry. I know the Spirit of God was in the sanctuary that day.

While participating as a singer or musician may not be for everyone, the willingness of CPC leaders to start new groups to meet diverse spiritual needs and uplift diverse voices supports its mission to welcome all.

Heritage of Faith recounts how three CPC musicians, after attending a music festival in summer 1978 held at Mt. Hermon in the Santa Cruz Mountains, started the tradition of handbell ringing at CPC. Once the three-octave set of bells were purchased in 1980, they began to see heavy use by junior high and high school ringers, as well as the Mission Bells adult group, along with the Chancel Ringers, another adult group that rehearsed in the evenings. By the mid-1990s the purchase of an additional two octaves rounded out the set. The Mission Bells were still ringing but the youth bell choirs had condensed into one—the BACH choir (for Bells in Christ's House), directed by Carol Honnold.[45] After a few years the BACH choir also folded, leaving Mission Bells as CPC's sole ringing group.

In September 2000, the Mission Bells had vacancies for two players. Musician Margo Scandella stepped in for one of the spots on the invitation of her friend Wilma McCammon. Recalling her start as a bell ringer, Margo said,

> I remember the day when I first got a glimpse of handbell music. The church orchestra was in the old McMillen Hall on stage to play and the bells were set up in front of the stage on the floor. I was sitting with my cello on the edge of the stage and I looked down at the bell music just below me. I was aghast! HUGE chords of 10–12 notes on each beat of a measure...I said

---

45 White, Herman, and Segur, *Heritage of Faith*, 143.

> to myself that I would never play in the bell choir with music
> like that. I thought it just completely impossible![46]

Margo soon picked up the needed skills to play handbells, though she resolved to stick with the same position in the bass clef for twenty more years.

The Mission Bells performed in several venues around Carmichael and the greater Sacramento area. They also attended bell conferences and music festivals as far away as Estes Park, Colorado, and Hawaii. Most players were from CPC's membership, though others from Northminster Presbyterian and Celtic Cross Presbyterian stepped in from time to time. On hearing feedback from prospective ringers who didn't read music, and those who needed an evening rehearsal time to be able to participate (as opposed to the usual time of 9:30 on Monday mornings), bell director Marti Wallace started a new group called Carillon in 2014. Carillon rang for CPC services several times each year until the COVID-19 pandemic.

In 2020 when the handbell ringers were forced to take a break, Marti sent an email of gratitude, extending "special recognition and love to Margaret Herman, Jimmi Mishler and Carol Piper, our three founding members of Mission Bells back in May 1980, and to all the directors through the years." The group was to have celebrated its fortieth anniversary in May 2020 with a special concert at church, but this had been canceled due to COVID-19.[47]

Music director Randy Benfield started the church orchestra in 1995 and kept the group going through 2013. At the first rehearsal only two volunteers showed up: Caron Honnold (Treon) and Brian Fair. But the group grew quickly to about twenty-five members at its peak, as the church had a rich pool of talent.[48] Instrumentalists Wayne and Barbara Reimers had deep-rooted music connections in the community, as did Duane Johnson, Vernon and Gail Bisho, and others. Starting in 1996 the orchestra played monthly in worship services. On the weekend before Memorial Day there was for many years a traditional jazz festival in Sacramento; parallel to that CPC also observed a Jazz Sunday in

---

46 Margo Scandella, personal communication, May 18, 2020.
47 Marti Wallace, personal communication, May 16, 2020
48 Benfield, interview.

May combining its own instrumentalists of all ages with other musicians from the community for a concert and swing dance in McMillen Hall.

Contemporary Worship

> *Liturgy is what happens in a worship service,*
> *and ceremony is the way we do it.*
>
> **—Rev. Jim Clark (paraphrased)[49]**

Chapter 1 mentions the launch of CPC's contemporary worship service under the leadership of the Rev. Dr. Gary Califf, Garrett Torgerson, and Mark Studer in 1997. According to Garrett, by the mid-1990s, the church was holding two regular Sunday morning worship services:

> The second service...was basically a rehash of the first service, except that the choir would get up and vacate after their anthem, so they didn't have to sit through the sermon twice. Remaining in the congregation after this departure had the odd feeling of being left behind after the rapture, if Presbyterians believed in such things. But that was an improvement over the previous incarnation, which featured a senior high choir [Carillon Choir] that had dwindled to the point it wasn't feasible to continue anymore.... The second service always had the feeling of an afterthought, at least as I remember it.[50]

Contemporary-style services were first held on Sunday evenings at 5:00 p.m. Mark Studer, who had originally come to CPC with his family as a teenager but had fallen away from the church for a few years, accepted the call from Pastor Califf to help start the new service. He said that the invitation from Pastor Califf "is what brought me back into the church" after a time of spiritual struggle. Mark made music selections, played guitar, and led the singing; his brother Chris played the piano. They were paid for their part in leading the new service. Describing their partnership, Chris Studer said,

---

49 Rev. James C. Clark, interview by Wayne MacRostie, June 12, 2002.
50 Garrett Torgerson, Evolution of the CPC Second Service, October 20, 2022.

> Mark and I worked together and when it came to worship, he was the leader. I was an accompanist. It was kind of funny because he did a lot of the logistics, but when it came to working out musical stuff in rehearsal, he turned to me a lot of the time. There were plenty of times when working out harmony parts or something he would ask me to take that part. Being brothers and working together was a lot better than I was anticipating.[51]

Chris said that the music they chose comprised a variety of contemporary genres, including some camp songs with roots in folk music and the Jesus movement of the 1970s, as well as worship songs and rock-pop hits on commercial Christian radio. According to Mark, attendance at the evening service was around thirty to forty; then after a year, contemporary service moved to the 11:15 a.m. slot on Sundays, taking over what had been the second traditional service. Attendance at the "new" second service grew to around 200.

Mark noted that the mid-1990s was the height of the so-called worship wars,[52] and that moving contemporary worship into the second service slot caused some conflict at CPC that mirrored the broader trend in Christian congregations. The conflict had partly to do with differences in philosophy over what worship should look and sound like—some, for instance, questioned whether music that mimicked what was popular on the radio could be considered reverent before God or appropriate for worship. Some questioned whether the lyrical content of the contemporary repertoire focused too heavily on individual spiritual experiences rather than the church's experience and calling as a community of faith. There was also conflict over whether the second service was "draining" children and young families away from first service.[53]

Was one service "doing it right," while the other was "doing it wrong"? Opinions among those interviewed for this book were varied and nuanced, but two main themes came through. Initiating the contemporary service opened the door to new members and helped retain existing members who

---

51 Chris Studer, interview by Susan Herman, November 3, 2022.
52 Barna Group, "Focus On "Worship Wars" Hides The Real Issues Regarding Connection to God," November 19, 2002, https://www.barna.com/research/focus-on-worship-wars-hides-the-real-issues-regarding-connection-to-god/.
53 Rev. Mark Studer, interview by Susan Herman, October 26, 2022.

wanted to refresh their faith life with music that felt relevant. It also created more opportunities for teens and young adults in the church to be leaders.

In terms of raw numbers, membership at CPC did not increase with the launch of contemporary worship. However, a few who joined the church during the early years of the contemporary service cited inspiring music as one of their reasons for coming. As one example, the Ludwig family joined CPC when they transferred their membership from Westminster Presbyterian in 2001. The youth music program at Westminster had petered out. Hannah Ludwig, then eleven years old, loved singing and had already begun voice and piano lessons with private instructors. When the Rev. Carol Pagelsen, also a trained vocalist, joined the church staff in 2002, she and Hannah sang the "Pie Jesu" duet from Andrew Lloyd Webber's 1985 *Requiem* mass. After that, Chris Studer invited Hannah to join the praise band. She sang with the band weekly from age twelve until she graduated from high school. On celebrating CPC's centennial with a solo concert in May of 2023, Hannah—who since leaving Sacramento had begun singing with opera companies and symphonies around the world—took time to discuss her musical beginnings at CPC. She described how being able to lead in worship had helped her grow as a leader and a person of faith.

Some people interviewed for this book expressed sadness and even regret over how the introduction of contemporary service "split the congregation." One who was a teenager at the time said her friends started attending second service but her parents wanted to keep attending first service, and that the change felt like a breakup. (It should be noted that there were already two services, so perhaps the difference was that attendance patterns became more firmly entrenched after the second service became the contemporary service.) Leaders on the Session and its Nominating Committee were aware that separate communities were forming at the two services and made a concerted effort to nominate elders and deacons who were regular attendees at first and second services to work together on these boards.

The Rev. Jim Clark, while expressing a personal preference for traditional ceremony, fully supported the start of contemporary worship at CPC. When interviewed shortly after his retirement in 2002, he said that "liturgical integrity" suffused both the traditional and contemporary services. In other words, no matter the format, worshippers were still gathering in God's name to praise God. They heard the Word proclaimed. They engaged in a meaningful response to the Word. The differences, he said, were in the ceremony "or what you might call style," of offering praise to God. While Pastor Califf's leadership was key in starting the contemporary service, maintaining its liturgical integrity over time was, according to Pastor Clark, due to the leadership of several children of the church—particularly the Studers, Garrett Torgerson and his sister Trina, and Pamela Jacobi.[54]

Mark Studer left the church staff to attend seminary at Princeton in 2001. Chris Studer continued to lead the contemporary service until 2007 when he left Carmichael for Berklee College of Music in Boston, Massachusetts. Jenny DeVries then filled in as interim director of the contemporary worship band for two years, and officially took over the role in 2009. She continued as director until 2022. Jenny, wife of Pastor Keith DeVries, had attended Westminster Choir College in Princeton, and was an avid listener of popular Christian artists. Of her fifteen years leading CPC's second service, Jenny said:

> When Chris headed to Berklee, I accepted the interim position because I had been singing and playing the guitar with the praise band for five years, and I was always willing to sing and play every other Sunday. After a few months, Jay Leek and Paul Zeman asked Keith to call off the search because we were satisfied with the way we had come together.... We could feel the Holy Spirit was alive and well when the children were dancing to the opening songs! I found myself praying for young musical leadership to join us. God was faithful! Gabe [Bisho] joined us and then Will [Condrey]. Musicians need positive feedback, maybe more than most, but we really loved getting thank you notes and positive affirmation on Sunday mornings. I had absolutely no idea that I would be leading music at the contemporary service for so long. But, I had the privilege of making music with really wonderful people![55]

---

54 Rev. James C. Clark, interview by Wayne MacRostie, June 12, 2002.
55 Jenny DeVries, personal communication, May 16, 2023.

Liturgical Arts

Quilted banners and paraments greet worshipers at CPC, evoking thoughts of how the sacred can be woven into everyday art that adds comfort to a family home. In 2002, several CPC members launched a liturgical arts group "with plans to embellish our sanctuary with the meaningful use of color and design."[56] That year Margo Scandella made an Advent quilt and matching paraments for the pulpit and lectern. The *Sacramento Bee* described her idea and artistry in an article in its faith series, excerpted here:

> "It was already August," says Scandella. "And we still hadn't settled on anything. So one day I said to the committee, 'I quilt. Maybe I could come up with something that would work.'"... Soon the retired medical technologist found herself completely absorbed in the Advent project, planning, cutting and stitching together in three months a quilt that normally would have taken six months to a year to complete.

> ..."Before I started on the Advent quilt, I thought a lot about what Advent means to me," she says. "I could imagine this deep blue, swirling sky and an enormous star. The sky is bright near the star. There is a lot of energy with meteors and other stars twinkling. Below the star is the peaceful town of Bethlehem. In the distance, shepherds are watching the star and wondering what it all means."

> To create the movement in the sky, she used more than 20 different fabrics, each in a different print and shade of blue. The pieces were carefully placed to give the sky a swirling, kaleidoscopic effect surrounding the magnificent Advent star. The quilting stitches are done in blue metallic thread that catches the warm glow of candlelight.[57]

Quilted paraments representing each liturgical season were added during 2003 and 2004 (purple for Advent and Lent, white for Christmas and Easter, red for Pentecost, green for Ordinary Time), and Sally Willey made the large wall hanging depicting the descending dove, a symbol of the Holy

---

56 Carmichael Presbyterian Church, *Annual Report 2002.*
57 Gwen Schoen, "The quilter's gift--Margo Scandella's Advent creation was a labor of love for her church," *Sacramento Bee*, December 21, 2002.

Spirit. Quilters also created a pair of banners to represent John 1:55: "I am the vine, ye are the branches." Members of the congregation donated a variety of green fabrics for the leaves, and a team of fifteen women met weekly for three months to applique, hand-bead, and hand-quilt the two banners. In 2004 Margo also created the butterfly Easter quilt. Dave Mauerman and Howard Willey built a storage closet and hanging racks to store all the fabric hangings. Thanks to their loving work all the quilts described were still in regular use in 2023.

CPC's Liturgical Arts quilters also made a large hanging for the Tallac Center at Zephyr Point in 2006. Margo Scandella based the design on a mountain scene with rows of evergreen trees rising from a lake to reach distant mountain peaks, a beautiful motif for the Center's setting at Lake Tahoe. Seventeen women volunteered to sew the modified log cabin squares needed to create the quilt. Margo and Betty Ekstedt sewed all the squares together, and Beverly Rogers did the quilting.[58]

Additional projects included:

- 2007: Lenten banner depicting Jesus in prayer; wedding banner with an image of two overlapping rings

- 2008: Adult-size costumes for a live nativity

- 2009: Praying hands quilt in the Parlor, dedicated to the memory of Maureen ("Mo") Beeby, daughter of quilter Chris Beeby, who passed away that year

- 2010: "Wooly sheep" quilt donated for the Planting Seeds of Faith auction; many more followed in different designs for subsequent auctions

- 2014: Eight Pentecost-themed fabric panels for the pillars in the sanctuary

Members of the middle school youth group, while on their February mission trip to Pacific Grove and Monterey Bay in 2016, created ocean-themed quilt paraments, which debuted on Youth Sunday that year. These were added to the liturgical arts collection and also made appearances for Earth Sunday starting in 2020.

---

58 Carmichael Presbyterian Church, *Annual Report 2006.*

To celebrate the church's centennial, CPC quilters created a new hanging about sixty inches wide by eighty inches long. It featured an image of the church building with a colorful sunrise behind it, and the words "Praising God 100 Years 1923-2023."

Worship and Music Ministry Leadership
From the 1990s to 2023

Randy Benfield started at CPC as the organist in 1995. He then took over the Sanctuary Choir and launched the church orchestra, as noted above. From 1998 until 2008 he also directed the Angel Choir, which was the children's choir. His wife, Marsha, co-directed the Angel Choir for a few of those years. In an interview with Karen Orlando, Randy noted that choir members Dick and Carol Piper volunteered for many years, Dick as choir chaplain and Carol as music librarian.

> The memories that stand out are with the choir and how they care for each other. The choir grew very close together, as a family.... I've had two extraordinary accompanists with Zorana and Trina. I feel very blessed. You don't get accompanists like that, and I've had two.

Listing his favorite people and moments at CPC, Randy said:

- The early staff: Jim Clark was an amazing leader. [Custodian] Jack Hatfield, I won't ever forget. My first Sunday as interim choir director it was cold. When I got into my office, Jack had come into the office earlier and turned on the heat so it would be warm.

- The Christmas Eve services at 11:00. They were very special.

- Singing the [Fauré] *Requiem* in April 2012.

- Taking a group of choir members rock climbing in the Consumnes River Gorge in 1997. It was an over-50 group with Darrell Torgerson and Dave Segur. I led the day trip and it was technical, with ropes. Then when we were all done and I was walking around, I tripped and sprained my ankle. I had to play at the church that night so I had to ice my ankle.

- The retreats. The first one at Marian Retreat Center in Auburn. We went to Zephyr for many and then lately at Leoni Meadows. Eating together and really getting to spend that time to grow closer. Then, of course, Carol Piper and Sally Willey zip lining at Leoni Meadows. And our spiritual focus. Meeting God and meeting each other at the retreats.[59]

As noted above, Mark and Chris Studer directed CPC's contemporary music team in its first years, and then Jenny DeVries led the program. In addition to her work at the church, she worked full time in the administration office at Mira Loma High School. In 2020, Jenny's father moved from his home in Spokane, Washington, to live with Jenny and Pastor Keith in Carmichael. Soon after that, Jenny stepped away from weekly worship leadership to devote more time to caring for her father. She returned to church music in a more limited role in the fall of 2022 as Mission Bells director, and moved its rehearsal time to Monday evenings so that she and others who worked during the day could participate.

From when the congregation reunited for in-person worship in late 2021 until the fall of 2022, music at CPC went through a tenuous time. Session had decided that with the return to in-person worship and attendance still low, a single Sunday morning service at 10:00 a.m. would suffice, and the music used would include both traditional hymns with organ, and contemporary selections with the praise band. When it became clear in early 2022 that the single Sunday worship service would continue indefinitely, Randy Benfield resigned from the church staff.

Soon after, Gayle Litz was hired as a worship consultant and as interim music director. She brought years of experience in both change management and music, having worked in a variety of church and community settings, and was eager to re-boot the choir. She consulted with the Session's Worship Division on how best to stitch two worship services, traditional and contemporary, into one. One strategy Gayle tried was to invite the choir to help lead vocals for the contemporary songs. To facilitate this, she found sheet music notation versions whenever possible, so that repeats and bridges were clearly indicated, and so the singers could read and learn their parts (the contemporary band and vocalists had been working exclusively

---

59 Benfield, interview.

from chord charts more appropriate for improvisation and playing by ear). She also chose a few choir-centric anthems that would incorporate percussion or other elements of the praise band. With a core of only about eight to twelve singers—the choir had lost many members to death in recent years—Gayle felt it was important to encourage congregational singing as much as possible. Thus, she leaned toward accessible selections that would work for a small group of leaders and would encourage those in the congregation to take part.

Easter of 2022 was to be the Sanctuary Choir's post-COVID-19 debut. However, at a midweek rehearsal right before Easter Sunday, several singers became ill with the virus. After a waiting period, they tried again. Over the summer Gayle participated in several discussions with Session's Worship Division, along with interested members of the congregation, on how to make the new "blended" worship accessible to all. One improvement, which was quickly implemented, was to add music notation to the lyrics for the praise songs printed in the worship bulletin.

Keith Atwater and Rick Schlosser joined the church staff in the fall of 2022—Keith as director of music, and Rick as organist. "Music Keith," as he distinguished himself from Pastor Keith, had previously served as CPC's choir director from Easter of 1985 through Christmas of 1987. His new position would include leading both the choir and the worship band.

During his time at Carmichael in the 1980s, Keith Atwater had completed a Master of Arts in Teaching Humanities from the College of Notre Dame in Belmont. He later earned another master's degree, and taught writing, humanities, history, and religion courses at Whitworth College, Sacramento State, and American River College until his retirement in 2021. He also taught music at the junior and senior high school levels and served as choir and music director at three other churches in the Sacramento and Auburn areas.

Reflecting on the many changes in music programming at CPC since his previous stint thirty-five years before, Keith said:

> There appears to be a trend in many churches that the tradi-
> tional, robed adult church choir is getting smaller and older.
> I have found that making extra efforts to put together small

vocal ensembles, locating and including instrumentalists (and vocalists not in any choir) of all ages, and broadening the role of the professional band quartet has paid off in fresh and meaningful worship music. I think the 21st century church music leader needs to be adept in composing, arranging, recruiting, and "thinking (musically) outside the box" in order to enhance everyone's worship experience. This task is made easier in some ways by the most current hymnals used by many churches that now include a very wide variety of styles of songs, many with guitar chords included, and are adaptable for many worship situations.[60]

Like Keith, Rick Schlosser also said he was "enticed out of retirement" to come work at CPC. A U.S. Air Force veteran and proud father, Rick earned bachelor's and master's degrees in music. He later completed both a Masters of Divinity (MDiv; Methodist Theological School in Ohio) and a PhD in Liturgical Studies and Jungian Depth Psychology from Graduate Theological Union and UC Berkeley. Rick was ordained in the United Methodist Church and served churches of many denominations in New York, Ohio, and California as pastor, and as minister or director of music. While at CPC he was also serving as the executive director/CEO of the California Council of Churches and an advocacy organization called California Church IMPACT.

Leaders of CPC's worship and music ministry are listed in Table 2.1.

Table 2.1. Worship Leaders of CPC, 1990s–2023

Position	Name	Years Served
Organist	Randall (Randy) Benfield	1995–2022
	Rick Schlosser	2022–present
Director of Music and Sanctuary Choir director	Randy Benfield	1996–2022
	Keith Atwater	2022–present

60 Keith Atwater, interview by Susan Herman, May 19, 2023.

Sanctuary Choir accompanist	Zorana Randjelovic-Flores	1996–2003
	Trina Spivack	2004–2022
	Rick Schlosser	2022–present
Celebration Singers	Zorana Randjelovic-Flores	Director, 1996–2000 Accompanist, 2000–2003 Director, 2004–2008
Angel Choir (children)	Randy and Marsha Benfield	1998–2008
Waterfall Singers (children)	Nancy Studer, director Kathy Phillips, accompanist	2008–present
Worship Band directors (Contemporary)	Mark Studer	1997–2001
	Chris Studer	2001–2007
	Jenny DeVries	2007–2022
	Keith Atwater	2022–present
Worship Band instrumentalists	Jenny DeVries, Jay Leek, Paul Zeman, Steve Parker, Jason Reed, Will Condrey, Trina Spivack, Gabe Bisho, Matthew Major, Michael Schwab, Merlyn Van Regenmorter	Overlapping periods from 1997 to present
Worship Band vocalists	Willie Wilson, Laura Leek, Tara Studer Calderon, Hannah Ludwig, Karen Gray, Bobby Brow, Lori Roberto, Chris Cameron, Julie Ueltzen, Jolie Crockett, Debbie Berke, Claire Aretsky, Beth Lindley	Overlapping periods from 1997 to present

Mission Bells directors	Ken Brown	1997–2001
	Arleen Michael	2001–2009
	Marti Wallace	2009–2020
	Tammy Sigl, interim	2020–2022
	Jenny DeVries	2022–present
Tech team members: video recording, tape and video copying, sound engineering, computers, projector, livestreaming	Chris Studer, Jeremy Sparks, Steve Parker, Bruce MacLean, Michael Gray, Patrick Sawyer, Daniel Cherry, Michael Aretsky, Josh Keaney, David Stoffel, Noor Bitar, Avonlee Janik	Overlapping periods from 1997 to present

Monday Through Saturday at CPC

Since its very first days, CPC has offered a variety of weekday ministries and hosted community groups on its campus. These include Carmichael Presbyterian Preschool, the Food Closet, and the Counseling Center, as well as the bathroom and shower ministry and gas card assistance. Carmichael Homeless Assistance Resource Team (HART) began holding its board meetings at CPC around 2019. In addition, members of the public have for decades been welcomed onto the church campus for self-help groups such as Alcoholics Anonymous and Al-Anon. All of those ministries are described in Chapters 5 and 6. This section names some of the other groups that have used CPC's campus and describes the church's member-led outreach to local artists.

Community Groups

Scout troops have met at CPC since the beginning. "Scout Troop 55 originally met at Carmichael School in the music room," reports *Heritage of Faith*. Carmichael School was also where the children's Sunday school met starting in 1918, and where a worshipping community formed that later became Carmichael Community Church.

> As early as 1923 the Scouts proposed that the [planned] church building be designed to provide space for them as well as other church functions.... When the church was built, unfortunately, there was no room in the building for the Scout troop. However, by early 1928 a Scout lodge was erected on church property with some materials salvaged from a wrecked building in Sacramento and rough siding from an old movie set.[61]

The Scout lodge is the log cabin pictured on the cover of this book. It was later called Stoner Lodge as a tribute to Irma Stoner, a church member and Sunday school teacher who died in a gas-leak fire at the family's home on Gunn Road. As of 2023, scout troops continue to meet and hold their ceremonies in classrooms and McMillen Hall.

Other community groups that used the facility over the years included the Christian Singles Network, a local group started in 1992, which hosted monthly dances in McMillen Hall well into the 2010s. Church member Michael Aretsky hosted a Wednesday evening Morse Code class for about ten years, attended mostly by amateur ham radio operators. Sports teams held registration nights and end-of-season celebrations in McMillen Hall, and, as of 2023, soccer teams affiliated with Capital Community Athletics (CCA) held weekly practices in the hall. CCA is a Sacramento-area league founded in 2020 for recently resettled refugee and immigrant children, mainly coming from Afghanistan, Syria, and Iraq.

Musicians have found the CPC sanctuary a welcoming space as well. The newly formed Sacramento Children's Chorus held events at CPC starting in December 1999.[62] With the building of the new music rehearsal space, the Kiwanis band also found a home at CPC. Likewise, many private music teachers in the area hosted recitals in the Gathering Place or sanctuary over the years. El Camino High School choral director David Vanderbout regularly had his choirs perform at the church, both in the sanctuary and McMillen Hall, beginning around 2015. "I've always appreciated how CPC connects to the community, and especially its young people," Vanderbout said. "I've been around here long enough to see that not all churches do this. It's rare, in fact."[63]

---

61 White, Herman, and Segur, *Heritage of Faith*, 25.
62 Walt Wiley, "Children's Chorus Offers Songs for the Ages," *The Sacramento Bee*, December 18, 1999.
63 David Vanderbout, personal communication, May 10, 2023

Weddings and Memorials

As part of the fundraising effort for the Legacy of Faith building campaign, CPC's Presbyterian Women in 1999 staged a bridal fashion show and donated the ticket proceeds to the building fund. An article in the *Arden Carmichael News* declared that the adobe chapel at CPC, built in 1946, was dubbed the "Wedding Chapel of Carmichael" because of the vast number of weddings performed there over the years, both for members and nonmembers. (The sanctuary saw hundreds of weddings, too.) Fashion show attendees were encouraged to come wearing dresses they had worn to weddings in the past. They were treated to a retrospective fashion show of bridal gowns and attendants' dresses, some of them family heirlooms dating back to 1887. Several children from the CPC preschool modeled clothing for flower girls and ring-bearers.[64]

In 1999 the demand for a traditional church wedding in CPC's intimate chapel or light-filled sanctuary was not particularly high—the annual report for that year records only six weddings. Perhaps in addition to fundraising, the Presbyterian Women hoped to fan the flame of interest in holding weddings at the church.

As of 2017 religious congregations nationwide hosted twenty-two percent of weddings, down from forty-one percent in 2009 and presumably a higher share in 1999. Reasons cited for this change include the fact that fewer people are being raised in the Christian faith, and that church attendance rates are lower than before, even among practicing Christians. People in the twenty-first century move frequently for work or higher education, making it harder to connect to religious congregations in a new town, and harder to stay connected to a congregation "back home." In addition, many young people coming of age after the 1990s "just do not see marriage (or sex or childbearing) as bound up with religious faith anymore."[65]

Church weddings at CPC reflected the nationwide down trend over the last twenty-five years. From 1998 to 2008 the average number of weddings CPC pastors officiated was 9.6; from 2009 to 2019 it was 4.1; including 2021 and

---

64 Bobbi Jones, "Carmichael Presbyterian Presents Bridal Fashion Show," *Arden Carmichael News*, May 6, 1999.

65 Jacob Lupfer, "Fewer people are getting married in churches. Does it matter?," June 7, 2018, https://religionnews.com/2018/06/07/fewer-couples-are-marrying-in-churches-does-is-matter/.

2022 the average was 3.6 (2020 is excluded because COVID-19 restrictions prohibited gatherings). Yearly statistical reports do not specify whether all weddings CPC pastors officiated took place in the church building.

Numbers aside, Pastor Ivan observed that "an interesting trend we've seen lately is requests from Christian immigrant couples to use our sanctuary. Often the churches they attend meet in storefronts or movie theaters, but for their wedding they want prettier surroundings." He noted that, per church policy in these cases, one of CPC's pastors must participate in the service, and that he and Pastor Keith usually do so by offering a prayer and extending a welcome to the officiant, couple, families, and guests.[66]

In the past twenty-five years the average number of memorial services at CPC each year has held steady at around twenty-three. One might think of this larger number as representing the congregation as it was in 1966, at its zenith. That population of church folk has been dying and will likely be gone in the next ten to fifteen years.

When confronted with the budgetary necessity of hiring only one new associate pastor instead of two in 2008, CPC leaders prioritized calling a congregational care pastor—someone who would shepherd the caregiving ministries of the church, visit members in the hospital and at their homes, and officiate memorial services. They chose not to create a new ordained position for children and youth. When Pastor Ivan joined the staff, he introduced to the Sunday service a moment to stand in honor of CPC members or friends who had entered the Church Triumphant. Soon the congregation was standing in memory every other week.

Art Ministry

Longtime church member Darrell Torgerson revived CPC's art ministry in 2002. According to *Heritage of Faith,* a regular program where works by local artists were shown in the church building had begun in 1965, and continued with some stops and starts through the 1990s. Church member Mary Kay Exstrom, who had been active with the art outreach in the 1970s,

---

66 Rev. Ivan Herman, personal communication, March 27, 2022.

maintained her own studio in Carmichael and had a thriving network of artist friends both in and outside the church. Darrell Torgerson launched the ministry's new iteration in part because it fed his own passion for art and his desire to share many types of art with the congregation. In an undated document he wrote describing the art ministry, Darrell said "everyone can enjoy being an artist, and we can all enjoy a variety of art... all people are artists just waiting to be discovered." He had been a chemistry teacher at Mira Loma High School for several decades and brought the growth mindset of a teacher to his interactions with adult artists, just as he had with teenage scientists.

Another reason for reviving the ministry was to provide community outreach. Artists of CPC wanted to share the brand-new Gathering Place gallery with other artists and art lovers, regardless of faith background (though they did hope some who came for the receptions would consider joining the church). The art displayed would not necessarily have God or spirituality as its main subject matter; rather, it would reflect each artist's joy in their gift. Over the years exhibits included woodworking, photography, weaving, needlework, quilting, painting, drawing, sculptures, pottery, and other media, created both by professionals and amateurs. Describing the launch of the art ministry, CPC member Priscilla Mauerman said:

> The first I knew of the art committee came from a call to our house from Darrell Torgerson. He wanted to know if Dave or I wanted to be on the new art committee that was being formed. I think he really wanted Dave, who is the artist, but I was the one that said yes.[67]

The group's first display was of paintings by Mary Kay Exstrom in February 2002.

The next month's exhibit was on a larger scale. The PC(USA) had designated 2001 as the Year of the Child and solicited artworks from children across the country as a way to "lift up the special needs and gifts of children." A collection of forty-five framed, 11 x 17-inch drawings made by children ages six to seventeen traveled from North Carolina to Carmichael in March of 2002 and was displayed in CPC's new art gallery from March 9 to March

---

67 Priscilla Mauerman, interview by Karen Orlando, December 4, 2020.

24. CPC was one of only three churches west of the Rocky Mountains to host the collection.[68] Reflecting on the first year of the new art ministry, Priscilla Mauerman said that after the Year of the Child exhibit:

> [W]e did seven more shows, and eventually I think it was Ron Standring who put up the molding that now makes it possible for us to hang all the art from high up near the ceiling. Shirley Neff joined our committee, had a show, and then spearheaded a fundraiser that was very successful; we had a used book sale that raised more than $1000. This made it possible for our work to become much easier as we were able to buy the equipment so that we could hang the art from adjustable wires instead of spending hours cutting fishing line the correct lengths so the art would be evenly displayed. We also then put up special lighting.

The group began hosting viewings and receptions open to the public in the Gathering Place on the second Saturday of each month[69] in coordination with Sacramento's Second Saturday evening art walks, which had started in the early 1990s. By the end of 2003 the gallery had exhibited the work of 114 different artists, and the monthly receptions had hosted a total of 465 guests from within the church and the broader Carmichael artist community.[70] Of the Second Saturdays, Priscilla said, "These were not well attended and took a lot of energy." The group changed its strategy—each month's featured artist would greet church members between worship services in the gallery on the first Sunday of the month. Community members were still welcome as always. Priscilla continued:

> Eventually, as we got older and lost key members of our committee such as Russ Franson, we started to hang shows that stayed up for two months instead of one. Because, in the early years, Mary Kay had an art studio open for artists in the community, we did attract wonderful creative people to help with our shows and they continue to be important contributors to our displays. And I count them as my friends along with the CPC members. Some of my fondest memories are of Russ Franson

---

68 "Community Events," *Carmichael Times*, March 5, 2002.
69 Carmichael Presbyterian Church, *Annual Report 2002*.
70 Carmichael Presbyterian Church, *Annual Report 2003*.

engineering creative ways to get light sources so that Jenny DeVries's stained glass would show well, and the open house with Darrell's family providing music. Darrell never stopped thinking of new ways to keep us busy.[71]

Prior to the COVID-19 pandemic, art shows changed every two months. During the time when gatherings were prohibited, Lori Keeney and others who came later to the art ministry created slideshows—sometimes of previous exhibits and sometimes new work—that would play at the end of each online worship service.

Continuing the art ministry into the church's centennial year, members of the Art Committee organized a six-month show of Clair Daugherty's photos depicting the demolition and rebuilding of McMillen Hall. The exhibit also had an interactive board, where viewers were invited to add photos of the church in prior eras from their own collection. In May of 2023 the artists' group hosted a plein air painting day at the church campus. Works begun on that day were then hung in the Gathering Place from July through December.

Membership Process

Heritage of Faith includes few details about the process of becoming a member of CPC and whether that process has varied over the years. It notes that as of the 1980s, potential members of the church took part in several classes to learn about CPC, its governance structure, and how Presbyterian congregations work together through the regional bodies of the denomination (presbyteries and synods) and the General Assembly.[72] Membership fliers from the church archives and descriptions in annual reports from 1998–2023 indicate the process has stayed consistent over the years. Prospective members attended two class sessions with the pastor and members of the Session's Membership Division, and were then formally received into membership in a brief ceremony at the next Sunday's worship service.

As of the 1990s and into 2023 (with classes held by videoconference in 2020 and 2021), the two class sessions typically took place on a Sunday afternoon

---

71 Mauerman, interview.
72 White, Herman, and Segur, *Heritage of Faith*, 146.

and the following Saturday morning. During these, prospective members shared personal stories about their own faith formation and any previous experiences as members or leaders in a congregation. Representatives from different ministries and social groups within CPC, such as Mariners (see Chapter 3), attended the classes to explain their activities and how new members could take part. After the Saturday class, attendees ate lunch with members of the Session and asked further questions. Session members could "examine" prospective members, as this is one of their duties outlined in the *Book of Order*; generally, their questions would revolve around why participants wanted to join the congregation and how they hoped to become involved in its life.

The *Book of Order* describes membership pathways for those desiring to join Presbyterian congregations. They can join by profession of faith, reaffirmation of faith, or transfer of church letter. Affiliate membership is also available to college students and others who may choose to retain their home church membership while living elsewhere on a temporary basis. If a prospective member has not previously been baptized—baptism at any age, in any Christian tradition, is recognized—they can be baptized at the same time they are received into new membership. When new members are presented to the congregation, they declare their intent to participate actively and responsibly in worship, life, governance, and the mission of the church. All worshippers in attendance at the service also reaffirm their baptismal covenants.[73] Tithing is not required of members, though pledges to the church's annual budget or other types of giving are encouraged, as is volunteering.

Other than the pathways noted above and its guidance to sessions on their responsibility to examine prospective members, the *Book of Order* does not stipulate how congregations should conduct member education. As such, it seems important to highlight certain choices CPC's Session has made with regard to the process. First, even though membership classes occur only at specified times (two or three times a year, according to annual reports), newcomers are offered all the same resources for pastoral care as members and, except for voting at congregational meetings and serving as deacons or elders, are also invited to participate in every aspect of the church's life. An undated brochure in the

---

73 Presbyterian Church USA, *Book of Order: The Constitution of the Presbyterian Church (USA), Part II.*

church archives lists eight specific privileges of both current and prospective members, including partaking in the Lord's Supper; receiving care "offered by the deacons, pastors, and other care-giving structures of the church;" attending education classes; attending congregational meetings; receiving the newsletter and all other communications; supporting the mission of the church with money or volunteer time; and presenting children for baptism, provided a parent holds active membership in another Christian church.

Second, encouraging prospective members to share their faith stories honors the diversity of religious backgrounds that characterized CPC's founders. Nothing is assumed about one's previous religious knowledge, experience, or skills in teaching or leading others in the faith. Inviting others to share their stories is an act of welcome.

Commitment to Continual Welcome

In the 1960s, church was the place to be on Sundays. People at your workplace would even ask, "Where do you go to church?" Church was an extension of your business network, just as much as it was a part of your social, family, and spiritual life. You'd build a new church building, open the door, and people would just fall right in.

Now, not so much.

—CPC member Clint Dahlke[74]

There can be no doubt that the Legacy of Faith building campaigns increased the capacity of Carmichael Presbyterian Church to do ministry, and to invite both the already-churched and the unchurched of the community to participate in programs of relationship-building, education, and service. Both physical space and programming are important for the vitality of the church, now and in the future. But as Clint Dahlke alluded to in the

---

74 Clint Dahlke, personal communication, April 2, 2023.

statement quoted above, the church is not the center of cultural life any more in much of US society. Functioning on the margins of the culture, or even as a countercultural force, the church is facing a future in which it needs to be more specific about what actions "welcome" entails, and what populations are included in the term "all."

A few key themes arose in interviews done for this book that may be helpful for readers who want to envision what "welcoming all" could look like in the future. Those themes were: welcoming unhoused neighbors, welcoming neurodiversity, and welcoming people whose faith communities have been *un*welcoming to them in the past.

"How can our Sunday worship be more welcoming to our neighbors experiencing homelessness? We offer care to them during the week but we don't often share our space with them on Sunday mornings." CPC member Paul Kinsella asked this question in an informal class called "Ask Pastor Keith" one Sunday after worship in February of 2023. Paul had recently joined the church and was active with a local advocacy group called Sacramento Area Congregations Together (Sacramento ACT), where similar conversations had taken place. Rather than continue to offer a passive welcome on Sunday morning, CPC's congregation could share its space in a more intentional way, Paul suggested. This might inspire more people to advocate. As a congregation, "we should be talking to our leaders about policies that prevent people from losing their housing in the first place," said Paul.

Pastor Keith responded that the PC(USA)'s Matthew 25 initiative (described in Chapter 1) is designed to help congregations address exactly this type of concern. He did not speak directly to the operational elements of Paul's question, since those would need to percolate through the Session and would likely take a while to do so. Instead, he shared some background information on steps toward greater welcome the congregation had taken in recent years.

He described how CPC's staff and volunteers, through weekday contact with the church's struggling neighbors, had worked hard to become informed and to change their own attitudes, as well as the attitudes of those around them, on poverty and related issues. He cited the church's long-standing partnership with the Sacramento County Sheriff's office and its work release crew that provides building and grounds maintenance once a month, under supervision by church volunteers. "We've also held one-off events like health and resource fairs," in partnership with the sheriff's department, said Pastor Keith (see Chapter 6), "and through these we've been able to model respect for the unhoused community." Making Sunday worship accessible and safe for all is a delicate balance, Pastor Keith acknowledged. But, he recommended, it is important to encourage church members to "learn individuals' names. That's where it starts."

Neurodiversity encompasses neurotypical brain functioning as well as variations such as ADHD, autism, mental health conditions, dementia, and developmental or intellectual disabilities. A child of CPC, Jen Boyd, who now lives in Colorado, noted in an interview that her brother struggled with depression and other conditions as a teen, and that this exacerbated family conflicts. Church was a sanctuary for her. Jen said that now, as a parent of non-neurotypical children, she wants her children to be able to participate in church. She knows how to deal with a range of challenging behaviors, and often educates others in her faith community on these topics. But, she said, she doesn't want to be solely responsible for imparting that education, as this is a burden for her and other parents in similar situations. She described her desire for churches like CPC to share the burden of education and welcoming, saying:

> I've spearheaded things like Parents Night Out for parents with children with special needs. And of course, the really hard thing with that is like, hey, if your kid is not used to our church—if you're taking a child that has developmental disabilities, and you're putting them in an unfamiliar place—that can be super stressful. So the church has to continually be welcoming. And I know from parent groups that I've been in, so many people feel not welcomed in places of worship, and so they just stopped going. And then of course, they get angry and resentful as well. Churches should be everybody's home and yet people don't feel welcome.[75]

---

75 Jennifer Boyd, interview by Susan Herman, October 27, 2022.

The Inclusion Task Force at CPC began its work in 2022 by identifying resources that would help the congregation be more welcoming and inclusive for LGBTQ+ people (see Chapter 1), with the intention that continual learning and skill-building in this area would transfer to other areas, such as greater inclusion of neurodiverse people and people experiencing homelessness. As church leaders apply those lessons, a helpful way to think about welcoming all may be to use the WISE framework: Welcoming, Inclusive, Supportive, and Engaged.

- A welcoming church offers safety and affirmation of all individuals as children of God.

- An inclusive church invites diverse voices into its leadership.

- A supportive church offers specific supports to individuals and families that make their full participation possible.

- An engaged church is involved in community problem-solving, education, and advocacy.[76]

A third way that CPC can welcome all is to reach out specifically to those who have been wounded in other churches. Rachel Carter, who served from fall of 2015 through spring 2019 as director of Carmichael Presbyterian Preschool (CPP, see Chapter 5), was a member of the congregation before joining its preschool staff. Friends invited her to CPC, knowing she needed support as her marriage was ending. Rachel said:

> I came from a church that was part of the CBA—the Conservative Baptist Association. I started to part ways with them when I wanted to leave my abusive marriage and I wasn't supported. The youth pastor's wife told me, "It's never so bad that you should leave." I was granted a permanent restraining order for me and my children. And [a pastor at that church] came to see me at work and said, "It's time to start talking about reconciliation with your husband." These are moments that fractured my relationship with that church. I couldn't keep going somewhere where I didn't feel supported...

---

76 "Becoming a WISE Congregation/Organization Toolkit," accessed May 8, 2023, https://www.mhn-ucc.org/wise-congregation-toolkit/.

I was loved at CPC when I was wounded. I want to be that for other people, and I feel like that's a value of the church: that we're here to love everyone, like Jesus. And Jesus doesn't judge—Jesus, you know, came for everyone. Rich, poor, white, Black, married, single, different people. So that was something I have experienced. It really transformed my faith and put love at the forefront in a way that had been kind of suppressed in me in the past by the evangelical churches I grew up in.[77]

Rachel also reflected in her interview that, in addition to the embrace she received from individual CPC members during a very difficult season of life, she also felt uplifted by the whole church, and empowered to serve. Diana West, another former director of CPP and Rachel's mentor, encouraged Rachel to start and complete a Bachelor of Arts in Child Development. Meanwhile staff member Lisa Torgerson, understanding the economic realities of Rachel's situation, "would roll up with her rolling cart loaded with food [from the Food Closet] and load up my car before I went home for the day. She was quietly blessing me."

Welcoming all is work. It is an intentional set of actions, customized to the needs of each person we seek to welcome. May the next 100 years of CPC be full of quiet acts of welcome, and public ones, that bring those on the horizons to the center.

---

77 Rachel Carter, interview by Susan Herman, January 27, 2023.

Chapter 3
Nurturing Relationships

"Therefore encourage one another and build up each other, as indeed you are doing." (1 Thessalonians 5:11) The letter-writer Paul knew that in order to serve God, the Thessalonians and other fledgling communities of Christ would need to nurture the relationships they had with each other. Christians today still know this to be true, and indeed, practices for nurturing relationships are as fundamental to faith formation for members and friends of Carmichael Presbyterian Church now as they were in 1923.

Good relationships helped build Carmichael Colony, making it a viable community. Through mutual support the congregation survived a diphtheria epidemic, schism, the Depression, and World War II. Early organizations such as the Ladies' Circle and Presbyterian Mariners provided landing spots for new members in the growing congregation, so they could more easily meet one another and get involved. These organizations also played key roles in supporting CPC's social outreach.

The deacons' ministry focused over time on hospitality and congregational care and it, too, included components of social outreach. By the 1990s, several specialized ministries had arisen to complement the deacons' work and to support specific needs for wellbeing within the congregation. For a little over a decade there was also a focused public relations effort to disseminate information about the church into the community. In the last twenty-five years both communications and community partnerships have begun to play larger roles in the nurturing of relationships in the church, presenting complex challenges and new opportunities.

This chapter explores the varied structures for nurturing relationships at CPC over the last 100 years, starting with legacy organizations such Presbyterian Women (PW) and Mariners, which serve a broad range of needs and purposes. Next, we look at the development of congregational care ministries within the Board of Deacons, and how some of these spun off into specialized ministries such as a cancer and faith group and prayer shawl knitting. Then we consider how CPC volunteers and staff used historical data and communication media to nurture relationships across time and space.

Mission and Social Organizations

Each chapter in *Heritage of Faith* includes a section on organizations within the church. Chapter 1 describes how in 1927, an adult Bible class began meeting in the back pews of the new white clapboard sanctuary. They called themselves the Loyal Students. Around the same time the Rev. Samuel Holsinger "brought strong leadership to the Young People's Society of Christian Endeavor,"[1] a nationwide, interdenominational youth movement founded in 1881 that still exists today. Its purpose in the 1920s and 1930s was to help keep older teenagers and young adults connected to the church, as Sunday schools typically served children only up to about age thirteen, by which time they would have finished their formal secular schooling as well.[2] Carmichael's Society of Christian Endeavor continued at least through the 1930s, and many other iterations of youth groups would follow. The Loyal Students became a social group in addition to an adult Sunday school and continued as such for sixty years.

1 Faye White, Margaret Herman, and Marie Segur, *Heritage of Faith: A 75-Year History of Carmichael Presbyterian Church* (Carmichael Presbyterian Church, 1998), 7.
2 Brian C. Hull, *A Brief Overview of the Christian Endeavor Society* (First Fruits Press, 2019). https://place.asburyseminary.edu.

Predating both groups was the Carmichael Ladies' Circle, founded in 1924 for "finding ways and means to build a church" for the congregation, which was then meeting at Carmichael School. In addition to fundraising for a church building they resolved to promote "sociability, community betterment, and higher spirituality." By 1938 the Ladies' Circle had also formed a "social issues arm," joining with a chapter of the international group known as Ladies' Missionary Society. One of its first local missions was organizing school lunches for children in the newly formed Carmichael School District. The Ladies' Circle was open to members of Carmichael Community Church as well as nonmembers.[3]

Around 1947 the Carmichael Ladies' Circle became known as Women's Council. It continued serving the fundraising needs of the church, as well as supporting local missions and the work of Christian missionaries abroad. In 1964 Women's Council adopted the Bible study resources of the denomination's national organization, United Presbyterian Women (UPW), and began formal affiliation with UPW. After the merger of Northern and Southern branches of the denomination in 1983, UPW also merged with its counterpart women's organization in the Southern branch, Women of the Church, and became known simply as Presbyterian Women.

Other groups within the membership of CPC included Crestriders, Golden Age Group, 39ers, Carmichael Men's Club, and Young Couples Club. These tended to be social in nature and tied to parishioners' stage of life. Some groups, like UPW/Presbyterian Women, also had a Bible study and prayer component, plus one or more service outreach projects.

Presbyterian Women

In recognition of the ninety-ninth anniversary in 2023 of CPC's Presbyterian Women, Carolyn McGregor wrote for the March issue of the *Mission Bell* that the "The Mmes (insert their husbands' names here)" raised funds for the first sanctuary of Carmichael Community Church. "Although denied equal partnership in the governance of the church they forged ahead with their mission." Women could not serve as elders in the Presbyterian Church

---

3 White, Herman, and Segur, *Heritage of Faith*, 56-60.

until 1930, and none served in pastoral leadership roles until 1956.[4] Over the years, Carolyn's article goes on to say, the Presbyterian Women of CPC

> [F]ashioned a quilt to raffle, held teas and fashion shows, organized fiestas, held luncheons with cookbook sales, and rummage sales—any activity that would be attended by members of the congregation and the community...when they saw a need within the church, they found a way to fill it.

> Over time women became equal partners, recognized with their own first names, in the governance of the church with all serving positions at CPC open to them.... I have been so blessed to have known so many of the women who have served CCC/CPC, both in [official roles] and quietly working in the background.

Well after women began serving at all levels of leadership in the PC(USA), Presbyterian Women continued to operate as its own entity, working in parallel with the other Louisville-based agencies of the denomination. In 2009, PW "incorporated, establishing itself as a publicly supported integrated auxiliary of the Presbyterian Church (USA). Then in 2016, the General Assembly added Presbyterian Women to the PC(USA) Organization for Mission as a related corporation."[5] Today it is a multifaceted ministry that includes scripture study, leadership development, fundraising for mission giving, and work that nurtures relationships between the PC(USA) and other denominations.

At CPC the Presbyterian Women were also part of the welcoming ministry of the church, most notably serving as memorial service coordinators. They eased the difficult journey for families that had lost loved ones. Their fundraising allowed them to purchase, among other things, "floor tiles, stoves, ovens, and many other much needed kitchen items" for McMillen Hall[6] where receptions for memorial services take place. Presbyterian Women were and are part of the church's nurturing

---

4 Rev. Dr. Rhashell Hunter, "PC(USA) Celebrates 60 Years of Women Clergy," (May 24, 2016). https://www.pcusa.org/news/2016/5/24/pcusa-celebrates-60-years-womens-ordination/.
5 "History," https://www.presbyterianwomen.org/who-we-are/history/.
6 Carolyn McGregor, "Happy 100th Anniversary From the Women who Baked the Cake and Lit the Candles," in *Mission Bell* (March 2023).

ministry as well, offering wholeness through maintaining contact with women experiencing health and life challenges.

In recent years the PW's budget has been around $5,500, half of which they spend locally. The other half is designated for worldwide mission and service projects through the denomination's own mission agency and through PW-specific grantmaking entities, as well as through ecumenical partnerships, such as Church Women United, Church World Service, and Fellowship of the Least Coin.[7]

Members of PW, whether formally serving on the Session, Board of Deacons, or in other areas of the church, have shaped the congregation's vision and mission in innumerable ways. Interviewees for this book noted how important PW was for helping them build leadership skills, as well as form friendships. "PW was really my place. That was where I felt the most comfortable [serving in the church]. I was a Circle leader," said Lisa Levering, referring to the smaller groups within PW that meet in between the monthly gatherings. She continued:

> [A]lso for many years I was the representative to Church Women United...they had monthly meetings and there were the Methodists, Lutherans, and everything. It was always downtown at the Interfaith Service Bureau on Folsom Boulevard. It really opened my eyes to what was going on around me.[8]

Church Women United is a social justice organization dedicated to fighting hunger, violence, and racism. Carolyn McGregor attended those meetings as well. She recalled one where the speakers, both Black women, shared stories of their upbringing in Sacramento. "The terrible thing to me was that they suffered more discrimination in Sacramento than did those ladies who grew up in Mississippi."[9]

Carolyn said one of the highlights of her many years in PW was attending its Churchwide Gathering in Louisville, Kentucky in 2006:

---

7 Presbyterian Women of Carmichael Presbyterian Church, 2017-2018 Handbook.
8 Lisa Levering, interview by Susan Herman, February 3, 2021.
9 Carolyn McGregor and Marie Segur, "Presbyterian Women at CPC," interview by Karen Orlando, January 30, 2020.

> There were just two of us from this church that attended. Jan Hendricks—she attended with me. But there were women from all over the United States, and different parts of the world. The biggest [non-US] contingency was from South Korea.... There were a lot of interesting things. During one of the breaks, I sat down with some ladies from a very small church in New Mexico. The ladies were all Hispanic. There were thirteen of them and they worked all year long making tamales and selling them at church on Sunday to pay for their tuition and travel.

Carolyn also spoke of how PW opened her eyes to the possibilities for women to make a difference, whether or not they were serving in formal leadership positions.

> I'm thinking back to the early 1960s when I became a PW member. We supported quietly under the radar: we supported those that got on the buses and went to the dangerous places in the Civil Rights movement in the South; the migrant ministries too, you know, the terrible conditions that many of the field workers were working under and the children that never got to go to school. Supportive of them all under the radar. All quiet. I'm not so sure we're quiet anymore about some of these social issues and that's good. To me, it's good...we worked in any way that we could to support these various social issues.

Speaking together of their experience with PW, Carolyn McGregor and Marie Segur agreed that the Bible studies they did with their PW Circles were foundational. The Circles "came together monthly for camaraderie and for learning where the Bible study will take us going forward," said Marie.

Marie also talked about how leadership in PW allowed her to find her footing as a leader in other contexts. In her early years with PW—the 1960s and 1970s—Marie also volunteered at Mission Avenue Elementary School's PTA. She eventually became a PTA counselor supporting schools in Carmichael as well as "Twin Lakes, Palisades, some of the schools way out almost to Folsom and Orangevale." In this role she made home visits to families of children in the local schools. Marie said, "I found a lot of homes with dirt floors, lack of refrigeration, and so brought a lot of that to PW to be aware. People [in Carmichael] felt like they were living in a good community, but they really didn't understand the community."

Marie reported back to PW and her small group, Rhoda Circle, about what she learned. Some of the information was hard for them to accept. "They just weren't ready" at the time to hear about topics like poverty and child abuse.[10] Still, Marie's efforts to raise consciousness prepared the ground for social outreach efforts that would come later for CPC.

Carolyn said, "You know, in the secular world I'm quite confident. And I think that confidence has come from my start in PW and the opportunities that were offered me." Both Marie and Carolyn noted that while PW raises money each year separately from the congregation's pledged operating budget and its connectional (denominational) giving, many of its members are "embedded" within CPC's core ministries. They serve as elders and deacons; they knit prayer shawls for church members and make lap robes for former foster youth; they serve in the Food Closet; they wash dishes for Supper on Saturday (see Chapters 5 and 6).[11]

Young women and girls growing up at CPC witnessed excellent models of women in leadership in the members of PW. As the Rev. Pamela Jacobi Starbuck put it, "Women spoke—there was no 'we *let* women speak.' And they served on the Session. My mother [Carole Jacobi], Marie Segur, and others I saw up front, spoke and were respected."[12] This was in the 1980s.

Aside from the leadership opportunities, Lisa Levering said the women of PW "are just great Christians." They showed their love and concern after Lisa's divorce:

> They were all my mother-in-law's [Cathy Levering's] friends, but they stuck by me. I didn't come to church for a year; no one knew where I was. I had been on the PW board for fifteen years and was no longer going to anything at all. So, they called. They called me, they sent me notes, you know, we miss you and I hope you're doing okay. They were just so wonderful and that was the biggest, most affirming thing for me.[13]

10 Marie Segur, interview by Jimmi Mishler, February 21, 1995.
11 McGregor and Segur, interview.
12 Rev. Pamela Jacobi Starbuck, interview by Susan Herman, May 26, 2022.
13 Levering, interview.

Presbyterian Mariners

> *Jim and I were very involved in the Mariner ship Skipjacks. I am pleased that they are still going strong. This group has been very supportive in joy and sorrow.*
>
> **—CPC member Carolyn Biggers**[14]

A child of CPC, Carol Honnold, said that her parents, Leroy and Roberta Wehmeyer, started the first chapter of Presbyterian Mariners at CPC.[15] That was in 1956, and the Wehmeyer's ship was one of the first five ships to be commissioned at CPC. However, an earlier iteration of Mariners had begun in 1950 as the Schooner Club. Members were married couples whose combined ages added up to less than seventy-five (this was later changed to eighty).

By 1955 the Schooner Club had become so large that it divided into multiple "Lifeboats," each with a crew of six to ten couples, which would take charge of duties such as programming, food, and keeping the log book. The Rev. Dr. Pyron McMillen brought leaders of the Lifeboats together in 1956 to formally organize as Mariner ships, using the national Presbyterian Mariners manual as a guide.[16]

According to David Staniunas of the Presbyterian Historical Society, the Presbyterian Mariners organization grew out of concerns over family stability, marriage, divorce, and the roles of partners within marriage. Staniunas elaborates:

> Searching for new means of strengthening marriages and support-
> ing families in the early twentieth century, a number of Southern
> California congregations organized Schooner Clubs, first among
> them one at Calvary Presbyterian Church (Wilmington, Calif.).
> In pastor Louis Evans' words, the clubs would support couples in
> "the Good Ship Matrimony on the Sea of Life." With the Church

---

14 Carolyn Biggers, interview by Kathy Lewin, February 8, 2021.
15 Carol Honnold and Caron Treon, interview by Susan Herman, March 1, 2020.
16 White, Herman, and Segur, *Heritage of Faith*, 114.

their Anchor and Christ their Pilot, other nautical-themed couples' clubs sprouted in the next few years. On June 22, 1936, the Schooner and Clipper clubs of Southern California gathered at Evans' next church, First Presbyterian Church (Pomona, Calif.), for dinner and fellowship as Presbyterian Mariners[.][17]

As noted above, Mariners caught on at CPC in 1950 and was formally organized in 1956, though its purpose was broader than couple and family support. At CPC the Mariner ships also functioned to help new members get plugged into the life of the church, to develop leadership skills, and to serve varying needs of the church, from maintaining the grounds to providing music at special events and much more. Moreover, they provided a social outlet and a way to channel members' creativity.

Phil and Jimmi Mishler joined the church in 1957, when the number of Mariner ships was multiplying. "We formed a ship for 'young marrieds' called the Monitor/Merrimac," said Phil. "This ship eventually became so large, it split into the two individual ships," that is, the Monitor and the Merrimac.[18] Through the years as many as thirty-three new ships were formed at CPC. After 1969, notes *Heritage of Faith*, decommissioning and merging of ships became more common than the formation of new ships. Still, interviewees for this book pointed to Mariners as a feature that attracted them to CPC and then later became indispensable to their faith life.

Dick and Carol Piper joined CPC in December of 1973. Their previous church had no small social groups for adults. Dick recounts their first visit to CPC: "I'm one to look at all the materials in the pew racks. I pulled out a card listing all of the Mariner ships. At that time there were eighteen ships listed in the Fleet. I poked Carol, pointed to the card and said, 'We found it!'"[19]

Jack and Carolee Roach spoke of being invited to the Skipjacks on joining CPC in 1981. From her conversation with them, Lisa Benadom reported that "involvement with Mariners has proven to be a lifeline for the Roaches." Lisa continued:

17 David Staniunas, "Marriage, Divorce, and Presbyterian Mariners," May 29, 2014, https://www.history.pcusa.org/blog/2014/05/marriage-divorce-and-presbyterian-mariners.
18 Phil Mishler and Jimmi Misher, interview by Kathy Lewin, August 5, 2021.
19 Dick Piper and Carol Piper, interview by Lisa Benadom, July 13, 2020.

> Members of Skipjacks have become their extended family with deep
> and abiding ties.... Many times they have served as officers in their
> ship as well as serving as Admirals for the whole Fleet. Some of their
> happiest memories are of Fleet events filled with joy, camaraderie
> and an opportunity to invite the entire congregation to participate
> and learn more about Mariners. Friendships built in Skipjacks have
> also provided traveling companions, which has further enriched
> their lives. It is while serving in Mariners that Carolee was able to
> put her gifts to use. Carolee had worked for an accounting firm, so
> her bookkeeping skills were put to great use as Treasurer.[20]

Don and Thelma Wever joined the Clipper ship on coming to CPC in the
early 1980s. "We became good friends with this group and came to rely
on each other personally," said Thelma. When Don passed away in 2013,
Thelma was glad for the support her ship gave. "I didn't feel as alone because
of the fellowship and comfort of my church friends who were there for
me—and are, even now."[21]

Nancy Studer, who joined the church with her husband Dave in 1984,
said, "We have experienced God at CPC through...our caring friends
in our Mariners group, Companionship." The Companionship liked to
sing—Nancy remembered singing Christmas carols with them at the
Eskaton Memory Care facility, and even putting on musicals for Mariner
Fleet events: *Joseph and the Technicolor Dream Coat*, a Broadway revue,
and a revue of songs by the band Train. She and Dave served together as
Skippers of their ship several times.[22]

Heritage of Faith mentions the dissolution in 1992 of the relationship
between the CPC Mariner groups and the national organization; however,
the Pinafores and Skipjacks opted to maintain their ties. At that time the
CPC Mariners also removed the Fleet level of the organization, so that
individual CPC Mariner groups could post their own "lookouts" and thus
take responsibility for integrating new members into the small groups.[23]
(Fleet events had been the primary vehicle for this before.)

---

20 Jack Roach and Carolee Roach, interview by Lisa Benadom, September 11,
2020.
21 Thelma Wever, interview by Kathy Lewin, April 14, 2021.
22 Nancy Studer, interview by Lisa Benadom, August 15, 2020.
23 White, Herman, and Segur, *Heritage of Faith*, 204-05.

As of 1997 sixteen Mariner ships were active in fellowship, Bible study, and service to the church. The Rev. Dr. Gary Califf reported that at that time, the Lightship and the Minnows played softball regularly at Capital Christian School.[24] Ships would often take charge of hosting large events, such as the all-church picnic. The Mariner ships also began supporting ministries outside of the church such as Loaves & Fishes or the conference grounds at Zephyr Point, calling these ministries their "cargo." Another example of cargo was the ships' regular cleaning and maintenance of their respective adopted areas of the church's buildings and grounds.

Mariners at CPC was so successful at helping its members form lasting friendships that it outlived the national organization, which folded in 2003. Mariner ships just kept on sailing and continued to do so at the time of this writing in 2023.

Upon dissolving the national organization, the Presbyterian Mariners Board created a perpetual fund to honor the Mariners' history. From this fund the denomination awards the Mariners Family Ministry Grant, which provides up to $2,000 of grant funding to PC(USA) congregations, camps and conference centers, and other related bodies of the church to "create or redesign opportunities for family ministry and provide measurable goals for evaluation."[25]

In addition, some remaining members regrouped to become Mariners in Mission, serving Presbyterian camps. In a 2022 article for *Presbyterian Outlook*, Barbara Taylor wrote that this group gathers to work at one of the camps two or three times a year: "[T]asks such as painting, landscaping, cleaning and sewing are performed... We have made countless curtains, T-shirt quilts and camp signs over the years."[26]

The most recent Mariner ships at CPC were formed in 2012: Kinship and Lifeboat. Kinship included many members from the former Lightship, which

---

24 Rev. Dr. Gary Califf, interview by Wayne MacRostie, May 27, 1997.
25 "Mariners Family Ministry Grant." https://www.presbyterianmission. org/ministries/theology-formation-and-evangelism/financialaid/pro-grams-for-institutions/mariners-grant/.
26 Barbara Taylor, "What's Right With the Mariners in Mission?," *Presbyterian Outlook*, February 18, 2022, https://pres-outlook.org/2022/02/whats-right-with-mariners-in-mission/.

had broken up around 2006. Lifeboat's members were mostly younger adults—single, married, and divorced—and parents of babies and toddlers, who felt that a fellowship group at church would offer a much-needed lifeline and spiritual buoy. Companionship member Wayne Williams attended one of Lifeboat's first meetings as a kind of mentor, explaining the Mariner framework and its merits. When choosing a nautical-sounding name, the new Lifeboaters were unaware of the Lifeboats that had first formed at CPC in the 1950s as subdivisions of the Schooner Club.

Like the other ships before it, Lifeboat took on cargo, which included de-cobwebbing the many windows, rafters, and light fixtures in the sanctuary during all-church workdays; serving as greeters for one or more months during the year; and bringing cookies for fellowship hour on designated Sundays. After Darrell Torgerson's passing in 2018, Lifeboat organized the 2019 all-church Kite Day and picnic in his honor. One of Lifeboat's best-remembered traditions was a Burns Supper, complete with a haggis, bawdy toasts, and readings of works by the eighteenth-century Scottish (and Presbyterian) poet Robert Burns.

Congregational Care

As an alternative to Mariners that would accommodate single parents, a group called Sojourners began at CPC in the late 1960s. With its creation we begin to see an evolution of models for nurturing relationships in the church. From groups that studied the Bible and served the community, who came together as women or as couples sharing a stage of life, there emerged in the 1990s and 2000s a variety of support groups and ministries that were narrower in scope and reflected certain changes in society at large and the culture of churchgoing.

As divorce began to carry less social stigma in the broader society, awareness gradually increased at CPC regarding how divorce shaped family life. For one thing, single parents struggled to find child care, whether because of financial limitations or their desire simply to devote more attention to their children. *Heritage of Faith* notes that the singles group Sojourners declined offers to merge with CPC Mariners; however, they did ask to join in some activities, and to bring their children along. Because of this Sojourners can be credited, at least in part, for inspiring more intergenerational gatherings for CPC folk, such as all-church picnics and family skating parties, beginning in the 1970s.

Social groups at CPC for single and divorced adults started up and petered out at various times, under varying models of leadership. In the 1980s one of the associate pastors, the Rev. Marjorie Wright, herself divorced, rebooted Sojourners.[27] In 2000 CPC members Trish Cripe and Ronnie Taggart initiated a singles group "to provide ongoing study, growth, and fellowship opportunities."[28] In 2002, the Rev. Carol Pagelsen formed a group for adults aged "twenty-something," to include both couples and singles. Phyllis Brewer, chair of Session's Fellowship and Nurture division, reported that a new singles group had started in 2005 for adults aged "thirty-five to sixtyish," and that the relatively new Dinners for 6, 8, or More fellowship program sought specifically to mix singles and couples in its get-acquainted groupings. (This program was later named Dinners for 6-7, or 8 to explicitly include an odd number.)

A nationwide survey in 2000 of Presbyterian members, elders, and pastors looked at stress levels in individuals' and families' lives, with the goal of teasing out ideas for new types of ministries that might help churches better support their members. A majority of respondents said that they or their families experienced at least a moderate amount of stress in the prior year, with "too much to do and not enough time" as the most significant family stressor reported. Other stressors named were: long work hours, economic hardship, the need to care for family members with illness or disability, work shifts that conflict with home life, and sports and other extracurricular activities for children.[29]

Recognizing these trends, pastor respondents in the study said programs they would most like to add in their church included "mission opportunities that families can participate in together," "adult classes that focus on parenting or

---

27 The Rev. Marjorie Wright was the first woman to serve on CPC's pastoral staff.

28 Carmichael Presbyterian Church, *Annual Report 2000.*

29 Presbyterian Church (USA) Research Services, *Ministries to Families and Same-Sex Issues in the PC(USA): Report of the August 2000 Presbyterian Panel Survey* (Louisville, KY, 2000), https://www.presbyterianmission.org/wp-content/uploads/panel10-aug2000.pdf.

other family issues," and "help on spiritual formation."[30] It was in this context of changing culture, along with the trend of declining church membership described in Chapter 1, that CPC leaders of the 1990s sought to focus attention on more targeted ways to nurture engagement of younger CPC members with the church and the life of faith. New relationship-focused ministries for older adults also got a boost in the 1990s and 2000s.

Family Ministries

Family and intergenerational ministries are covered in more depth in Chapter 4; however, it is worth noting here that the Rev. Sherry Sauer was ahead of the curve in this area when she served as associate pastor in the 1990s. Well-informed regarding the stressors families faced, Pastor Sherry initiated a program through the Session's Fellowship and Nurture Division called Building Caring Families. One of its major outgrowths was the Labor Day Weekend family camp at Westminster Woods, which started in 1992 and continued for about twenty years.

Building Caring Families, Pastor Sherry explained in a 1997 interview, "emerged out of a group called Parenting for Peace and Justice out of St. Louis." Mariner groups had gone on camping trips before and included their children, but with the Westminster Woods trips, Pastor Sherry sought to infuse family discussions with spiritual formation content.[31]

Deacons' Role in Congregational Care

> *I served as a deacon years ago and learned a lot about the workings of the church. I think everyone should be a deacon at least once to learn how much "behind the scenes" goes on; to see and know how many people it takes to keep the church running.*
>
> *—CPC Member Thelma Wever*[32]

---

30 Presbyterian Church (USA) Research Services, *Ministries to Families and Same-Sex Issues in the PC(USA): Report of the August 2000 Presbyterian Panel Survey.*
31 Rev. Sharon Sauer, interview by Wayne MacRostie, May 29, 1997.
32 Wever, interview.

The office of deacon as we know it at CPC in 2023 is introduced briefly in Chapter 1 as a ministry of hospitality and caring for the church family. The deacons' hospitality role is further explained in Chapter 2 in terms of welcoming worshipers into the church building and helping them feel comfortable; Chapter 6 describes their role in community outreach. Here I trace a little more of the history of CPC deacons as leaders in congregational care.

In CPC's earliest days it did not have a Board of Deacons. The first deacons began serving in 1931. The small board was made up of four to six people—most of them women—who were elected from among the congregation. They made house calls to members of the congregation who were sick or elderly, and they visited newcomers to invite them to church. They also prepared the bread and juice for communion on Sundays when the Lord's Supper was observed.

In 1950 the board bifurcated into a Board of Deacons and a Board of Deaconesses. The Board of Deacons, now all men, was fashioned as a kind of training ground for future elders. Their main duty was ushering during worship services. This was the state of affairs Doris Beckert described when she joined CPC in 1968 and became a deaconess:

> The men did the ushering; we served the church school classes. We served the Kool-Aid and cookies. And we served the con-gregation in the fellowship time. Coffee and cookies, nothing much. We took charge of the silver service. And I remember I had to take it to a silver repair man. We'd polish and get the tarnish off and all of that...and we all wore dresses.
>
> We had to deliver flowers, well there for a while they were silk flowers. Somebody in the congregation did them for seasons. We put the stock season floral arrangement up. Then later they had fresh flowers.

Deaconesses continued to prepare communion. They also invited newcomers to sign the guest book (which as of 2023 still resides in the narthex atop a handsome carved wooden stand). *Heritage of Faith* describes a careful-ly-choreographed Sunday morning routine from the deaconess's handbook, prescribing that once a deaconess copied the names of visitors from the guest book onto a separate piece of paper, she would hand it to the choir director, who would be waiting in the narthex with the choir for the processional hymn. The choir director would then lead the choir up the aisle during the opening hymn and discreetly pass the list of visitor names to the pastor, who would announce them during the greeting time.

In 1980 the deacons and deaconesses merged into a single board again. While the reconstituted Board of Deacons retained its hospitality functions, it also added the visitation ministry from earlier years, now called Care and Share, back into its repertoire. Carol Honnold remembered that she and Ann Kerr were the first women nominated to the new unified Board of Deacons.[33] The Rev. Marjorie Wright encouraged the deacons, in addition to Care and Share, to offer care for members in assigned geographic areas, or parishes. Each parish had approximately five CPC families living there. Within their respective parishes, called Agape Pods, the deacons would organize social events or other means for the families to get to know each other and become more aware of any special needs.

The Agape Pod model got some traction but never really took off. By 1988 the parish boundaries were dropped and the deacons again turned their focus to visitation and maintaining telephone contact with members who were caregivers, suffering from illness, or shut in. Around this time deacon teams were formed to handle regular visitation, crisis calls (e.g., visiting the family when one of its members was in the hospital), and transportation to Sunday services for those who didn't drive. All the while they continued their stewardship of the sanctuary space and communion elements; and, as described in Chapter 6, they became involved in care for refugees and people experiencing poverty in the neighborhood. There were sixty actively serving deacons in 1988.

During the 1990s the number of deacons was reduced to a more manageable thirty-six. They continued making regular contact with homebound CPC members, and periodically were provided training in how to serve communion to people in their homes. The Rev. Carol Pagelsen played a strong role in this training in the early 2000s. Presbyterian Women's circles aided deacons in identifying members of the congregation who were homebound, ill, or bereaved. Kathy Lewin, who coordinated deacons' in-home communion service for a time, reflected:

---

33 Honnold and Treon, interview.

Serving someone at their home is very different from serving communion at church; it is so much more personal. I found that the people I served were more interested in conversation than just receiving the elements. You cannot rush serving people in their homes. I always allowed at least an hour.[34]

In 1999 CPC members Joe St. Clair and Carol Jones compiled a booklet called *Prayers and Poems to Comfort the Soul*, which pastors and deacons handed out to those they visited in their homes. That year the deacons reported assisting members of the congregation with transportation to medical appointments and shopping in addition to Sunday church services.[35]

Speaking about her experiences serving in-home communion, Beth Lindley told of her monthly visits with an elderly church member, Mildred Riley, at her care facility, which took place over a few years.

I was not impressed with that facility. To me, it had an air of defeat about it and a stench that went with it. I don't know how else to describe it. But Mildred was kind of a light in her little room. [Another patient would often be] shouting and screaming… it'd be hard to have some kind of peace about you, in a facility like that. But Mildred didn't seem to mind; she would say, "Oh, it's just so and so, it's okay." She didn't seem to let it bother her.

One Sunday I went in, and she was lying in the hospital bed, and I could tell there was something drastically wrong…. The staff always knew I came with communion, and they told me she was dying. She couldn't have water or take communion, but something had told me earlier that day to pack some other things. I had some bubbles with a wand, and so I said "Mildred, it's springtime outside, it's beautiful. I brought some bubbles for you." And I blew the bubbles up near the window and the bubbles were shining with all the rainbow colors, and she was just enjoying that.

I left there feeling like she had some lessons to teach me that probably would take me a long time [to learn]. And on the way

34 Kathy Lewin, personal communication, June 1, 2023.
35 Carmichael Presbyterian Church, *Annual Report 1999*.

home there was a part of me that was happy for her and there's a part of me that was really sad. Part of that sadness came from knowing that [my husband] Harry was getting close to the end of his life, and knowing that something like this could happen with him. But I was also grateful that Mildred was the example that she was there at the nursing home.[36]

Deacons provided ushering for memorial services at the church, and in 2002, began to take a more active role in coordinating memorial service receptions, which Presbyterian Women circles and Mariner ships had done previously. In the 2000s the deacons also took over hosting the annual Sundae Sunday ministries fair. Later called Friendship Sunday, the September event featured ice cream refreshment. Different toppings were strategically placed at tables around McMillen Hall, where people were invited to partake and to ask the table hosts about their area of ministry and how to get involved.

Training for deacons at CPC has taken various forms and, since about 1962, has been supplemented with a detailed handbook. In 2000 the Board of Deacons and members of the Session jointly attended a spiritual leadership retreat led by the Rev. Joanne Hines at Celtic Cross Presbyterian in Citrus Heights. At the retreat, "Reverend Hines discussed the ever-changing cycles of society and culture and its influence on the church in both positive and negative ways. The forty participants were challenged to look for new ways that inspire and enrich the growth of the church through deacon and elder service."[37]

Other special speakers at deacon and elder trainings included the poet Ann Weems in 2005 and author Diana Butler Bass in 2008. Beth Lindley described the joint board retreat weekends as more of a spiritual enrichment and relationship-building time, rather than a run-down of every "job" that needed to get done.

According to Bill Dunn, around 2015, "the deacons realized that our congregation was getting older and there was more of a need to help members with meals when one or more in the household were sick or having surgery."[38] Kathy Lewis and Kate Eisel began investigating online

36 Beth Lindley, interview by Susan Herman, June 5, 2023.
37 Carmichael Presbyterian Church, *Annual Report 2000.*
38 Bill Dunn, personal communication, October 23, 2020.

signup platforms for "Healing Meals" (Karen Gray's idea for a program name). They found one called Meal Train, which was user-friendly and more efficient than relying on Mariner ships, which had limited pools of meal-bringers. With a single coordinator to contact, anyone in the congregation could opt in and be added to the email list. Michael Aretsky began coordinating Healing Meals while on the Board of Deacons, and kept doing it once his term of active service was over. Caron Treon took over the task after Michael's passing in 2022.

Kathy Lewin served as moderator of the Board of Deacons during "the COVID years" of 2020–2022, having served previous terms in 2000–2003 and 2017–2019. Shortly after the church stopped holding in-person worship and meetings in March of 2020, the deacons undertook a phone canvass of the entire congregation, both to learn of any pastoral care needs and to share information on how to stay connected via phone, email, the church's YouTube channel, electronic giving, and so on. "What an undertaking! Not only did all the deacons participate in calling on people, but others as well," Kathy said.

Moderators of the CPC Board of Deacons from the congregations' early days through 1998 are listed in *Heritage of Faith*. Moderators from 1999 through 2023 were:

Mary MacDonald, 1999	Nonye Kamalu, 2010–2011
Jeff Hanson, 2000	Ernest (Ernie) Chard, 2012
Joe Martin, 2001	Laura (Garwood) Meehan, 2013
Barbara Scott, 2002	Hal Holland, 2014
Lisa Benadom, 2003	Kathy Lewis, 2015
Daniel Cherry, 2004	Lynette Ledesma, 2016
Kathy Crow, 2005	Laura Janik, 2017
Jenny Davini, 2006	Ernie Chard, 2018
Janice Hill, 2007	Laura Garwood, 2019
Judi Stewart, 2008	Kathy Lewin, 2020–2022
Tracie Hewitt, 2009	Deb Sweetman, 2023

Stephen Ministry

The Rev. Dr. Gary Califf served as pastoral resource to the deacons during the 1990s. He noted in an interview that Birgitta Ellis, who had been coordinating Care and Share for some time, in 1995 proposed that the congregation adopt Stephen Ministry as an adjunct to its existing methods for congregational care. Stephen Ministry had started in St. Louis, Missouri in 1975. Its founders were a husband and wife who had professional experience in pastoral ministry, clinical psychology, and health care. From there Stephen Ministry expanded nationwide to offer resources and training for lay people to provide "high-quality, one-to-one, Christ-centered care to people in the congregation and the community experiencing life difficulties."[39]

CPC's first Stephen Ministers completed their training in 1997. That year Pastor Califf reported that:

> We have seven active [Stephen Ministers] who are ministering to between four and six people on a weekly basis. We screen very closely the people that they are visiting because we do have an active deacon Care and Share group led by Birgitta Ellis, and they have been very successful over the past year in keeping in contact with people...in retirement homes—people needing that regular long-term contact from the church.
>
> ...We have had Stephen Ministers helping people through legal cases and legal challenges, problems with their children, loss of a spouse. These are all intense relationships that have a definite beginning, definite goals, and an end to walk people through.... We are meeting tonight, and I am doing a module on depression for their continuing education.[40]

In 1998 a second class of six Stephen Ministers was commissioned, bringing the total to thirteen certified Stephen Ministers and one Stephen Leader. Allison Cagley, in her report for the Fellowship and Nurture Division,

---

39 "Equipping God's People for Ministry since 1975," https://www.stephen-ministries.org/default.cfm. Stephen Ministry is named after the martyr Stephen in the Book of Acts, whom Christians commonly recognize as the first deacon.
40 Rev. Dr. Gary Califf, interview, May 27, 1997.

noted that "the program effectively filled a need in the church community for care and support in a quiet, confidential manner."

In 2010 CPC's Stephen Ministry team, with John Wallace as coordinator, hosted a regional workshop in Northern California. Their preparations included doing all the publicity, which paid off, as 133 people attended the March 6 event. Joel Keen, the presenter from St. Louis, had positive feedback for CPC; according to John, he was "completely impressed with the church and the turn-out." John noted that this was a great bonding time for the Stephen Ministry team at CPC.[41]

John Wallace's notes include names of trained Stephen Ministers and Stephen Leaders: seventy-three in total, as of 2020. The ministry remains active as of 2023. Since its beginnings about 100 to 115 people have received care—some for just a few months and others for up to three years.

Being a Stephen Minister can get tricky, noted Misty Dunn, even when you've been well trained on when to refer people to a professional and how to define boundaries between personal friendship and Christian care. "Some people are lonely and just need someone to talk to."[42] Speaking of his experience as both a Stephen Minister and Stephen Leader, Len Tozier said:

> What was most valuable about Stephen Ministry? I think it was a matter of being able to work with people in a very personal one-on-one basis. A lot of things in the church are group kinds of things. And to be able to have that one-on-one contact was very meaningful. Learning through Stephen Ministry how to listen, actively listen, and avoid jumping in and fixing—because I think our natural tendency is [to say] let me fix that for you. And very often, when people are going through a critical time, they've already thought of all the fixes, and they want to get the stuff off their chest.... I think learning to do that was very important and that has been helpful in life in general, trying to remember those lessons. When people approach you casually

41 John Wallace, CPC History Notes: Pastors, Mission Trips, Stephen Ministry Leadership, Microassistance Program, June 19, 2020.
42 Misty Dunn, personal communication, June 4, 2023.

with an issue to try to put on that listening ear and not just do all the talking and try to fix it.

Initially Stephen Ministry was made available to members of the congregation, and I think almost all of our care receivers were members of the congregation. Over the years, a lot of nonmembers have found out about it [thanks to the cards in the pew racks].[43]

Len said that another component developed by the Stephen Ministry team at CPC was to offer a time for prayer at the end of each worship service. Two members of the team stand by the Stephen Ministry banner each Sunday for a few minutes during and after the postlude. "There have been many Sundays where no one comes over," he said, "and that's okay. And then there'll be a Sunday when someone does come—sometimes it's someone from outside who has never been in the church before. And they're just really in a crisis and to be able to talk to them and then pray with them is really meaningful."

Health Ministry and Care Visitor Ministry

Faye White reported for *Carmichael Times* that during 1997–1998, CPC member Deborah Young, RN, PHN, had begun assembling a task force to start a health ministry at the church.

The nine-member planning committee of doctors, nurses, and lay people has developed programs to provide increased awareness about health-related issues which can lead to earlier, more effective treatments...while providing the personal caring and attention that is often lacking within health care systems.[44]

Health ministries and parish nursing had been gathering steam in the US since the 1970s. The Rev. Granger Westberg, a Lutheran minister from Chicago, popularized the idea of health ministries for low-income congregations, and for other congregations as well.[45]

---

43 Len Tozier and Viki Tozier, interview by Sharon MacLean, November 16, 2020.
44 Faye White, "To Your Health," *Carmichael Times*, June 18, 1998.
45 Ann Solari-Twadell, "Health and wholeness: Granger Westberg," *Christian*

In low-income contexts or communities of color, health ministries tend to revolve around cultural and socioeconomic needs. They may focus on people whose health issues reflect challenges such as being undocumented, lacking access to care, living in "food deserts," or having low levels of trust in the medical system.[46] At Carmichael, however, the health ministry and parish nursing program (later called faith community nursing) took a different shape. Most CPC churchgoers had ready access to medical care. Their needs had more to do with aging—for example, fostering healthy acceptance of the aging process and building awareness of signs that more support is needed.

Deborah Young, and later, Sue Bowington, Charleen Lee, and others involved in the health ministry organized monthly blood pressure checks at CPC. They presented Sunday adult education classes on fall prevention, nutrition, CPR, recognizing signs of dementia, and planning for end-of-life care. They also accepted donations of used walkers, wheelchairs, commode seats, and other durable medical equipment to loan out to families.

Because falls and medical emergencies sometimes happened during church services, members of the health ministry team, including Dr. Richard Frink, a physician, and Jan Olson, a registered nurse, collaborated with the deacons to increase sanctuary safety. They stocked first aid kits in the narthex and offered mobility aids for worshippers who needed them.

Another important aspect of the health ministry at CPC was that it encouraged people of all ages to connect physical health and wellbeing to stewardship of the spirit and the social mission of the church. Partnering with a blood donation agency, Blood Source, and having church members participate in an agency-sponsored church donor club was for many years a key component of the CPC health ministry, as was the collection of used eyeglasses, hearing aids, and cell phones, which were given to community organizations for distribution. "Darrell Torgerson and I were blood buddies," said Glenda Perrou, explaining that she and Darrell regularly signed up to donate blood together when the Blood Mobile came to the

---

Century, March 17, 1999, https://www.christiancentury.org/article/2012-01/health-and-wholeness.

46 Pam Chwedyk, "Come All Ye Faithful: Diversity in Faith Community Nursing," *Minority Nurse*, June 26, 2014, https://minoritynurse.com/come-all-ye-faithful-diversity-in-faith-community-nursing/.

CPC campus.[47] From about 1998 until 2011 the Blood Mobile came two to four times per year, with some disruptions due to construction on the church campus.

When Samaritan Counseling Center (see Chapter 5) closed in 2010 and moved out of its upstairs corner meeting space, CPC's health ministry moved its meetings to that room, and renamed it the Wholeness Center.

In 2014 CPC member Joan Hurlock, a nurse, initiated a faith-based caregiver support program called Care Visitor Ministry, and secured grants for its development through the Synod of the Pacific. Joan wrote a program manual and made presentations locally and at regional and national-level conferences to encourage other congregations to adopt the program. St. Mark's United Methodist church in Arden-Arcade began implementing the program soon after.[48] At CPC, ten care visitors completed training in 2014, including the Rev. Ivan Herman. By 2017, nineteen had been trained.

Over that period the care visitors made monthly home visits to caregivers, with the goal to "help sustain the caregiver's wholeness, share the care burden, and extend the love of Christ into the caregiver's life with the aid of stronger connections with CPC."[49] Pastor Ivan reported that the visits were positive, but that it was hard for some care visitors to take on a new assignment once the person they had been visiting died, or lost the loved one they had been caring for. He also observed that the ministry overlapped somewhat with Stephen Ministry. And, in 2018, Joan Hurlock moved out of the Sacramento area. The Care Visitor program did not find a new "champion," and ended.

As mentioned earlier, CPC's health ministry included adult education classes. In addition to topics like end-of-life care, some classes nurtured the creative mind as well. The Rev. Judy Davis of Bethany Presbyterian in Sacramento gave a six-week class at CPC on life story writing. Tony and Glenda Perrou spoke about how the Amherst Writers and Artists Method class helped them get in touch with their own grief from having lost their grandson in a car crash, and how it helped them learn the stories of fellow church members. "We were just fascinated," Tony said. "Bep Van Der Mik

---

47 Tony Perrou and Glenda Perrou, interview by Susan Herman, May 14, 2023.
48 Carmichael Presbyterian Church, *Annual Report 2015*.
49 Carmichael Presbyterian Church, *Annual Report 2017*.

wrote about how her family in Amsterdam had to house Nazi soldiers during World War II, and somehow keep it quiet that her brother was part of the Dutch Resistance."

Tony and Glenda also said that they struggle sometimes to understand how their children's and grandchildren's generation has so decisively fallen away from the church. The health ministry class gave them tools, they said, not necessarily for analyzing or solving matters of faith, but for continuing the conversation about faith in ways that help them relate to their younger family members.[50]

During the COVID-19 pandemic, CPC's faith community nurse Sharleen Millering served on the church's Re-opening Task Force to implement measures for guarding against infection once in-person worship and meetings resumed. By October 2020 worship services were conducted outdoors on the large playing field by Robertson House; Sharleen conducted temperature checks with a no-contact infrared thermometer as attendees entered the space. Later that year and through most of 2021 worship services took place in McMillen Hall, with doors open for ventilation and pairs and small clusters of chairs spaced six feet apart. Once the HVAC unit in the sanctuary was replaced and worship resumed there, Sharleen organized stations at sanctuary entrances stocked with disposable face masks and hand sanitizer gel.

Later in 2021, Sharleen relinquished her duties as faith community nurse, and the health ministry began a period of re-evaluation. By then the Blood Mobile was no longer making stops at the church campus. Training on the AED and other safety procedures was now integrated into the ushers' and deacons' preparation. (Their training also began to include discussion of protocols in the case of an active shooter in the building.) In-home visits of any kind were slow to resume following COVID-19. Had the needs of the congregation shifted? What might next steps be?

One possible new direction for CPC's health ministry, as indicated in the Fellowship and Nurture Division report for 2021, might be to offer

---

50 Perrou and Perrou, interview.

community health fairs on the church campus, similar to the Homeless Outreach Partnership Events (HOPE) that CPC co-hosted with the Sacramento County Sheriff's Department (see Chapter 6). As of 2023 the question remained open.

Prayer and Bible Study Groups

One outgrowth of CPC's health ministry, or perhaps a parallel development, was the prayer shawl ministry, which began in 2002. Other churches were starting similar groups at that time, as a way to share "the unconditional embrace of a sheltering, mothering God."[51] As of 2023 the making and sharing of knitted and crocheted prayer shawls continues to nurture relationships, both among members of the CPC community and between individuals' physical and spiritual selves.

Debbie Berke, a member of CPC since 1975, started the prayer shawl ministry. Not long after hatching the idea and starting to talk about it, Debbie asked Viki Tozier to join in. Soon there were eight or nine women meeting once a month to work together on their creations, meeting in the Wholeness Center. Speaking of their time together, Viki said:

> There's some real sacred air there, and it's just comfortable. We start every meeting with a devotional. And we pray...over our yarn and pray for the people who will be meant to receive [the shawl], because we don't have any idea where it will go.[52]

The shawls are made of varied yarn colors in rectangular patterns, and measure roughly the length of an arm span, about fifty-eight inches long. They are stored until needed, and a few times a year any shawls still waiting to be distributed are brought into the sanctuary during a Sunday service for the whole congregation to pray over and offer a blessing on their eventual recipients. News of those requesting prayer—people experiencing grief, illness, or recovering from surgery, for example—would come from friends or family members through the church office, or through other groups such as Mariners. As of 2020 when Debbie and Viki shared their stories, over 500 prayer shawls had been gifted to members and friends of CPC.[53]

---

51 "About the Shawls," 1998, accessed June 6, 2023, www.shawlministry.com.
52 Tozier and Tozier, interview.
53 Debbie Berke, interview by Sharon MacLean, September 26, 2020.

As of the late 1990s two men's prayer groups met regularly: the Men's Covenant Group and Men's Prayer Breakfast group. By 2006 only the prayer breakfast group was still meeting, Thursdays at 7:00 a.m. at the Waffle Barn on Fair Oaks Boulevard. When the Waffle Barn closed in 2014, the group moved to a Denny's restaurant nearby. To guide their discussions they used a publication called *The Upper Room*, which follows Bible readings from the Revised Common Lectionary.

In 2010 Harry Lindley reported that one of their older members, a 94-year-old Pearl Harbor survivor, Bob Hargis, had taken leave from the prayer group upon moving to a skilled nursing facility. Harry's report continued:

> Our discussions [are]...peppered with anecdotes and experiences as well as comments on the programs and activities of our church. One cannot leave our breakfast time together without taking some mental, emotional, and Christian spiritual "food" to help sustain us in the coming week. Many of us older members marvel at the work of the Holy Spirit among [us]. It is very rewarding to see persons share their experiences, share their faith stories, and grow in the openness of our group.[54]

In 2020 as restaurants closed in keeping with the COVID-19 restrictions, the group moved to the Zoom platform and was able to incorporate members with transportation or health challenges. Living in a care facility was no longer a barrier, as it had been for their friend in 2010, so the group continued to meet online. Tim Farley noted in 2022 that online attendance averaged eight members, and that the Zoom "door" was always open to new participants.

Women's Bible studies, as noted above, were and are an integral part of Presbyterian Women. Outside of that structure, a few other women's groups have formed at CPC. Sharon MacLean spoke of a women's Bible study that grew out of a series of conversations at a Women's Retreat in the mid-2010s. As of September 2020, she said,

---

54 Carmichael Presbyterian Church, *Annual Report 2010*.

> The Women's Bible Study [now online] is going strong and growing. I think the community support and digging deeper into scriptures and our faith is something we all longed for and need right now.... And I think once we can meet again and go back to church, things will be even more different, and we'll have to re-define things again. How do we teach about and bring Jesus to a hurting world? We are always evolving and need to be flexible and try new things.[55]

Women's Retreats

Women of CPC began holding yearly retreats at Zephyr Point Conference Center on Lake Tahoe in the early 2000s and continued through 2019. These spring weekends were always well-attended and intergenerational; photos on the Friends of Carmichael Presbyterian Facebook page from the 2010s show groups of thirty to forty women, spanning in age from late teens to ninety-plus. The Rev. Carol Pagelsen reported leading as many as sixty-five women at the 2004 gathering.[56]

Leaders for the retreats over the years included CPC member Kathy Daigle, who introduced women to the concept of spiritual direction and incorporated contemplative practices into prayer times and worship. The Rev. Jerilyn Dahlke, a pastor in the presbytery who attended CPC with her family when not working elsewhere, led the 2014 retreat on the theme of hope. Other retreat speakers over the years included the Rev. Diana Bell-Kerr and author Marilyn McEntyre. Before its cancellation due to COVID-19, plans were underway for the 2020 retreat, which the Rev. Peggy Krong, a retired pastor active in CPC's congregation, was set to lead on the theme of Celtic spirituality.

In addition to scripture study and prayer, the women's retreats included both structured and unstructured time for art in multiple media—everything from poetry and acting to chalk painting and collage. Kristen Zeman served for many years as the retreat organizer, not only booking rooms at the retreat center, but also infusing the weekend's programming with playfulness and opportunities for women in different seasons of life and from different

---

55 Sharon MacLean, interview by Susan Herman, September 11, 2020.
56 Carmichael Presbyterian Church, *Annual Report 2004.*

areas of church involvement to know one another and engage deeply with spiritual themes. Jenny DeVries and Trina Spivack led the group in singing Christian music: folk and campfire-style songs as well as hymns and meditative refrains from the Taizé community.

Kristen Zeman and others involved in leadership invited attendees to imagine the retreats as a "soul vacation," that is, freedom from obligations and doing for others, and freedom for the Holy Spirit to seep in during times of stillness and laughter. Women who worked in demanding careers or gave generously of themselves at church sometimes found themselves feeling open and vulnerable at the retreats, speaking freely about difficult topics like illness and chronic pain. Victoria Bush shared this story:

> A memorable time for me was the "laying on of hands" at the Zephyr Point Women's Retreat. At that time, I was recovering from having cancer four times in eight years. At the Women's Retreat, I felt the love and energy of my Christian sisters as they lay their hands on me and others, saying and praying prayers of recovery for me. The experience was overwhelming, spiritually enriching, and energizing.[57]

After 2020, members of the Session's Fellowship and Nurture Division began researching new options for locations to hold the women's retreat. Some who had year after year traveled the winding road (US Highway 50) to the Zephyr Point facility, located at an altitude of 6,225 feet, now had health and mobility concerns that the high altitude and hillside terrain did not accommodate. As of 2023 a new retreat spot had not been identified; still, as mentioned above, women who longed for ongoing connections over scripture and conversation found ways to keep that going.

Support Groups

The Widows or Widowers (WoW) group started in 2004 under Pastor Carol Pagelsen's leadership and was faithfully led by Ramona Stubblefield and Margo Scandella from 2007 to February 2014. The Holy Scow Mariners became the group's sponsors in October 2014. WoW's main activity was eating together and enjoying entertainment. Attendance

---

57 Victoria Bush, interview by Kathy Lewin, March 12, 2021.

averaged twenty-five participants at each of three themed lunches during the year. Entertainment or education often followed the meal. Some examples of this included poetry readings by members, travel slide shows, and performances by a banjo band and the Sacramento chapter of Sweet Adelines. The El Camino High School Madrigal Singers were featured one year. Attendance gradually fell, however, and the last WoW event was a Valentine's Day luncheon in 2016.

Misty Dunn started the Cancer and Faith Experience (CAFÉ) group in 2005. It was an outgrowth of Stephen Ministry, and included cancer survivors, those undergoing treatment who could attend on their "good" days, and caregivers of people with cancer. In 2011 it expanded to include people with other chronic illnesses. Seven to ten attendees participated in the early years, though numbers dropped in later years. Misty said that the twice-monthly meetings "frequently filled with laughter as we told about many humorous experiences. We found that the prayers, support, stories, and information we shared...have fortified our faith, courage, and positive attitude."[58]

Most participants in CAFÉ were members of the church; a few were referred to the group by the American Cancer Society. Due to low attendance, CAFÉ's last year was 2012.

Nurturing Relationships Between the Spirit and Self

Since its inception, Carmichael Presbyterian has been an outward-looking church, seeking always to serve its community. Even weekend events described as "retreats" often centered on service of some kind. Choir retreats were for learning new music to share with the congregation in worship; deacon and elder retreats were for creating a vision and discussing how certain aspects of the church's ministries could be improved. Of course, relationship-building was the main purpose of such retreats, with the same being true of mission trips and other activities where church folks were serving together. Still, aside from the women's retreats, there have been relatively few opportunities for CPC members to nurture their relationships with themselves or with their souls.

---

58 Carmichael Presbyterian Church, *Annual Report 2006.*

A few members of CPC—Marsha Cook, Kathy Daigle, Wyn Cane—as well as the Rev. Sherry Sauer and the Rev. Peggy Krong, completed formal training to become spiritual directors. Spiritual direction has its roots in the monastic traditions and resurged in popularity across broader swaths of Christianity in the 1990s and early 2000s. Richard Foster, a pastor and teacher of spiritual formation based in Denver, describes spiritual direction as an interpersonal relationship. It is not the same as pastoral counseling or therapy, as these more often seek to solve problems or examine things that are going wrong in one's life. Rather, it is a structure for discernment or tuning in more closely to God's intention for one's life.[59] Similar to Stephen Ministry, spiritual direction is confidential, so while it is unclear how many CPC members have benefitted from such a relationship, one can say that many have experienced moments of deep exploration or openness to God when spending time with spiritual directors in workshops or other contexts.

Kathy Daigle and Jenny DeVries brought Taizé-style prayer and worship to the congregation in the early 2000s. Together they offered an hour-long contemplative service in CPC's chapel on Wednesday evenings as part of the Wednesday Works program (see Chapter 4) until 2019. About twenty worshipers would typically attend the loosely structured service, either joining in the singing or dropping out to quiet their minds.[60]

In 2016, following the vision of Jenny DeVries and Lisa Torgerson, the chapel was transformed as a place of prayer and meditation. The pews were removed and replaced with individual, upholstered chairs. During the Advent season and at other points during the year, Lisa would create prayer stations where individuals were encouraged to light candles and engage in contemplation of scriptures or images. From the perspective of 2023 when many are processing grief and trauma from COVID-19 and other sources, it may be that contemplative practices have much to teach for CPC members and the community.

---

59 "What is spiritual direction?," accessed June 7, 2023, https://renovare.org/articles/what-is-spiritual-direction.

60 Songs with just a few words, such as *ubi caritas et amor* (live in charity and love), characterize Taizé worship as it is practiced at the Taizé commune in France—an ecumenical Christian community founded in the 1940s that continues to host international peace-seekers today.

Staying Connected

Since 1989, CPC's Heritage Committee has worked to nurture relationships across time, helping to keep the congregation connected to its own past and to its Presbyterian heritage. Likewise, various teams focused on internal and public communications have also sought to keep the congregation connected in the present.

Heritage

> *History is an ever-present and ongoing part of our lives.*
>
> *—CPC member Jimmi Mishler*[61]

CPC formed a Heritage Committee in 1990 as a way of continuing work begun in 1988 to celebrate the denomination's bicentennial. *Heritage of Faith* notes that the denomination's *Mission Yearbook for Prayer and Study* for 1988–1989 highlighted the 200th anniversary of the first Presbyterian General Assembly in the United States and included "ideas to help local congregations celebrate this milestone." During those years,

> Carmichael Presbyterian Church was entering a period of being served by interim staff: the Reverend Deane Hendricks, interim pastor; the Reverend Aart van Beek, interim associate pastor; and Jimmi Mishler, interim director of education. It seemed a good time to channel congregational energies into a new creative venture, celebrating the local history while participating in the national bicentennial observances.[62]

From Reformation Sunday on October 30, 1988 through May 21, 1989 (the denomination's first designated Heritage Sunday), this new committee planned several special observances that included inviting as guest preacher the Rev. James Comfort Smith, who had served as CPC's pastor from 1943–1954.

---

61 Carmichael Presbyterian Church, *Annual Report 2007*.
62 White, Herman, and Segur, *Heritage of Faith*, 147-48.

Congregants had previously assembled mini-histories and scrapbooks on topics such as the church buildings and Presbyterian Women's activities; however, as of 1990, no comprehensive archive of key documents yet existed. The Session of CPC commissioned a seventeen-member committee to do exactly this, and to establish a central location for the records along with an index and storage and retrieval system. Another goal, carried out steadily over the next fourteen years, was to conduct and transcribe oral interviews of longstanding members of the church, members of its lay leadership, and pastors. The results of this faithful work are hours of audio tape and two large binders containing a total of fifty-seven interview transcripts, plus additional written reports on selected topics.

The Heritage Committee, under Jimmi Mishler's leadership, published CPC's 75-year history in 1998. CPC member Bill Davis, a retired archivist for the State of California, led a massive effort to curate the church's records. Thanks to his expertise the Heritage Committee was able to offer guidance to other congregations in their handling of historical records.

To keep congregational history alive throughout the year, members of the Heritage committee rotated displays of photos and memorabilia periodically in a dedicated cabinet, which had been established for the purpose early on. They also began a tradition of recognizing forty- and fifty-year members of the church on Heritage Sunday each May. This tradition continues as of 2023 and now includes a category to recognize those with sixty or more years of membership as well as new members who joined during the previous year.

Bill and his wife, Ruth Davis, completed the initial archive collection in 2002 along with an index to its contents and a system for ongoing collection and assessment of church-related documents. In recognition of their service, the archive storage room in the sanctuary's bell tower was named after Bill and Ruth Davis in 2008.

In 2003 Carol and Dick Piper, along with Jimmi Mishler, spent several days at Montreat Conference Center in North Carolina, learning from Presbyterian Historical Society's national staff and from other church historians about best practices in preserving congregational history. Back in Carmichael, they advised the Session on document retention and helped develop a policy of committing all important records to microfilm every five years. Microfilm was used through about 2011; starting in 2012 records were stored on CDs and USB flash drives, and later, on both physical media and cloud servers. To preserve paper records, particularly newsprint with its high acid concentrations, members of the committee applied de-acidifying sprays and purchased acid-free paper for making photocopies.

The Heritage Committee made annual gifts to the Presbyterian Historical Society. In 2013 they made their donation in honor of Wayne MacRostie, who had served the congregation for sixty years as an historian and in many other capacities.

"May of 2019 brought transition to the Heritage committee with the dissolution of the founding group chaired by Jimmi Mishler and lovingly tended by Dick and Carol Piper, Carolyn McGregor, Wilma Boland, and Bonnie Hard."[63] With these words, new Heritage Committee chair Kate Erlich offered thanks to those who had maintained the church's records of weekly, seasonal, and special events for more than thirty years. By that time, planning for the centennial had begun and a team was forming to bring the plans to fruition. A new Heritage Committee would reckon with curating digital photos and more going forward. But first, the congregation would celebrate their centennial. Along with the publication of this book, centennial-related recognitions were sprinkled liberally throughout 2023. These are listed in the Appendix.

Communications

Internal and public communications at CPC have been handled in a variety of ways over the years. The Communications Network, called ComNet for short, began as part of the Session's Stewardship Division in 1991 to review and plan local media releases that would tell the story of mission outreach and other projects of the church. Marie Segur coordinated the committee as of 1997 and served as liaison to Stewardship (later Administration Division). Other ComNet members included Bobbi Jones, Features editor of the *Carmichael Times*; as well as Wilma Boland, photographer and historian; and Faye White, who submitted news releases. Dick Piper attended monthly meetings of the Carmichael Chamber of Commerce, beginning in 1995, offering the invocation for most meetings.

---

63 Carmichael Presbyterian Church, *Annual Report 2019*.

A conundrum that arose in ComNet's early years was where to place advertisements for the church and deciding "What is the story we want to share?" Marie Segur spoke about this in a 1995 interview with Jimmi Mishler. The *Sacramento News and Review*, a local news and culture paper that included content for gay and lesbian readers, had approached the committee with an offer to advertise in their weekly publication. After they determined the price was too high, Marie nevertheless kept scanning the *SN&R* church page regularly. Rev. Sherry Sauer, she said, thought the *Sacramento News and Review* could be an appropriate outlet for ads about CPC. However, Marie noted, as a congregation, "we haven't made that switch to say, 'Hey, we can welcome some lesbians, we realize we have some in our midst.'" Most in the congregation at that time, she reflected, would rather not include any messaging, positive or negative, about same-sex relationships. "I think we are in a restless place. Some of us are on the fence...we prayed about it."[64]

Meanwhile, the *Mission Bell* newsletter, published monthly since 1949, anchored the church's internal communications. Dick Piper began editing it in 1992. He retired from the post in 2001, then resumed it a few years later and continued through 2009 when Amy Lerseth took the reins. Pastor's Secretary Karen Gray took over from Amy in 2023.

The pastor's secretary continued to prepare the Sunday worship bulletins and Parish Notes; Fellowship and Nurture Division published an annual adult ministries directory with information about each Mariner ship, including its officers, members, and which charitable organizations they supported. Other groups and divisions created brochures for the pew racks where visitors could easily take them.

By 2002 the first iteration of the CPC website was live, thanks to the efforts of webmaster Phil Mishler. Recognizing a need to coordinate internal and public-facing communications into a unified strategy, that year members of ComNet and others responsible for church communications created the Information Policy Committee, later simply called Communication Committee. ComNet dissolved, and Margaret Herman chaired the new committee through 2010. Marie Segur led it after that until 2013.

---

64 Marie Segur, interview by Jimmi Mishler, February 21, 1995.

This group took charge of working with the county authorities on signage and banners. They also had, for a time, a communications calendar to aid in organizing news releases, purchasing ads, and placing stories with various print outlets. They continued the relationship with the Carmichael Chamber of Commerce. Further, the Communication Committee developed guidelines for what would go on the website. They analyzed the data on website visits and most popular content areas of the website, and reported on this data to the Session.

As businesses, churches, and government entities were quickly establishing their online presence through the first decade of the 2000s, traditional news outlets, unable to compete with the internet, began to cut their budgets and largely eliminated coverage of church events. Social media platforms where users could share their own content began to proliferate, and by 2012 CPC had launched its Facebook page. Soon after, some groups within the church created private and public accounts on various social media platforms to share news. As of 2013, the functions of the Communication Committee had been absorbed into other areas. Membership and Outreach took on most of the public relations-type functions.

A member of the worship tech team, Steve Parker, volunteered in 2013 to refresh and take over administration of the church website. Steve uploaded sermon videos; the church secretaries kept the home page and calendar information up to date; leads from various bodies within the congregation were also given logins to add their content. As one might imagine, some pages on the site grew thick with outdated information. And, with increased popularity of internet use on mobile devices, it soon became clear that a pared-down, refocused, mobile-friendly website was in order.

In 2021, the Session's Administration Division assembled a website task force from within the church's membership and hired an outside company called Landslide Creative, based in Nashville, Tennessee, to create the new website. Consultants from Landslide met with the CPC task force via Zoom to come up with a design and navigation structure that would complement different patterns of typical website user behavior, known as "skimming, swimming, and diving." With these guidelines and other tips—such as how to write short bits of informative text containing search terms—Susan

Herman and Karen Gray got to work updating the site. Sharon MacLean, who with her husband Bruce had unofficially assumed Wilma Boland's mantle as visual chronicler, provided a trove of digital photos to use on the new site, which launched in December of 2022.

Heritage of Faith includes an appendix on the history of pictorial directories at CPC, noting that these have been produced every few years since 1964. Starting in the 1980s the church worked with photography studio Olan Mills on several directories. Under their business model, church members would sit for their directory photos and would have the option to purchase packages of print photos for their personal use. The sale of portrait packages subsidized production of the directory, which was then offered free of charge to church members. CPC continued to conduct business with Olan Mills throughout the 1990s and early 2000s. LifeTouch purchased Olan Mills' church directory division in 2011, and CPC worked with Lifetouch on subsequent directories through 2019.

LifeTouch closed its church directory business in 2020. By that time many churches had begun to house member photos and contact information in an electronic "church management system" or database. Members could access their friends' photos, names, and any personal data they chose to share, through a mobile app or by logging in to their church's website. As of 2023 CPC's website did not have a user login function (though its designers did offer this as an option). So, CPC's office staff created the 2024 pictorial directory in-house. No large-scale commercial services comparable to LifeTouch existed anymore. In 2023 and 2024 CPC secretary Julie Ueltzen collected member-submitted photos and updated contact information. Members also had the option to sign up for a sitting with photographers Bruce and Sharon MacLean. Julie used the member database and design software to generate the pages, and printed professional-quality new directories on the office copy machine.

Commitment to Nurturing Relationships

Relationships make service as the body of Christ possible, and for this reason nurturing relationships remains a core part of CPC's mission. Some of the challenges facing CPC in the future that interviewees for this book identified might constructively be thought of in terms of relationships. I will share a few examples here.

Numerous interviewees voiced concern about younger adults and families not being as involved in church life as they themselves were, both in terms of social activities and service. In terms of raw numbers, there are indeed fewer young adults and families in CPC's congregation now than in decades past; this age demographic also makes up a smaller percentage of CPC members than in decades past. When it comes to degrees of involvement, it is true that some families are deeply involved while others are less so, though it's difficult to draw direct comparisons between proportions of involved to less involved people over time.

Here I think we can look to the PC(USA) Research Services survey results cited earlier in the chapter for some clues about church involvement among younger adults and families, as the trend extends well beyond CPC's congregation. Families are under stress, due in part to changing economic conditions. They need to work more—often, two or more adults in the household need to work—and thus have less time available for church. This, combined with parenting philosophies that emphasize spending more time with children, means that the most inviting church activities for families today may be those that nurture intergenerational relationships.

As for their involvement in service, perhaps a question worth exploring is this: How can some functions of CPC's boards be modularized, as with the Healing Meals signup? Would this make service more accessible, or provide a kind of on-ramp for someone who might later say "yes" to a higher level of involvement? Adults of all ages go through seasons of life that limit their bandwidth for time-intensive volunteer work like visioning and maintaining ties with other groups. Likewise, those who are available and willing to do that systemic work may need more assurance that they will not be expected to do it forever, or that there is backup for when they need time off.

Another comment that came up in interviews had to do with adult education: Why aren't as many adults willing to attend Sunday or Wednesday evening classes on the Bible or other faith-related topics? While Christian Education is explored in more depth in Chapter 4, it may be helpful to wonder here whether the desire to build relationships may again be a factor.

For adults with caregiving responsibilities, their priorities may lie with family, thus limiting the time and energy they can devote to attending classes or reading. For others it may be that simply chatting over coffee feels like a more valuable use of time, as it allows conversations to unfold that might not happen in a structured class setting yet might still get to the heart of a faith concern.

Discussing her time on the Board of Deacons in 2014, Kathy Lewis said that moderator Hal Holland (a member of Generation X, that cohort born between 1965–1980) made a point of asking deacons to file their reports online prior to each meeting so that information-sharing would not take up the bulk of the meeting. That way, the focus could be on relationship-building within the group.[65] Social science research has shown that Generation X adults and Millenials, who began turning forty in 2021, tend to pursue learning for specific goals, rather than for learning's sake. They also see relationship-building and interaction as an integral part of the learning process[66] and perhaps even as a prerequisite for embarking on volunteer work together. Content, after all, can be retrieved when needed. And, in the 2020s—an age of extreme political and cultural polarization—perhaps learning how to build relationships and trust should in fact be a primary goal.

---

65 Kathy Lewis, personal communication, March 15, 2021.
66 "Meeting Different Generational Needs for a Strong Adult Learner Experience," updated March 25, 2022, https://universityservices.wiley.com/meeting-different-generational-needs-for-a-strong-adult-learner-experience/.

Chapter 4
Growing in Faith Together

On May 2, 2004, the Rev. Carol Pagelsen preached on the story of the apostle Peter raising the seamstress Dorcas from the dead in the port city of Joppa (Acts 9: 36–43). For her sermon, Pastor Carol chose to focus on Dorcas, who is called by the Aramaic name Tabitha in the text. Dorcas's life was irreplaceable, she said, continuing:

> One person, and one person's gift, can change the world—can change a community—can change the church. Think about that one person who was there at just the right moment when you needed help, whose presence changed your life. Who could replace that one person? Likely no one. Think about yourself and the things you have done, known only to God. Who could replace you? Who could replace them?

> The significance of Dorcas's life was that she blended together her professional ambition and her Christian compassion. She didn't compartmentalize...toiling over her tunics for forty hours a week and then performing isolated acts of charity with whatever time she had left over. The text reports that she was devoted to good works and acts of charity, meaning that these activities played a central role in her day-to-day life. She may have turned

some of her sewing work into mission work, creating tunics and clothing for the widows and orphans of the community. She kept the professional and spiritual sides of herself together, united in a single seamless existence. What are the chances that we could do that today?

...Young people today are discovering that true happiness cannot be found in the culture of materialism. Nor can it be discovered in the patterns of the past—the lives based on a fantasy world of the 1950s sitcoms. Young people want something different... they want a good life, real happiness, and the opportunity to do something worth doing. They want to make a difference. They want to be able to live their lives and even offer them, if required, for something worthy of sacrifice. They want a good life, not just a good living. They want to be like Dorcas, combining professional and spiritual skills, abilities, and service.

We can pursue our goals by following the example of Dorcas, who turned her sewing work into mission work and had a powerful, positive effect on the community around her. We can keep our professional and our spiritual sides together by [seeing our work] as an opportunity to use our God-given abilities to treat every human being as a child of God.[1]

Pastor Carol's sermon on Dorcas demonstrates how CPC has always valued its children, teens, and young adults. In her sermon, Pastor Carol clearly had young people in mind, and she invited all in the congregation to briefly adopt what we might call a Millennial's[2] perspective on life, work, and faith. Growing in faith together at CPC has always meant affirming oneself and others as children of God, learning from God's Word, and directing new knowledge and skills toward action in God's world.

---

1 Rev. Carol Pagelsen, *Dorcas Lives!* (Sermon at Carmichael Presbyterian Church May 2, 2004), VHS Recording.
2 The Pew Research Center uses birth years 1981–1996 to define the Millennial age cohort.

This chapter emphasizes CPC's beginnings as a Sunday school. Before the worshiping community we now know as Carmichael Presbyterian Church was founded in 1923, it was a Sunday school for the children of Carmichael Colony. For 100 years the congregation has placed a high value on faith formation for all its members, but particularly for its young ones.

In this chapter I describe CPC's Sunday school and youth programs, foregrounding this with a brief history of the Sunday School Movement. I also discuss adult education and intergenerational programs. Throughout the chapter I include several stories from children of CPC who came of age in the 1980s, 1990s, and 2000s (Generation X and Millennials) and who are today, like Tabitha/Dorcas in the Book of Acts, doing God's work both inside and outside of the church.

Sunday School for Children

In recounting the 1918 beginnings of Carmichael Presbyterian Church as a community Sunday school for children, *Heritage of Faith* notes:

> The Sunday School Movement that began during the religious revival after the Civil War had revived following World War I. Many churches viewed Sunday schools as a most important means for reaching the unchurched. Often families could be reached through their children.[3]

The ecumenical Sunday School Movement may also be traced back a little farther, to late eighteenth-century England, when the layperson-taught schools were mainly a vehicle for providing basic literacy to children from poor families. In the years before child labor laws, Sunday schools met on Sundays because they were serving children who worked in factories during the week. In the United States, Sunday schools built upon that foundation and also provided civic and moral lessons that were oriented toward upholding national ideals.

Multiple waves of religious revival swept through the US during the nineteenth century and, as noted above, again after World War I. At this

---

3 Faye White, Margaret Herman, and Marie Segur, *Heritage of Faith: A 75-Year History of Carmichael Presbyterian Church* (Carmichael Presbyterian Church, 1998), 47.

time, content taught in Sunday schools became more religious in nature. During the decades prior to World War I, "[c]hildhood began to be treated as a distinct category of life when individuals received their most formative and lasting impressions."[4] Sunday schools thus began to take on a more evangelistic purpose.

Though the Sunday School Movement was cross-denominational, scholar Page Putnam Miller notes that from its first decades in the US, Presbyterian women in particular "provided significant leadership."[5] One of these, Joanna Bethune, co-founded the Female Union Society for the Promotion of Sabbath Schools in 1816, and quickly found herself administering a large urban organization with over 3,000 students. "She supervised a large budget, established policy, oversaw the publication of curriculum, and coordinated an enormous staff" of around 250 teachers.[6]

Another model of Sunday school leadership that more closely resembles the beginnings of CPC might be found in Margaretta Mason Brown. In 1819 Brown created a Sunday school in her small Kentucky community, which at that time was on the country's western frontier, as California would be 100 years later:

> The Sunday School Movement opened up a whole new array of opportunities for women. Besides offering women the opportunity for a few hours of classroom teaching experience, involvement in Sunday schools had the potential for including social work, theological study, preparation of curriculum materials, establishment of libraries, innovation of teaching methods, organization of local schools, and experience in a national network. The participation of women in the Sunday School Movement dramatically altered the generally accepted pattern of female behavior.[7]

---

4 K. Elise Leal, "'All Our Children May be Taught of God': Sunday Schools and the Roles of Childhood and Youth in Creating Evangelical Benevolence," *Church History* 87, no. 4 (2019), https://doi.org/doi:10.1017/S0009640718002378.
5 Page Putnam Miller, "Women in the Vanguard of the Sunday School Movement," *Journal of Presbyterian History* 58 (1980), https://jstor.org/stable/23335341.
6 Miller, "Women in the Vanguard of the Sunday School Movement."
7 Miller, "Women in the Vanguard of the Sunday School Movement."

Thus in 1918 when Carmichael's Sunday school began—with Mrs. Lena Cowan, Mrs. Elinor Champlin and Mrs. Ellithorpe[8] at the helm—a foundation and philosophy was already in place and the idea that children from the entire community should take part together, regardless of their parents' religious denomination, was widely accepted.

Sunday School Memories of CPC

Heritage of Faith includes many recollections from people who were children in the 1920s and walked the dirt roads of Carmichael to Sunday school, or caught a ride in a neighbor's wagon. Families pitched in with pennies so the teachers could purchase song books and other resources. Once the church had its own building in 1927 (classes and worship previously met at Carmichael School), children crowded onto the porch for Sunday school, or in the basement, their classes partitioned by tables set on their sides.

During the baby boom of the 1940s and 1950s, Sunday school classes took place not only in the church basement and porch and in the rustic Boy Scout lodge on the property, but also at the Carmichael Irrigation District building and the county library. Even the church bus—an old diesel purchased from the City of Sacramento, named Ermintrude by members of the youth group—served as a classroom. *Heritage of Faith* notes that during the building phases from 1946 to 1951 (chapel, parlor, west wing classrooms, sanctuary) and from 1955 to 1963 (two-story classroom units, McMillen Hall, kitchen), construction was constantly "playing catch-up" with the growth in church membership and Sunday school attendance.

By the 1970s CPC's Christian Education programs, under the direction of Jimmi Mishler, were categorized by age group—pre-communicant (elementary school age), youth, and adults—with subcommittees for each in charge of curriculum, teacher recruiting and training, and activities. As mentioned in Chapter 3, while Sunday school was highly age-differentiated, this era also saw the beginning of intergenerational activities such as family skating parties, Easter Week activities, and a One Great Hour of Sharing art project connected to the denominational giving campaign by the same name (see Chapter 8).

---

8 No first name is given in sources used for this book

Heritage of Faith also notes that the Advent Family Breakfast, in which the congregation met for worship and communion on the first Sunday of Advent around tables in the social hall, began during the 1970s. So did the tradition of a Stone Soup supper following a Sunday of creative workshops for families. As in the children's story "Stone Soup," families would each bring an ingredient for a stew, which would cook all day and be served for supper.

Marsha Cook, a child of CPC, who for a time directed a parent co-op preschool on the CPC campus, shared these reflections on Christian Education in the 1970s:

> Carmichael Presbyterian Church has given me an outstanding and grounding base for my faith. When I was in high school, I volunteered to help in the Sunday School Department when Jimmi Mishler was the director. I stayed for fourteen years, and through her many and careful workshops on how to teach lessons I became totally grounded in the many Bible stories and in teaching them; they became a part of my life.... I ended up searching for an even deeper relationship with the presence of God. My seminary education solidified my thirst for the living God. It made my faith stronger when learning the history of the Bible stories, and the depth of the Greek and Hebrew Bibles. I grew a passion for serving, helping, and supporting in the Church.[9]

Sunday morning chapel time was a feature of the elementary-age Sunday school program from 1979 through 1986 to provide music education. The Rev. David Templin, an associate pastor, led the chapel time with Mary Torgerson, Jean Brown, and Roberta Gaston.

A major development in the 1990s was the adoption of a child abuse prevention policy. In her annual report to the congregation for 1997, the Rev. Sharon Sauer expressed her gratitude for CPC leaders' work in writing the policy. "I see this as a sign of growth and health," she wrote. California Assembly Bill 3354 had become law in January 1997 and required all clergy to become mandatory reporters of suspected physical or sexual abuse of children. The church policy

---

9 Marsha Cook, personal communication, January 25, 2023

was updated several times. Implementation steps during 1998 and continuing as of 2023 included fingerprinting and criminal background checks for all paid staff and all volunteers who worked with children.

Interviewees for this book shared Sunday school memories—particularly of Barbara Parshall, who in 1996 received special recognition during worship for her forty-eight years of continuous teaching in CPC programs.

In 1983, Barbara Parshall and her co-teachers, Oscar Ritter and Steven Floyd, initiated a time capsule project with their students. Describing it, they wrote:

> Our junior high curriculum has concentrated on the history of the church along with detailing the difficulties the early Christians had to overcome. Studying these situations generated the time capsule idea, especially since we are living in rapidly changing times. Everyone agreed that providing current information on the mission of our church and other happenings would be of great interest to the Christians of the next generation. All junior highs plan to be here in the year 2000 when the capsule is unearthed.[10]

Forty students worked together to gather the items. These included issues of *Time* magazine and *Popular Mechanics*, as a reminder of the news and technology of the day. Also included in the time capsule were:

- Newsletters from the Youth Advisory Council, listing activities of the Fellowship of the Carpenter (high school youth group) and Free Spirits (junior high youth). Their calendar included a planned trip to see the film *The Empire Strikes Back*, the much-anticipated *Star Wars* sequel.

- The June 11 issue of the *Sacramento Bee* that included articles about the closing of La Sierra High School in Carmichael, and about the reunification of the Northern and Southern branches of the Presbyterian Church and formation of the Presbyterian Church (USA)

- Audio recordings of sermons by the three pastors serving at

---

10 Barbara Parshall, Our Junior High Sunday School Time Capsule, June 1983.

that time: the Rev. Dr. William (Bill) Johnson, the Rev. Larry Jung, and the Rev. Marjorie Wright

- An audio tape of the children describing the time capsule project

- The 1981 CPC pictorial directory

- A pocket-sized New Testament, Good News for Modern Man translation

- A written prayer by eighth-grader Debbie Cox

- Copies of the June 1983 *Mission Bell* and the May 29 Sunday bulletin

- A proposed church budget for 1983

The time capsule also included a write-up describing the work of the CPC Food Closet, then just ten years old, and the Sacramento Food Closet Coalition. It closed with these words: "Hopefully, as you read this in the year 2000 the food need will no longer exist and will be only a matter of history."

Pamela Jacobi (later the Rev. Pamela Jacobi Starbuck) was in the class that made the time capsule. She attended the May 2000 unearthing ceremony, along with classmates Karen Tozier (Gray) and Garrett Torgerson. Of her Sunday school teacher, Pamela said:

> Barbara Parshall did ministry while "broken." She would invite us to her home to bake cookies while her husband was in a hospital bed in the living room. She cared for her great-grandchildren, and all the time would still teach us. She had a great big map in the Sunday school room. She showed us all the places where people were serving Christ around the world. She was never "cool." She always wore those housecoat dresses. But she loved us so much. She lived out un-self-consciousness while doing her youth ministry.

The Rev. Christa Brewer also remarked on Barbara Parshall's lessons about mission work abroad and living a Christian life:

> In junior high Sunday school with Barbara Parshall (1991–1994 for me) we supported the American Bible Society with our offerings. We were asked to bring at least fifty cents a month.

We had a chart up front with our names and how much we'd given. She would give us an update each month and divide the total by three dollars, because that was how much each Bible cost. And she'd tell us every time a shipment of Bibles went somewhere. We were always excited by how many Bibles we were able to give to others in the world. This was a great way to incorporate stewardship and mission outreach into junior high Sunday school.

...[Mrs. Parshall] must have been in her seventies at that time. No one misbehaved in that class because we just revered her. You had so much love and respect for her because you'd been dying to get into her class since the second grade. She respected us as intelligent people. We were not talked down to. She expected a lot of engagement from us and got a lot of engagement from us. We actually read a book together one year and talked about it. It blows my mind that we could do this. She had some magic in her or something. We ended each class with a prayer circle by the exit door. This was some powerful prayer time, just holding hands in a circle and so deeply appreciating that moment. She knew us inside and out.[11]

Christa spoke fondly of other teachers too:

Martha Hatfield and Mary MacDonald were my first-grade teachers. My parents [David and Phyllis Brewer] taught my third-grade class, when we had to memorize all the books of the Bible. Pat and Gene Chaney taught fourth grade. I had surgery that year, and they followed up and checked in on me. [All the teachers] took us seriously. And every single Sunday after first grade we'd go and give Martha and Mary hugs. I remember that we were loved and how much fun we had.[12]

Following on the success and congregation-wide enthusiasm for the time capsule's opening in 2000, the junior high Sunday school class in 2001

---

11 Rev. Christa Brewer, interview by Susan Herman, June 7, 2022.
12 Rev. Christa Brewer, interview.

created a new time capsule, on the theme "Year of the Child," which the entire denomination observed that year. They buried the sturdy metal box on June 17, 2001, in the same corner of the courtyard where the 1983 time capsule had been laid. Several members of that 2001 class joined with the next generation of CPC children on May 21, 2023 (Heritage Sunday) to open it.

The 2001 time capsule contained photos and class lists from each of the seven classes then meeting at the church's weekday preschool (see Chapter 5). It also included a photo of the thirty-two member Mexico mission team and a blue Amor Ministries t-shirt (see Chapter 7), a photo of the children's corner in the Bea Durley Library, and a series of photos taken by Wayne MacRostie of the seventy-two children ages two through twelve who participated in the June 3, 2001, Children's Sabbath. There was also a set of wooden characters from Godly Play, scripts from two Kid's Connection skits, a t-shirt and promotional materials from the Summer 2001 Vacation Bible School, a Bible presented to the 2001 third-grade class, and a Presbyterian Planning Calendar for 2000–2001 featuring art by children from PC(USA) churches across the country.

Godly Play and Faith Stepping Stones

In launching its Godly Play ministry in 1996, Christian Education at CPC was embracing Montessori-inspired practices and constructivist streams of thought that were being implemented in some public and private schools at the time, particularly for young children. Maria Montessori (1870–1952), an Italian physician, had developed her educational curriculum to create "opportunities for student movement and interaction in a structured environment that supports children's natural curiosity." In Godly Play, as in Montessori, teachers "accompany the child in a careful and respectful manner,"[13] introducing content through hand-size wooden figures and other props that children can touch, such as pieces of colored felt and small basins of water.

Godly Play encourages children to wonder about God and God's relationship

---

13 Emel Ultanir, "An Epistemological Glance at the Constructivist Approach: Constructivist Learning in Dewey, Piaget, and Montessori," *International Journal of Instruction* 2, no. 2 (2012): 203-04, https://files.eric.ed.gov/fulltext/ED533786.pdf.

with people. Teachers create models of wondering for the children during the story time, asking questions such as "I wonder what part is most important? I wonder where you are in the story/what part of the story is about you?" Children play with the simple wooden pieces and hear stories representing three main topics:

- Sacred Story—Old Testament stories such as Creation, Noah and the Flood, the Ten Best Ways, and Abraham and Sarah beginning the Great Family

- Parables—New Testament stories of Jesus

- Liturgical Action—explanations of the symbols and rites of the church and the actions used in Christian worship

As mentioned in Chapter 1, the Rev. Sharon Sauer introduced Godly Play to CPC in 1996. In doing so, she first needed approval of the Session. Of that time, elder Dave Studer said:

> She brought it before the Education Division, and they were not so sure about it. I remember meeting with her afterwards. And I said, "Do it again. But this time, don't tell us about it, *show* us how it works." And then they embraced it. And it's still part of the program.[14]

Pastor Sherry recruited Mary MacDonald to teach Godly Play. Mary had joined CPC in 1979 and began teaching Sunday school shortly after. Bonnie Paxton and Paul Shultz teamed up with Mary for Godly Play, and the three continued teaching the program together for twenty-five years. Mary noted that the "wooden story pieces were made by Paul Shultz, Bob Beckert, and a friend of mine who is actually a Jewish carpenter!"[15]

Over the years, Mary MacDonald said, she and Bonnie Paxton modified the structure of the class somewhat, adding in the PC(USA)'s *Belonging to God* catechism cards, a set of sixty question and answer cards that teach children about God's relationship with humanity and our relationship with each other. The children's catechism begins with, "Who are you?" to which the children respond, "A child of God."

---

14 David Studer, interview by Susan Herman, August 25, 2019.
15 Mary MacDonald, interview by Susan Herman, March 8, 2022.

Mary continued:

> It is amazing how engaged the kids are with the stories. There
> have been times when I saw kids practically crawling in Bonnie's
> lap to get closer to the story. Often kids want to continue working
> with the story instead of the craft project. The parable of the Great
> Pearl [Matthew 13: 45–46] is one that leaves them quiet. They are
> amazed that someone would even give up their bed and house to
> get that pearl. The other story that always brings questions is the
> Good Samaritan. Kids want to know just how bad someone can
> be and still have God love them. They always asked if God loved
> robbers, and bad guys and criminals and finally one boy asked if
> God even loved [President Donald] Trump! I had to choke down
> my laughter but assured them yes, even Trump....
>
> Over the years I have had older kids who want to come back for
> a bit. We tell them they are our helpers and can help show the
> little kids how to sit in the circle and listen quietly to the story.
> I always find these older kids are looking for something. They
> always enter the stories at a new depth. They don't stay many
> weeks, but we always let them come. We never discourage them
> from finding a special time to come close to God.[16]

Godly Play was for a short time used with all age groups up through high
school, but by the early 2000s, it continued for ages three through six
(kindergarten or first grade) while other curriculum series were adopted
for children ages seven and up. Some of these were designed to follow
the Sunday Bible passages used in worship from the Revised Common
Lectionary, while others had their own internal organization. For example,
Expressions of Faith, used for upper elementary grades, combined acts of
service with Bible conversations. On some Sundays the students would
sort and stage items in the Food Closet, re-packaging rice and other food
from large containers to smaller bags appropriate for one or two meals.

In 2002, Lynn Shultz, who had earlier served as CPC's interim director of
Christian Education, took a position with the Presbytery of Sacramento
as its Resource Center director. After her stint with the presbytery, Lynn

---

16 MacDonald, interview.

remained involved in Christian Education at CPC, serving on the Session's Christian Education Division in various roles for another fifteen years. In an interview Lynn spoke about meeting Rich Melheim, whose company, Faith Inkubators, created the BibleSong curriculum. CPC adopted BibleSong in 2007 and used it for seven years.

> He had developed a program that we used for a little while at CPC: "incubating faith every night in every home." He was a Lutheran, but anyway, there were different forms of [his program being used] all over the place. And there were also some Presbyterian educators that were adding it too. He asked me to come back to their headquarters in Stillwater, Minnesota. I realized once I got there that I was *the* Presbyterian representative. He had people from all the different faiths that were going over his curriculum so that they would mesh with all these different churches. I felt very inadequate. But I guess I had asked the most questions about it. Anyway, it was a very nice trip![17]

The BibleSong curriculum included sign language as well as art and singing to help children learn Bible stories and tenets of the Christian faith. It also included a robust take-home component that encouraged families to discuss "highs and lows" of the day, read a Bible verse or story, and pray together. The congregation hosted Rich Melheim in 2009 for a teacher training.

In addition to the school year-based Sunday school program, CPC offered the Faith Stepping Stones program (also by Faith Inkubators) starting in 2002 and continuing through the time of this writing in 2023. Each of the seven "stones" represented a step or a stage of development in a child's faith journey: baptism, entry into Sunday school, learning about the Lord's Supper, first Bible, entry to youth group, confirmation, graduation/entry to adulthood. The two- or three-session classes associated with each stepping stone were offered to students as they entered the appropriate age range. Lynn Shultz introduced Stepping Stones to the Christian Education Division. For many years she took the lead in extending invitations to parents of infants to join the baptism classes. She tracked each cohort of children through the seven rites of passage, up through high school graduation.

---

17 Lynn Shultz, interview by Susan Herman, February 14, 2023.

Lynn taught the First Communion class for second graders for ten years, handing it off to ElizaBeth Phillips in 2013. This class included education for both children and parents about the sacrament's meaning, and an exploration of Jesus's last supper with his disciples. It also featured a baking session in the church kitchen. The children then presented the communion bread they had baked for use in the next Sunday's service.

When Lynn's longtime Stepping Stones teaching partner Christine Dorf stepped down in 2008, Michael Gray took responsibility for the First Bible class for third graders, partnering with Terry Barto for a few years, then teaching it on his own. Parents were also included in the First Bible class, and often said they appreciated the refresher on Bible history and the different types of literature found in the Bible. The ceremony for presenting first Bibles, held on a Sunday during worship, included reading aloud this inscription from the inside front cover:

> In celebration of your faith journey, this Bible is hereby presented to [Name] and comes with a Lifetime Guarantee. Should this Bible ever become lost, destroyed, or just plain worn out, this congregation promises to replace it so that you will never be without the Word of God in your daily life! With love from Carmichael Presbyterian Church, Carmichael California, [Date], Signed by Keith L. DeVries, Pastor.

In March 2023 as part of CPC's centennial celebrations, everyone in the congregation was invited to bring their first Bibles on the day the third graders received theirs. Then in June during the Youth Sunday service, the congregation had a chance to make good on its Lifetime Guarantee. Bruce MacLean, who had grown up at CPC and at age sixty misplaced his Bible, received a new one. Fourth grader Aiden Westbrook and seventh grader Robin Herman, who were helping to lead Youth Sunday worship, signed the Lifetime Guarantee and read the inscription aloud to Bruce.

As Lisa Torgerson's leadership in Christian Education evolved over the 2000s and 2010s, she coordinated with youth leaders and volunteer teachers to form confirmation classes every few years. These sometimes followed a curriculum guide, but not always. At its core, confirmation was a series of one-on-one conversations about the life of faith between each confirmand

and an adult mentor from the congregation. Confirmands were formally recognized in a worship service by answering the four membership questions from the PC(USA)'s constitution:

- Trusting in the gracious mercy of God, do you turn from the ways of sin and renounce evil and its power in the world?

- Do you turn to Jesus Christ and accept him as your Lord and Savior, trusting in his grace and love?

- Will you be Christ's faithful disciple, obeying his Word and showing his love?

- Will you be a faithful member of this congregation, share in its worship and ministry through your prayers and gifts?

Mary MacDonald, who in addition to teaching Godly Play also coordinated Youth Sunday worship for several years, stayed abreast of which children were entering their senior year of high school. At the beginning of their school year, Mary would ask the high school seniors their favorite colors, so she could sew each one of them a quilt for their families to wrap them in during the final Stepping Stone recognition in worship. Between 2003 and 2023 she made over 160 quilts.

The quilt idea was not part of the official Faith Stepping Stones curriculum, Mary explained. Lynn had come back from an Association of Presbyterian Christian Educators (APCE) conference feeling excited about the new program and began brainstorming with Mary and others about gifts they could use to recognize each of the Stepping Stones. Mary remembered:

> We were not sure what to do about graduation from high school. A few days after our meeting I was watching an episode of the *Carol Duvall Show*. She had on two women from a church in the Midwest who were describing these easy-to-make "striped" lap quilts. I knew it was perfect. We began the year [Pastor] Keith's youngest daughter graduated high school. We kept it a secret from everyone except Rev. Carol Pagelsen.[18]

---

18 Mary MacDonald, personal communication, June 14, 2023.

Worship Hour Pull-Out Classes

Children's Sunday school at CPC was for many decades taught during the worship services, mostly out of necessity to manage large numbers, and partly because worship services were quite formal, and some adults preferred not to hear children's noises. The outlook on children in worship began to shift during the 1990s, and the Sunday school hour was eventually moved to 10:00 a.m., between the two worship services.

Still, some families still wanted an option for their children to do age-appropriate worship activities, rather than stay in the sanctuary for the sermon and prayers. Around 1998, Kristen Zeman—whose mother Mary Torgerson, had been very involved with children's ministry—began leading a second service pull-out class called Kids' Connection. After the children's sermon, children ages three through eleven were invited upstairs to Kids' Connection. Other classes were added in and out of the rotation for the next fifteen or so years. These included Jesus and Me (JAM) for younger children and Reader's Theater for third through fifth graders. There was also a puppet storytelling class from 2005–2007, led by Martin Bass. Kids' Connection and Readers' Theater were high-energy, interactive classes involving a mix of music, Bible-themed games, and skits.

Several of the families who began attending CPC in the early 2010s gravitated to the 8:45 a.m. traditional service. In 2012 an additional pull-out time was added for their children, using a preschooler-friendly, lectionary-based curriculum called Spark published by Sparkhouse, the publishing house of the Evangelical Lutheran Church in America (ELCA). In addition to Bible lessons the pull-out classes allotted plenty of time for free play with train sets and building blocks in the well-appointed room.

Kristen continued her second service pull-out until 2015. Other volunteers stepped in afterwards, using the Spark curriculum. Soon the 10:00 a.m. Sunday school hour was also using the Sparkhouse materials for grades two and three and four and five, with Godly Play continuing for the younger children. Infants and toddlers rested or played in the nursery under Paul and Mary Camozzi's loving care. The Camozzis began providing Sunday child care at CPC in 2001 and continue to do so at the time of this writing in 2023.

Bea Durley Library

A library was first established at CPC in 1955. Its initial collection consisted of books for children and youth. Over time the collection grew to include church history and doctrine, world religions, Bible study resources, biographies and memoirs, theological and cultural scholarship, fiction, and audio and video recordings. *Heritage of Faith* traces the location of the CPC library from the church office to the Session room on the east side of the chancel in 1957 (now the sacristy, used for communion supplies and preparation), and then, in 1967, to a room between the parlor and the sanctuary.

Bea Durley was librarian by that time, and Doris Beckert, who had recently joined CPC, quickly became her assistant. Doris spoke of her history with Bea Durley and the church library:

> I was a professional librarian. So, I took note that there was a library here and offered my services to Bea Durley. It was down there where the Gathering Place is now. I aided Bea Durley in cataloguing and minor things [starting in] 1967.

> ...I aided in the library for years and years, and even got my Mariner ship to take the library as their cargo. For many years we've had the library as our cargo, but mostly now it's just financial aid. Before we used to be painting, making curtains, all sorts of detail, taking inventory. Then Bea died in 1993 and it was a big shock to everybody. And so things came to a grinding halt there for a few months until Education Division named me librarian in January 1994.... In 1995 they named the library in honor of Bea Durley—there's a plaque.

> Then they were planning to have this big redevelopment here and they had to move the preschool into the library. So the library was moved and put in storage in one of the preschool rooms. And there was a fire in that room.

> I thought everything was gone. But no, the shelf list, which is the data for the library—the cards were all singed but readable. That was 1998. It took a long time to go through the insurance process. It was a really dark time. There was no library the

whole year of 1998. And most of 1999, while the new wing was being constructed, it was all on hold. I remember going to the fire people's place where they oxygenated the books in a vat. Took the smell out. I had to go and weed out anything that we didn't want to waste time treating. And there was a whole warehouse full of books being de-smoked. So everything was on hold. It was really a little bit chaotic because I lost some things. A lot of books were stored in a desk and then they got rid of the desk.

Then in 1999, the wing was done. And that's when the new library was opened, and new life has begun.... What you see is the result of a lot of people working to try to furnish it with insurance funds or with free donations. The children's table and two chairs were bought by insurance and the bookcases were all insurance money. And the rest was donations. That credenza and the desk, it's all donations. The media center was planned and purchased with funds from the church.

The media center had a television and VCR. It housed a collection of video recordings of sermons and special church events for checkout, along with donated videos in a variety of genres, including the children's series *Veggie Tales*.

Doris Beckert became involved in the National Church Library Association based in Stillwater, Minnesota, and led its local chapter for many years before the association closed in 2012. Her assistants in the CPC library included her husband Bob, Carol Piper, Kate Erlich, Rob Axell, and Ernie Chard.

Each year since becoming CPC's librarian, Doris reported statistics on books and other items in the collection. As of 2022 the library collection included 3,670 books. Doris contributed updates to the *Mission Bell* on new titles, both purchased and donated, and encouraged readers to visit the library. She also began a long project of data entry for the Resource Center of the Presbytery of North Central California, which moved onto CPC's campus in 2021.

Youth Ministries

> *[In the 1950s] Chi Sigma was the place to be!
> On any given Sunday night, there would be upwards
> of 100 plus high schoolers here having a mini church
> service, activities, refreshments (of course) and just
> enjoying fellowship. Chi Sigma became "my group"!
> I felt an identity there. It was a place to grow in
> Christian faith, to be accepted, loved, and supported.
> It was a place to learn leadership skills as Chi Sigma
> officers and to become a part of a larger Christian
> community as we were encouraged to become youth
> presbytery and synod officers. I was privileged
> to be able to serve in those offices.*
>
> *—Jan Olson*[19]

Youth ministries for adolescents and young adults at CPC have taken various forms over the years, changing based on the needs of the participants, the culture of the time period, and who was leading. As mentioned in Chapter 3, the first youth group at CPC was called Society of Christian Endeavor. During Jan Olson's time in the 1950s, the youth group took the name Chi Sigma. Later iterations were called Agape, The Beach, Fellowship of the Carpenter, Free Spirits, and Miraculous Catch of Fish. (According to Jennifer Boyd, this name was conceived of as a kind of parody of Fellowship of the Carpenter.[20]) In 2011 it was re-branded once again as Upper Room Student Ministry, a name still in use in 2023.

Since the 1990s youth ministry at CPC has emphasized, to varying degrees, Bible study, outreach, relationship-building, leadership development, worship, and mission. Topical discussions had to do with friendships, parents, school, money—all the subjects you might expect—plus matters of personal and sexual ethics and what it means to take the Bible seriously, if not always literally.

---

19 Jan Olson, Faith Story presented to the CPC congregation during worship, November 17, 2018.
20 Jennifer Boyd, interview by Susan Herman, October 27, 2022.

Leadership and leadership structure for youth ministries underwent multiple changes over the last twenty-five years (see Table 4.1), from having an ordained pastor in charge, through having paid directors for both junior and senior high with a Director of Christian Education overseeing the program, to having a single staff member handling all the planning, communication, and execution. By the mid-1990s a Young People's Discipling Committee steered the program and advised the staff. This committee was absorbed into the Session's Christian Education Division in 1998.

Table 4.1: Youth Ministry Leaders of CPC, 1998–2023

Position	Name	Years Served
Director of Youth Ministries	Mark Studer	1997–2001
	Chris Studer	2001–2004
	Abby Fox	2009–2011
	Ronnie Slimp	2011
	Jeremy Meehan	2011-2013
	Lisa Torgerson	2013-2021
Youth Ministry Coordinators	Chris Studer	2004–2005
	Laura Janik	2005
	Brett Bowers-Smith	2005
Pastoral Assistant/ Associate Pastor for Youth and Family Ministries	Rev. K. C. Wahe	2003–2006
Director of High School Ministries	Megan Kays	2006–2009
Director of Junior High Ministries	Laura Birdsall	2006–2009
College Ministry	Mark Studer	1997–1998
	Rev. Sherry Sauer	
	Rev. Pam Jacobi	1999–2001
	Scott & Sharon Rathburn	2009
	Garrett & Lisa Torgerson	2010
Youth Ministry Interns	Katherine Sawyer	2015–2016
	Matthew Lillie	2018–2020

Up until the 2010s, the Christian Education Division included eight to a dozen members. They provided youth directors with program guidance. They also recruited volunteers, such that CPC's youth had regular contact with many caring adults each year. Most of the time the volunteers did not have children in the youth group. As church membership declined and personnel costs for hiring youth staff became ever more prohibitive, volunteer support also waned and the Christian Education Division itself contracted considerably.

Lisa Torgerson, who had taken over leadership of youth programs in 2013 on top of her work with children's and family ministries, excelled in event planning and developed deep, trusting relationships with many teens and families. Because of this she was able to run a high-quality program, with assistance during a few of those years from paid interns. However, the pool of volunteers slowly dried up.

After Lisa's resignation in 2023 CPC's Personnel Committee launched a search for a new director for youth and children's ministry and began to explore ways it might alter staffing structure or otherwise re-envision the church's ministry to children and youth.

Learning, Meaning-Making, and Truth

Chris Studer related that in 1998, when he was in college and his brother Mark was youth director at CPC, they both attended a college group at Fremont Presbyterian in East Sacramento. Its leader, Chris said, "was really good at the exegetical approach toward scripture." They had encountered the historical-critical method of interpreting the Bible in Sunday sermons at CPC but hadn't previously understood "where to turn if we had questions about scripture." Because of this experience they chose to follow a Bible- and lectionary-based curriculum for both their Sunday school classes and midweek evening youth group meetings.

"I think we could have done more topical lessons," Chris said. However, the Bible discussions paid off when youth group members knew the passage that was going to be preached on the next Sunday. "They showed up at church and worship. It was easier for them to engage if they already knew something about the passage." Chris went on,

Just knowing that Scripture is layered and complex and sometimes scary—it's a beehive of issues at times. But there are ways of navigating through all of this that can be talked about and explored, rather than having to read something and think you're being forced to believe things in exactly this way. That was important to me.[21]

Likewise, Jennifer Boyd said she was glad youth ministry at CPC taught her to view the Bible in a nuanced way. She was in the youth group when Mark Studer was the leader:

I really do credit [Mark] for a lot of my intellectual interest in theology. He opened that world up to me and allowed me to pursue the intellectual side of my faith instead of just the spiritual [though] both are important. That allowed me to approach theology as a study—as a subject—instead of just, "Oh, you should *feel* God now."

...Most of the Bible wasn't written as it was happening, right? It was written in the post exilic period. It was a group of people who were trying to figure out who they were in relationship to the fact that they had just lost their state and were then exiled and were now coming back—it's basically a constitution, it's defining who they are as a nation, but they don't have a state.... For sure, the Spirit can influence how you hear things or how you interpret things. But it's not as if the prophets were writing to me personally.

I was being taught these things when I was in high school. The Bible is not a book about God. It's a book about people's relationship with God. How could we write a book about God? God's too big for that.

Jennifer went on to say that looking more deeply into her faith was especially helpful in confronting the "purity culture" movement. Many Christians in the 1990s put outsize emphasis on teaching teens to avoid sex at all costs, not just for reasons of healthy development but because God wanted them to save themselves for marriage, to remain pure. Jennifer said that her youth leaders, by teaching how to reflect critically on God's Word, helped her

---

21 Chris Studer, interview by Susan Herman, November 3, 2022.

understand that while they should protect themselves from risky situations, ultimately "boys and girls are worth more than what they've done. They have innate value."[22]

Katherine Sawyer, who was in the youth group from 2006–2013, shared her experience of coming to church for the first time as a fifth grader:

> John Wallace brought my family [to CPC]. My dad knew him through Boy Scouts. My grandma had passed away and my dad was kind of looking for a church after that... and my dad went one Sunday, and then the next Sunday, it was like, "Everybody's coming."

Katherine had not grown up with Christianity but said her Sunday school classmate Ryan MacLean helped her get up to speed. "We were always so glad when Ryan was on our Bible quiz team!"

As a middle schooler, Katherine went to summer rafting camp at Rock-n-Water with her church friends and youth leader Laura Birdsall. "I think I went two or three times as a camper. And then when I was sixteen, I was a volunteer for a summer at Rock-n-Water. And then after that, I became an official guide. I worked at Rock-n-Water for four years." In addition to being a river guide, Katherine's job was to have campfire talks about faith with the campers. Since then, she said, "I've gone through a deconstruction, kind of. I don't know if I believe that I'm specifically Christian anymore." Explaining, she said:

> I believe in love. And I think that's what Jesus was trying to teach us. That's what I hold on to, and I credit CPC for that a lot, because of the service that they taught me and the loving the community and being welcoming to everybody.... All the finer details of religion and Christianity just get so complex. Working at Rock-n-Water I got groups from every denomination. So I was getting mixed messages from all these different groups.... That was educational, but also stressful because I did feel like I was being compared to other people. Like, am I Christian enough? Am I reading my Bible enough?... I think there needed to be more structure for the younger group of us that were there.

---

22 Boyd, interview.

Talking about her faith life today, Katherine said that she hadn't been able to find a church she feels comfortable attending in the Tacoma, Washington area, where she lives now and works as a nurse:

> I miss the people aspect and the community aspect of a church. But I actually see my work now as my method of acting out my love and service. I had an interesting interaction with a patient when I was in nursing school. I was washing her feet after she had soiled herself and I said, just making conversation, "Do you know the lessons Jesus taught when he was washing his disciples' feet? I'm not comparing myself to Jesus or anything, but it came into my mind as I'm sitting here washing your feet," and she was like, "Oh, yeah, interesting connection." And that was a moment [when I thought] even if I'm not attending church, even if I'm not working at a church, I am still acting out my Christianity in the way that I live, in the way that I work.[23]

Outreach, Mission, and Evangelism

Youth groups at CPC had a regular practice of teaming up with groups from other churches for mission trips, and for special activities within the presbytery. The door was always open to friends who needed something other than sports, family, or school to think about.

During Jeremy Meehan's time as youth leader from 2011 to 2013, he emphasized the outreach facet of the ministry by hosting fun events—lock-ins, messy games on the field, holiday parties—and by taking groups on such outings as the Dixon Corn Maze and an ice rink to play broomball. Jeremy did a lot of work himself to upgrade the youth rooms and found low-priced or donated furnishings to make them inviting. Over the summer of 2012, he renovated the three-room suite to create a study lounge with café-style seating; several conversation areas with shelving for Bibles and board games; a video gaming spot with oversized bean bags; and a recreation room with a table tennis, foosball, air hockey, and a pool table. When all the work was done, the youth hosted an open house for the whole congregation to come and admire the refurbished spaces.

---

23 Katherine Sawyer, interview by Susan Herman, April 28, 2023.

Aside from the Mexico missions described in Chapter 7, CPC youth groups were engaged in local missions and hunger awareness campaigns such as the Sacramento Food Bank's Run to Feed the Hungry race at Thanksgiving, World Vision's 30 Hour Famine, and the Souper Bowl of Caring (collecting money for food closets on Super Bowl Sunday). Alongside CPC deacons, members of the youth group helped stage and deliver Christmas Baskets. They also pitched in as servers at Supper on Saturday and helped set up beds in classrooms for when the congregation hosted families from Family Promise of Sacramento (see Chapter 6).

Mission trips inside the US varied widely in terms of the types of communities the youth groups would interact with and the topics of focus. For a few years the junior high youth traveled to Ceres, California to the Heifer Ranch, where they learned about the work of Heifer International on food security and helping farmers in developing nations use their livestock to create income streams.

In 2016 junior high students spent a three-day weekend in Pacific Grove learning how plastics in the ocean affect marine life and cleaning a beach while collecting data for a scientific study on types of garbage left on local beaches. Senior high students spent a week in April of 2017 doing cleanup and restoration work in rural Middletown, California, after it had suffered wildfire devastation.

Other trips included visiting a Navajo reservation in Arizona, and several urban locations where students spent time with unhoused people and assisted with existing local ministries offering food and shelter. Often the mission was a combination of meeting new people and hearing their stories, worshiping and praying in diverse Christian settings, and physical labor (e.g., painting, digging, simple construction, serving food, and washing dishes).

John Wallace, a longtime volunteer with CPC youth groups, shared about some of the trips:

> Our 2010 youth mission trip was to San Diego doing inner-city mission with Event Source Ministries (the same organization we used last year in Arizona). Kenny May was the organizer. Our group of eighteen did Vacation Bible School with local children,

and home projects (porch railing, patio, fence, concrete step and backyard grading) in La Mesa as well as feeding the hungry and homeless in downtown San Diego. There was a small mulch project at the church where we stayed in Lake Murray and a fence-painting project at the VBS church.

Jeremy Meehan was from the Portland, Oregon area, so the high school youth mission trip in 2012 was to Portland (twenty-two youth, eight adults). The ministry program we partnered with was Second Stories, located at the Lents Gilbert Church of God. Their ministry focus was with the urban campers (homeless) and those in government-subsidized housing. The CPC Mission team also worked with Adorning Grace, a ministry program for women pulled from the sex-traffic trade. The projects accomplished included: yard work around two Adorning Grace buildings, surveying/fellowshipping with people at three light-rail stations, doing VBS/serving hot dogs at three government-subsidized housing projects, yard work at several senior citizens' homes, building a property fence at Lents Gilbert Church and serving hot dogs/chili on two street corners to the homeless. The team had a Seder meal on Maundy Thursday at Lents Gilbert and a Good Friday worship service at Jeremy's old church. Friday was the group's "fun" day so we drove to the Columbia River Gorge and hiked to the top of Multnomah Falls. We ate at Voodoo Donuts and Kennedy School restaurant. This trip taught us how to minister "with" people (being in relationship) rather than just "for" people (little to no relationship).[24]

John also wrote about work the high schoolers did to help renovate a fellowship hall in an early twentieth-century San Francisco church building, one where a few CPC folks had personal connections. For years after that 2013 trip, the church's website included photos of CPC youth placing tiles and painting walls, giving the space new life, so the church could better carry out its mission.

---

24 John Wallace, CPC History Notes: Pastors, Mission Trips, Stephen Ministry Leadership, Microassistance Program, June 19, 2020

Personal Growth and Leadership

Many youth at CPC served as deacons while still in high school or were nominated to serve on the Session shortly thereafter. Bruce MacLean and his daughter Whitney both had this experience, about thirty years apart. Alex Cavalari, who grew up at CPC and now works as a pharmacist in Rocklin, California, also served in leadership roles. When Alex entered the youth group, he had a difficult time transitioning. On top of normal sixth grade struggles, he had just lost his older sister in a tragic accident. 'I would not have made it if it were not"I would not have made it if it were not for Chris Studer!... He was an inspiration and mentor over the years," Alex said.

> I became highly involved in the youth group and pretty much just stayed. I mean they couldn't get rid of me. I came on as a [volunteer] junior high youth group leader in 2005 and stayed until 2019 when I got hitched.... I'd like to think I made an impact on the youth program. I also served on a few committees while I was at CPC: the van task force, and another membership committee that met monthly with Pastor Keith and was a part of a larger group in the Sacramento Presbytery.[25]

Jennifer Boyd also served as an elder shortly after graduating college and remembered going to presbytery meetings with the Rev. Carol Pagelsen:

> Carol Pagelsen was really important to me because she challenged me a lot in my faith as in, "Okay, so if you don't like this in the church, what are you going to do about it?" You can either sit back and complain or you can make a change and you know, that essentially is what dared me to go to seminary.
>
> I was upset. I think one of the things that really got me upset is I went to the presbytery meeting, where we elected representatives to go to General Assembly. There were some women on the ballot, but none of them were selected. And I was speaking with [Pastor Carol] about it, and I said, "You know, it makes me really mad because I voted for the women...women's voices need to be heard too." And she was like, "So what are you going to do

---

25 Alex Cavalari, interview by Susan Herman, March 2, 2022.

about it?" All right, I thought, I'm gonna be a woman's voice in the church then.

Jennifer did go to seminary, graduated, and later chose a different career—teaching. Similar to Katherine Sawyer's story, Jennifer said that she, too, finds ways to enact the lessons she learned about God every day in her work.

Another child of CPC, Caron Honnold (Treon), shared her experiences with attending a youth conference and helping to plan one. In 1995 she attended Presbyterian Youth Triennium[26] at Purdue University in Indiana—a gathering of around 5,000 youth from across the country.

> When I was young, in junior high, I went to Discovery, which was a weekend. And we had that up in Tahoe. It was a youth conference, and I loved it. I loved it. And we had a guy talk and that was the first time I had experience with someone who was LGBT. He was gay and he used to be a minister and they booted him out.... That was very eye opening, and I put my name down as somebody who wanted to organize the next one.
>
> I was very shy, not very into any of this stuff. But I was so taken with this conference that I wanted to be on the team to design it.
>
> And I did it! A whole year we worked on it. I went all over California. We had a meeting in Fresno, we had a meeting in Modesto, this little nucleus of about twenty people. It was my happy place, my belonging place.
>
> [As a conference planner I had to phone] all these people and ask them if they'd be willing to lead workshops, and willing to come up with a little blurb about what they were going to do. And that was terrifying! But I did it. I got really good at it, too.
>
> Then we put on the conference, and I wish they'd had Fitbit then, because I went up and down those stairs at Zephyr Point about a bazillion times over the weekend.

26 Deana S, "Presbyterian Youth Triennium," July 14, 2016, https://www.history.pcusa.org/blog/2016/07/presbyterian-youth-triennium.

> And then I went to Triennium...about four or five of us from
> that design team for Discovery went. I have a picture, here
> we all are in the airport, Chicago O'Hare, sitting on the floor
> waiting for our bus or flight or something. And we just had
> the greatest old time at Tri, and I've always wanted to go back
> and facilitate a workshop. I don't have to wait until I'm old
> enough anymore![27]

These experiences, Caron said, set the stage for her to make CPC her own
church, not just the one her parents brought her to as a child. She felt
empowered to lead and secure in her own identity as a Christian.

Summer camps at Calvin Crest and Westminster Woods were a highlight
for CPC youth over the past four decades, as was Rock-n-Water during
the past fifteen years. Dozens of former campers from CPC also worked at
summer camp. Chris Studer and his wife, Aimee, worked at Westminster
Woods for five summers, and then served as camp directors there from 2010
to 2020. Katherine Sawyer, in reflecting on her summers as a river guide, was
surprised at how well the job prepared her to be a health professional—not
only in teaching her safety and first aid, but also how to communicate with
different types of people.

To raise funds for mission trips and to defray the costs to families of summer
camp tuition, CPC youth groups had traditionally performed plays and
musicals and put on pancake breakfasts. Each May, during the years 2000
through 2002, the Pinafores and Nautilus Marinerships sponsored a talent
show, raffle, and dinner event for this purpose. Parents from the Lightship
coordinated the acts. Many of the performers were Lightship children,
who were all of camper age, though others pitched in as well. Darrell
Torgerson reported for the *Carmichael Times* that Roberta (Bert) Gaston
played the harmonica. "She says that her air is giving out, driving her to
play smaller and smaller harmonicas. She performed one number with
her "Little Bitty Harmonica," to gales of laughter from the crowd.[28] Lisa

---

27 Carol Honnold and Caron Treon, interview by Susan Herman, March 1,
2020
28 Darrell Torgerson, "Carmichael Presbyterian Church Rasis Funds for Chil-

Torgerson solicited donations from grocery stores and restaurants, while other sponsors obtained raffle items.

The talent show was the seed for Planting Seeds of Faith, a live and silent auction event that continued in 2023 as an annual fundraiser for children and youth of CPC. From modest beginnings—Darrell reported the 2002 event raised $1,400—the auction in later years would raise $27,000 or more. The Rev. Keith DeVries was an accomplished auctioneer. His fast-talking skills were a perfect match for the re-envisioned event. Planting Seeds of Faith attracted members and friends who lived locally, and even some who had moved away from Carmichael, to come for the luncheon and to donate generously.

Adult Christian Education

Like children's and youth education, adult Christian Education at CPC has been a consistent thread of ministry that has assumed different shapes over the years. As mentioned in Chapter 3, at least one adult Sunday school class from the early years became both a social group and a group of co-learners that met weekly for decades, while periodically changing topics and areas of focus on scripture.

This model of cohesive group studying over the years continues in many churches today, but not at CPC. A Sunday service bulletin from 1975 lists nine topical classes for adults. Their titles: "New Life in the New Testament," "Isaiah," "Understanding the Fullness of Life," "Christian Doctrine," "Creative Singlehood," "Inquiry into Faith and Church Membership," "The Bible Speaks to Human Relationships," "Let's Serve," with option number nine being "Coffee and Conversation in the Mahogany Room." Aside from coffee hour, which was on offer every Sunday, the classes were generally designed to last six to twelve weeks.

Fast forward nearly twenty years, and the eleven-member Adult Education Committee was mailing out a twenty-two-page course catalog listing classes that would take place on Sunday mornings and Wednesday evenings as part of the Wednesday Works intergenerational program (see below).

---

dren's Camp," *Carmichael Times*, May 14, 2002.

The faculty list included pastors and missionaries both active and retired, as well as a veterinarian (Marsha Birdsall [later Benfield]), an engineer (David Brewer), a legislative advocate (Margaret Herman), and multiple professors and public-school teachers with specialized skills in counseling, chemistry, music, and other fields.[29]

In the early 2000s adult education classes focused on three main areas:

- Basics of Christian doctrine and practice, designed for an audience of "seekers," or people new to the faith. Topics included the sacraments and worship. (Why do we sing so much? Is worship entertainment, or something else?)

- "Spotlight" classes focusing on hot topics of the day, e.g., science and Creation, labor and Sabbath rest, the latest news on welfare reform, Israel-Palestine issues

- Deep dives into the Bible, e.g., Paul's letters, the Gospels, Revelation

At times there was also a sermon discussion class exploring themes the pastors had brought up in their proclamation of the Word.

Even after well-received visits to CPC by acclaimed Christian writers Anne Weems in 2005 and Diana Butler Bass in 2008, by the early 2010s, interest in adult education seemed to have fallen off precipitously compared to previous decades. The trend was playing out beyond CPC as well. In 2010, researchers Cynthia Woolever and Deborah Bruce reported that, nationwide, the majority of church goers experience their congregation only through worship services. "Less than half of all worshipers (45%) are involved in small groups organized through the congregation," including Sunday school, prayer groups, Bible study groups, and social or fellowship groups.[30] Considering the other small group outlets for adults in addition to education, CPC was doing comparatively well.

Exploring new options for connecting study to the congregation's mission, leaders in Christian Education collaborated with the Mission Division. For seven years beginning in 2012, they offered a speaker series called Connecting

29 Carmichael Presbyterian Church, *Adult Study Center* [booklet] (1993-1994).
30.Woolever and Bruce, A Field Guide to U.S. Congregations: Who's Going Where and Why, Second edition, 50-51.

to Our World. The idea was to expand the audience to include thoughtful adults from across the community, Christians and non-Christians alike. The speakers' visits were advertised in local media and funded largely through a CPC endowment fund held by the Presbyterian Foundation and designated for special speakers. The speakers included:

- Ying Ma—immigrant, lawyer, and policy advisor on China-US economic relations and author of *Chinese Girl in the Ghetto*

- Father Gregory Boyle—priest in Los Angeles, founder of a gang intervention nonprofit called Homeboy Industries, and author of *Tattoos on the Heart*

- David LaMotte—singer/songwriter and Rotary World Peace Fellow, author of children's book *White Flour*, about how Knoxville, Tennessee, citizens peacefully disrupted a Ku Klux Klan march

- Dr. Michael Lodhal—theological scholar and author of *Claiming Abraham* and *Reading the Bible and the Qur'an Side by Side*

- Dr. Marilyn McEntyre—expert on chronic illness, healthy aging, and author of several books on "dying well"

- Rev. Kate Taber—PC(USA) mission coworker in Israel and Palestine serving at the invitation of Palestinian churches in Bethlehem

- Rev. Dr. Yvette Flunder—pastor of City of Refuge United Church of Christ in Oakland, California and author of *Where the Edge Gathers: Building a Community of Radical Inclusion*

- Imam Kamran Islam—imam based in Sacramento, Program Director for Sacramento Academy for Muslim Youth and CAIR Muslim Youth Leadership Programs

In addition to the Connecting to Our World series, Sunday morning and Wednesday evening programming for adult education, when it was offered, continued to feature both Biblical and topical studies. Dick Piper was perhaps the most faithful in offering his time to lead these. Hal and Kelly Holland led a relationship-themed class on *The Five Love Languages*; Susan Herman shared a book study on mental health in the church. In late 2020, four small groups took to Zoom to study *How to be an Anti-Racist* by Ibram X. Kendi, and in 2023 the Revs. Keith DeVries and Ivan Herman, in collaboration with the Session's Inclusion Task Force, led a six-week discussion on a book called *The Bible's Yes to Same-Sex Marriage*.

Partly in response to questions about why attendance and volunteers for adult education had declined, and partly to spur discussion about the future, Pastor Ivan wrote an article for the *Mission Bell* about "flipping the script on education." Referring to Paolo Freire's *Pedagogy of the Oppressed*, the Civil Rights-era Citizen Education Schools of South Carolina and Highlander Folk Schools, he wrote that education "sets us free to take action" and "has been part of Christian teaching and practice since Jesus called twelve disciples to follow and learn by his example."

> Rather than waiting for students to absorb the information handed to them by their masters/teachers through the memorizing of verses, charts, historical dates or mathematical algorithms, a liberation pedagogy treats students as sources of wisdom and learning to be shared.... From the open invitation for our kids to explore wonder in Godly Play, to the interactions in WhatsApp between Afghan women learning English, to the caregiving role play of Stephen Ministers... we are liberating and educating one another....We fulfill our mission to grow in faith together every time we witness the moving of God's Spirit through the gifts of experience, story, and loving relationships.[31]

Intergenerational Ministry

The Rev. Christa Brewer said that while she was an undergraduate, she got involved with the college-age group at Menlo Park Presbyterian.

> We had a designated college pastor who led Sunday morning worship just for us, and activities on campus Wednesday nights. There was something missing, though...at Carmichael I knew everyone from birth to death, all ages. So I started going to church in the sanctuary with more age groups. That was better. But I still felt something was off. When I started getting involved with service activities too, then it finally felt like "this is church!"[32]

---

31 Rev. Ivan Herman, "Education Is Liberation," in *Mission Bell* (November 2022).
32 Rev. Christa Brewer, interview.

Vacation Bible School

The first summer Vacation Bible School (VBS) at Carmichael Church was in 1925. Over the decades the tradition carried on, sometimes in partnership with other churches in the area and sometimes with groups of children specifically invited from neighboring apartment complexes. Its purpose has stayed the same: to reach out to neighborhood children and children of the congregation and provide them a fun and creative place to learn about God and to build relationships with one another. Until the COVID-19 pandemic, numbers of participating children and adults were surprisingly consistent. In 2002, Christian Education chair Mary MacDonald reported that 110 children attended VBS week and ninety adults volunteered. July 2019 saw 176 child participants, plus around fifty teenagers and forty adults as volunteer leaders.

CPC members and friends went all-out to provide a fun experience for children at VBS. For example, in 2002 Randy Benfield provided a demonstration of rappelling for the river adventure-themed week. Glenda Perrou, who volunteered for many summers, commented that she was impressed at how many men took part. Darrell Torgerson, Bob Beckert, Kim Drake—they were all wonderful playground attendants and "VBS grandpas," she said.

Due to the pandemic, in 2020 Lisa Torgerson and about a dozen teen volunteers put together "VBS to-go" bags filled with scavenger hunt lists, coloring pages, and family activity suggestions. Families came to McMillen Hall's curbside to pick up the bags. In 2021 VBS was offered in-person, but much scaled back from previous years. In 2022 no VBS was offered, as the Christian Education Division was reevaluating its programming, staffing, and volunteer needs.

ElizaBeth Phillips and Julie Ueltzen revived VBS in July 2023, this time as an evening program offering dinner. Twenty children participated, along with thirteen teenagers and twelve adults as leaders. The VBS band—complete with drums, bass, guitarists, and vocalists—was entirely led by children ages fourteen and under.

Wednesday Works

In 1989, Jimmi Mishler, in collaboration with youth activities director David Carroll, started an intergenerational weekly dinner and activity night.

They called it Wednesday Works, and it continues as of 2023. Volunteer chefs shopped for and prepared the food; diners paid up to five dollars per person to defray the cost. Chef duties rotated among Mariner groups and volunteers who liked to cook. Sherri Johnson and her team served up an impressive number of dinners for nearly thirty years. After Sherri, Mike Aretsky and his wife Lynette Ledesma took the lead.

After dinner there were Bible studies for adults, choir rehearsals, youth group meetings and games, and contemplative worship. After COVID, it took time to restart these activities, but the dinner portion of Wednesday evenings remained a priority.

Early on, Wednesday Works included skits. Jimmi Mishler described one slapstick episode involving herself and the Rev. Jim Clark. Pastor Clark "asked me to come on stage with my mouth full of water," she said. "He was going to ask me a question—I don't remember what about—and I was supposed to spit an entire mouthful of water at him."[33] In a similar vein, Pastor Gary Califf shared a memory of a dinnertime skit where Pastor Clark was supposed to be a burger-flipping tough guy. "My role was the complaining customer. I went up and told the cook, 'Hey, there's a hair in my burger!' Then [Clark] whapped me hard with the metal spatula!"[34]

Family Outreach and Spiritual Enrichment

For many years CPC members enjoyed an annual picnic at Carmichael Park. The picnic in 2000 featured balloon creations, face painting, and a tree planting. ComNet (see Chapter 3) donated a red oak, which they had received permission to plant in the park. They dedicated it to "our PC(USA) emphasis on the Year of the Child and to our grown CPC children who helped plant and water the tree. Dirt, water, and children—what a great combination!"[35]

Another fun family event was Kite Day, which was held annually at Ancil Hoffman Park in a spot with ample space to fly kites. The Pinafore Mariners

---

33 Jimmi Mishler, personal communication, May 21, 2023.
34 Rev. Dr. Gary Califf, *Future Nostalgia* (Sermon at Carmichael Presbyterian Church May 21, 2023).
35 Carmichael Presbyterian Church, *Annual Report 2000*.

and Darrell Torgerson would present prizes for Most Original Kite, Longest Flight, and the like.

The Family Advent Breakfast and Stone Soup traditions continued, though beginning in 2002 these were combined into one and re-made as an evening craft-making event called Family Advent Night.

The first Harvest Festival at CPC took place in October of 2003. Both the Harvest and Advent events continue as of 2023. Harvest Festival is an outreach event for the community, featuring bounce houses, a costume contest, and a "trunk-or-treat" (where owners of theme-decorated cars give out candy from the trunks of their cars).

For a few years (2010-2012, and 2014) Christian Education staged an elaborate Advent live nativity festival called A Night in Bethlehem. It was intended as a community outreach, similar to Harvest Festival. In its first year the "market stalls" of the recreated Bethlehem village drew 300 attendees. Although successful, Sharon MacLean and others involved determined that with the forty or so volunteers it required, the event was too labor intensive to sustain.

Drama Ministry

Following the tradition of VBS—which always involved skits and acting out stories from the Bible—along with Wednesday Works' onstage dinnertime antics and the Advent nights in Bethlehem village, it seems quite logical that CPC would also have a drama ministry.

Sharon MacLean said that she started the Drama Team in 2000 at the request of Pastor Jim Clark.[36] In the following year's annual report, the Worship Division reported that this team, directed by Karen Orlando and supported by Sharon MacLean and Lisa Benadom, "presented two full-scale drama productions this year." The report continued:

> The first was an Easter drama performed on Maundy Thursday, called *Living Lord's Last Supper*. The second production was on December 9th called *Lost and Found: The Hope of Christ's Birth*.

---

36 Sharon MacLean, interview by Susan Herman, September 11, 2020.

These two productions were an outreach to the community and a blessing to all of us.

When Karen Orlando first saw the Sunday bulletin blurb soliciting members for a drama team at CPC, she ignored it. "I had four kids at home, two of whom were under the age of six." But the idea stuck around, Karen said, continuing:

> Well indeed, God did ask me to step up and that darn blurb in the bulletin was still there [a few weeks later]. I went to the first meeting, and it was just Sharon and me. Little did I know or suspect God was preparing me for a journey of twenty years.... I had never written or directed a drama before, but God provided, repeatedly.

To create a stage that would fit the contours of the renovated chancel space and extend it outwards a bit further, Karen's father drew a design and Ron Standring, a former CPC choir director, got the stage built. "We were on our way to the Last Supper. The next obstacle was we needed thirteen men. Sharon cajoled and wrangled and ultimately had thirteen guys committed to the project." Karen said,

> Every year [since 2001] we have done something during Holy Week. It has been an important part of our ministry. Even with COVID in 2020 we managed to figure something out. Beth Lindley wrote and directed in 2015 our Good Friday drama. It was her gift to Harry, her late husband who had been an instrumental member of our core group.

Dramas at CPC often included children and teenagers. "The kids always brought such gifts to the table," Karen said.

> The Tomlinson kids, Jolie Crockett, and Sarah Spivack—each one was worthy of being the center of one of our dramas. Even if it did get a "no thank you" from Dave Mauerman when Derek Tomlinson and his Shepherd Boyz band took a traditional hymn and turned it into rap music. These kids are so talented. The MacLean kids and my kids were often part of our acting troupe. They could not escape it. Carolyn Biggers and Dick Piper played

grandparents when we did "Gloria, the Christmas Angel," which I adapted from a children's book my sister gave the kids. We had a write up in the *Sacramento Bee* about the drama, because Jenny DeVries wrote an original song for the play. All those great musical backups, writers, singers, and support people. When we asked, they always said yes.[37]

Family and intergenerational ministry is not a new concept at CPC. Just like all other types of ministry, it requires constant renewal, recommitment, and re-examination. As the congregation faces leadership transitions in education, perhaps a way forward with hope lies in strengthening intergenerational opportunities to teach one another and grow in faith together.

---

37 Karen Orlando, Drama History at CPC, November 6, 2020.

Chapter 5
Connecting With and Serving
Our Community:
Children and Families

*Responding to God's love through Jesus Christ,
We connect with and serve our community*

The Carmichael Times, on December 21, 1999, published this Christmas message from CPC's senior pastor, the Rev. Jim Clark:

Recently, the Barna Research Group conducted a random sample poll of over 1000 people, as to what they consider the most important part of Christmas. Eighty-eight percent of those sampled identified themselves as Christians. Forty-four percent of the participants listed family time as the most important part of Christmas, while only 37% said the birth of Christ was most important. This order of importance was of concern to those reporting the study results.

But I wonder if there isn't wisdom to this ordering. How is it we should celebrate the birth of Christ? Somehow, I picture our Lord being pleased to see families together in his name and his honor. Celebrating and expressing their love for one another. After all, it is in the family that we are most likely to experience the kind of unconditional love which Jesus came to share with us.

The next thought that occurred to me is this: What about those whose families are not centers of genuine love, or those who have no family with which to celebrate? Would not Jesus, friend of the friendless, want us to enlarge the circle of love as we celebrate the holy birth? If that is how we Christians celebrate the birth of Christ, it will indeed be "Joy to the World."

Previous chapters in this book have described the family-oriented ministries of Carmichael Presbyterian Church, while also pointing to the many ways in which the CPC family has been set free by that love and care to serve others. Experiencing love within the fold of one's biological family, or one's family of choice, pleases our Lord, noted Rev. Clark in his Christmas message. Jesus was born to teach us how to demonstrate love, so that in doing so, we may help others feel that sense of belonging and embrace. This chapter continues the theme of family, while shifting the focus to CPC's family-oriented outreach into the community and emphasizing the capacity-building and "serving alongside" aspects of that outreach.

Connecting With a Changing Community

Heritage of Faith describes how, in its early decades, CPC primarily served the needs of pioneering farmers and other new residents of Carmichael Colony. The church provided Biblical instruction, spiritual encouragement, and a gathering space for the sharing of ideas as its people developed the land and built out community assets, such as schools, roads, plumbing, and sewers. Once Carmichael Colony became less of an outpost and more of a suburb to Sacramento, with a few key employers driving its growth, CPC's mission focus turned to giving families a place to thrive and build social networks. In the 1960s and 1970s, different needs emerged that the church also sought to fill. Among these were hunger, housing challenges, and changes in patterns of labor and family dynamics necessitating child care outside of the home and more concentrated forms of relationship care than a church's pastoral counseling or fellowship programs could provide.

Following nationwide economic trends from the 1980s until today, well-to-do California residents saw a gradual rise in their incomes. Those who were struggling began to have even more difficulty making ends meet. A 2022 report by the Public Policy Institute of California noted the trends during this period:

> Driven by increased global trade, technological advancements that have favored more educated workers, and other factors, top incomes have grown 60 percent over the last 40 years (reaching $270,000 for families at the 90th percentile). Meanwhile, bottom incomes have suffered several large downward swings, only increasing about 10 percent ($25,000 at the 10th percentile).[1]

Carmichael and neighboring Arden-Arcade exemplified this trend.[2] CPC members, whose relatively high levels of education and employment buffered them somewhat from economic downturns, nonetheless took notice of hunger and precarious housing situations in their midst. Welfare reform, and how the church could respond, was a prominent conversation around CPC in the late 1990s.[3]

In the 1980s and 1990s, and continuing into the 2020s, Carmichael became home to successive waves of refugees—from the former Soviet republics, East Asia, Central Asia, and the Middle East—and the church stepped in to support them in various ways. Homelessness in Carmichael also emerged as a top concern, while food insecurity, even among families with one or more income earner, increased as well. Musing on her fifty-plus years of membership at CPC, Carol Honnold noted how the emphasis in her childhood on worship and Bible study (while still important) had shifted: "We are a community center. I think we had to become that because Carmichael needed it."[4]

Acknowledging the challenges in dealing with community change and staying relevant within Carmichael over time, church historian Jimmi

---

1 Sarah Bohn et al., *Making Sense of California's Economy*, Public Policy Institute of California (2022), https://www.ppic.org/publication/making-sense-of-californias-economy/.
2 Anita Chabria et al., "State's fastest poverty increase in a year was in Arden Arcade," *Sacramento Bee*, September 14, 2017.
3 Betsy Turnbull, "The Place of Carmichael Presbyterian Church in Welfare Reform," *Mission Bell*, November 1998.
4 Carol Honnold and Caron Treon, interview by Susan Herman, March 1, 2020.

Mishler also affirmed that "CPC hasn't become stagnant."[5] Rather, it remains dynamic.

Education and Social Support Outreach

Carmichael Presbyterian Preschool (CPP) was the church's core education outreach ministry from 1986 until 2019. The other activities mentioned in this section illustrate additional ways individual CPC members and fellowship groups have chosen to provide social support to children and families in the community.

For thirty-three years Carmichael Presbyterian Church was home to a community preschool, known as CPP. The program welcomed its first young students in the fall of 1986. In brochures and reports, 1985 is sometimes cited as its founding date, as that is when the commitment was made to establish a preschool. The preschool, while functioning as an independent 501(c)(3) organization, complemented the church's other outreach ministries for children, including Vacation Bible School (described in Chapter 4), a recreational program at the nearby Woodland Towers apartment complex, and tutoring at Deterding and Carmichael Elementary Schools.[6]

In 1989, Karen Banker, a CPC member, founded Mustard Seed School in downtown Sacramento to give unhoused families support and a safe, caring, transitional environment while assisting them to enroll or re-enroll their children in public school. Mustard Seed School continues today, serving children ages three to fifteen. It is an integral part of Sacramento Loaves & Fishes, which in 2023 marked its fortieth year of providing "an oasis for adults and children experiencing homelessness."[7]

In 1999, a volunteer team from CPC was trained to begin tutoring and other activities at the North Area Teen Center, a youth center organized by the Sacramento County Sheriff's Department. And, in 2004, CPC members began participating in another outreach to older adolescents: furnishing

5 Phil Mishler and Jimmi Misher, interview by Kathy Lewin, August 5, 2021.
6 Faye White, Margaret Herman, and Marie Segur, *Heritage of Faith: A 75-Year History of Carmichael Presbyterian Church* (Carmichael Presbyterian Church, 1998), 173-74.
7 "Loaves & Fishes 40th Anniversary," https://sacloaves.org/.

"emancipation baskets" to smooth entry into independent living for those aging out of the county's foster care system.

Carmichael Presbyterian Preschool

> *The joys were incalculable and laughter was my daily bonus. There is nothing I can compare to the joy of witnessing a child's enthusiasm in play, the mastering of a skill, the building of friendships and the development of self-awareness and empathy.*
>
> *–Diana West, CPC preschool director from 2002–2015*[8]

The seed for the CPP was a weekday nursery school started in 1957 by Jessie Glasse, wife of one of CPC's associate pastors at the time, the Rev. John Glasse.[9] Marsha Cook, a current member of CPC, remembered working at this nursery school. After it had ceased operation for some years, Marsha started a parent co-op preschool and served as its director. She left in 1979 to pursue further education and the school once again closed.[10]

In the early 1980s, CPC member Lynn Shultz operated a home preschool. As her children entered public school and Lynn shut down her home business, she began contemplating what to do next. "God put it on my heart that we could have a preschool or a child care at the church," she said. The next step was to find out whether there was demand for either type of service.

Lynn, together with Sue Holman, conducted a survey. Participants included parents of young children who were members of the church as well as parents whose children attended toddler programs provided by the San Juan Unified School District at the time.[11] The Child Care Task Force that formed to administer and analyze results of the survey "reported that they had found very little interest in day care but found a strong interest in

8 Diana West, interview by Susan Herman, January 25, 2023.
9 White, Herman, and Segur, *Heritage of Faith*, 106.
10 Marsha Cook, personal communication, January 25, 2023.
11 Lynn Shultz, interview by Susan Herman, February 14, 2023.

offering a midweek preschool program."[12] With $2000 in seed money from the congregation, walls were repainted and child-size toilets were installed. Some parents expressed concern about there not being a door to the toilet area, Lynn recalled, chuckling, but once she explained about the need to ensure child safety (i.e., adults assisting children in the bathroom could always be observed), these concerns quieted.

Other than the toilets, upgrades to the rooms were fairly simple; some shelving and other furnishings were already in place from the earlier programs. Lynn remembered the "funky little chairs someone had made out of wood pieces and rebar." With all in place, CPP opened its doors on September 2, 1986,[13] offering classes for children aged three, four, and five. Parents were given the option of signing up for a two-day, three-day, or five-day program for their children, which would run from 9:00 a.m until noon. Later a fourth class was added, as well as an extended day option called Lunch Bunch, which allowed children to stay until 2:30 p.m. for an additional fee.

Over the years the preschool's board of directors always included at least one member representing the church. The school served around seventy children each year, usually maintaining a long waiting list: "The waiting list for 2003 alone has in excess of 95 names," read the 2003–2004 CPP annual report. That year various options for expanding the school were under consideration. Ideas included "afternoon classes, expansion of the number of classrooms available, as well as an increase in the number of children per class with the addition of a full-time teacher's assistant per classroom."

Directors of Carmichael Presbyterian Preschool were:

> Laurel Lyda, 1986–1987
>
> Marty Cox, 1987–1991
>
> Lynn Shultz, 1991–1997
>
> Wendy Burri, 1997–2002
>
> Diana Foote (West), 2002–2015
>
> Rachel Ratliff (Carter), 2015–2019

---

12 White, Herman, and Segur, *Heritage of Faith*, 157.
13 White, Herman, and Segur, *Heritage of Faith*, 131.

Laurel Lyda came to CPP from Carmichael Parks and Recreation, Lynn Shultz explained, and brought an aide with her from that program as well. "At the time, people were surprised that I didn't want to be the director," Lynn said, "but I really wanted to teach in the program because I was concerned how that would go." Lynn observed that the curriculum Laurel Lyda was using was more academic than play-focused. Because of this difference in philosophy, Lyda departed after one year. However, Lyda was responsible for getting the preschool licensed, and did an excellent job completing that task, said Lynn. "She should get all the credit for that," as licensure was a heavy lift and required a lot of business skills on top of expertise in early childhood education.

Marty Cox came from Merryhill School as did classroom aide Joette, Lynn noted. "She and Joette were wonderful teachers...ultimately Joette ended up being the director of the [child development] program at American River College." Lynn continued,

> [We] were really into helping our teachers upgrade their skills. And we helped them with tuition. All of the teachers, and at one point, all of the aides, actually had enough credits to be regular teachers. So when we had spaces open up for teachers, we would move the aides into those. My big coup is that we actually got one of our teachers through getting a Master's.... What was interesting is that Brenda [Descalso] didn't leave our program. She loved our program. So even after she got all those credentials, she stayed with us.

One of Lynn Shultz's favorite stories of her time as preschool director concerns the playground upgrade that took place around 1994. After multiple rounds of fundraising, she said, "we had saved up" and bought the playground equipment.

> It was a winter when it rained and rained and rained. And we had to put the equipment in storage and wait until it was dry enough to finally install it. We had all these trees out there that were messier than sin. And someone had arranged with a company to bring a tractor to take the trees out. We took all the kids out on the deck to watch this happen. Well, this guy was trying so hard to get it just right to take these trees

> out, that finally the hard part of the ground let go and [the
> tractor] started sinking into the hole. He backed up so many
> times, it just sank. So finally he came over and said, "Well,
> I guess I'm gonna have to call my dad." [Then his father]
> brought this huge tow truck and backed it in to pull the
> tractor out of the mud.
>
> Then when we went to put the play structure up—and we had
> waited a long time—we brought it out, and the parents were all
> over it, putting all these pieces together. And when they went to
> lift up the platforms, a lot of people were holding them, pushing
> them up where they needed to be. And THEY started sinking!
> Up to their ankles in mud.

Lynn Shultz so enjoyed being the director of CPP that she got her whole family involved in supporting it. Her son, Teddy, built all of the classroom lofts, she said, earning service points that would eventually help him get into the Air Force Academy.

"My faith is very grounded," said Lynn, because of the time spent around children, both in the church's programs and through the preschool.

> [C]hildren are very direct. They understand what they believe.
> And they can tell you about it, if you give them the words....They
> notice things that we don't see. You know, when they pick the
> tiny flowers? And they see the seasons change, and all those
> things. They're very pure about how God gave them all that, if
> we give them the words to express it.

Wendy Burri began her tenure as director of the preschool in January 1997 after working as a teacher for four years. At that time the rooms were not air conditioned, so the summer preschool sessions held during July and August mornings were very hot. And the church was under construction for much of that year, so one of the classes met in the church library, which was located on the first floor where the Gathering Place is now. In addition to the director, the preschool at that time employed five teachers and three instructional aides.[14] Construction on the church campus continued during 1998 and 1999, at times displacing the preschool. One class met in the church parlor for a while.[15] Burri and her husband moved to Yuba City in 2002 and Diana Foote (now West), who had already worked on the preschool staff for several years, succeeded her as preschool director.[16]

Diana had come initially to CPP as a parent. Her son, Alex, was not ready emotionally for kindergarten, she said, but his previous preschool would not allow him to stay in the program past the age of five. On the advice of a past CPP parent, Diana made an appointment to talk to Lynn Shultz, "and the rest is history," she said. As director, "I always felt great support from the governing board and church members. I always felt they took great pride in the work we were doing at the preschool."[17]

Citing an often-voiced desire among church members in the early 2000s to build strong liaison relationships with the preschool, associate pastor the Rev. K. C. Wahe proposed a monthly chapel time with the children, which was enthusiastically approved and begun in 2004. With Pastor K. C. and later with Pastor Jack McNary and Pastor Ivan Herman, the monthly chapel time continued.

The first time the preschool had vacancies was in 2009, likely an effect of the recession.[18] Not long afterwards, Diana West remembered,

> San Juan School district began to offer an excellent, free Pre-K program. Our preschool as well as many others in our area began to see a dramatic drop in enrollment. Despite extensive efforts by CPP staff to adapt the program to area needs, advertising, and enrollment incentives, the drain of students increased dramatically.... The other thing I felt was impacting our enrollment was the natural aging of our surrounding community. I was aware of a great number of preschools in our area closing, but was not seeing a great influx in enrollment from those closures. Initially we increased advertising and offered

14 Carmichael Presbyterian Church, *Annual Report 1997*.
15 Carmichael Presbyterian Church, *Annual Report 1999*.
16 Carmichael Presbyterian Church, *Annual Report 2002*.
17 West, interview.
18 Carmichael Presbyterian Church, *Annual Report 2009*.

enrollment incentives like discounts. By the 2016 school year major changes were taking place like early drop-off and late pick-up for working parents.

Rachel Carter's letters in the church's Annual Reports from 2015–2019 do mention various adaptations the school made to increase sufficient enrollment numbers and keep the school going. One was aligning the preschool calendar with the San Juan Unified School District system calendar; another was increasing capacity in the five-day-a-week program. Rachel herself returned to teaching, on top of her leadership duties. She remained upbeat, affirming that a local kindergarten teacher "who has been teaching for over thirty-five years named CPP as the very best for kindergarten readiness." Despite this, by the fall of 2018, enrollment had dropped to twenty-four students, well under its capacity of seventy-two. Reflecting on the decision to close the school at the end of the spring 2019 session, Rachel wrote:

> [Our legacy] is in those once-little people who showed up curious and unsure and left us confident, capable, secure, beloved, and still curious enough to soak up the knowledge their next teacher imparted, hopefully sitting crisscross applesauce with their hands in their lap.[19]

In an interview, Rachel reflected on the many "champions" of CPP who supported its staff, recruited other families through word of mouth, and built key linkages between the preschool and the church. Among those champions were Mary MacDonald, Mike Aretsky and Lynette Ledesma. She also included Megan Kays—a preschool teacher who also worked with CPC's youth program and recruited Rachel into volunteering with that ministry—and Lisa Torgerson, who was the church's director of children's and family ministries during Rachel's tenure. Lisa "created events...that brought our preschool families to the church and that brought the church to the preschool," Rachel said. Church members were always included in invitations to the Spring Sing fundraiser and Christmas Pageant. By all accounts the preschool outreach was tightly integrated with the church—and even, as Rachel put it, "beloved" by the church.

---

19 Carmichael Presbyterian Church, *Annual Report 2018*, 21.

CPP's dedicated staff also loved the children. In her interview, Rachel also spoke of her younger son, who attended CPP in Leslie Evans's class. Like many children transitioning to public school, he had unique learning needs that were documented in an Individualized Education Program or IEP. "Mrs. Evans came to IEP meetings with me for at least the first couple of years and she continued to show up for his school plays, presentations, and awards," Rachel said.

While the church's weekday preschool primarily served middle-class families in Carmichael, CPC folks were acutely aware of families that were economically marginalized. Welfare reform in the late 1990s, as noted above, was a hot topic of discussion at the church. One of the reforms enacted was limiting welfare aid payouts to sixty months over the recipient's lifetime. There was thus a sense of urgency for those who would soon lose their social safety net benefits. As it turned out, the church was able to play a role in helping families in this situation.

CPC served as a training site for a state-funded pilot program to train stay-at-home mothers on CalWORKS to become licensed family child-care providers. The two-year, $136,000 pilot project was sponsored by the Sacramento County Department of Human Assistance, the Los Rios Community College District and Child Action Inc., a nonprofit advocate for quality child care. Approximately 140 students attended the program from January 1999 through June 2000. According to a report in the *Sacramento Bee*, more than eighty-five percent of graduates from the Child Care Provider Training pilot program got jobs in child care or another field, or began attending community college to continue beyond their initial twelve units in early childhood development provided in the training.[20]

Mustard Seed School

Mustard Seed School is a program of Sacramento Loaves & Fishes. It is not a CPC ministry but was founded in 1989 by a CPC member, Karen

---

20 Carey Peterson, "Class bridges welfare-to-work gap," *Sacramento Bee*, July 6, 2000, Arden/Carmichael Neighbors.

Banker, who served as Mustard Seed's non-salaried "director, janitor, and volunteer" for about twelve years. Karen then transitioned into community liaison work and fundraising while serving on the board of Loaves & Fishes, until stepping down in October 2022.[21]

Just as the church leadership has periodically re-examined its ministries, individual members who volunteer their time (led by their faith but serving independently of church groups) also speak of moments when they need to step back and evaluate how their specific skills and concerns might be focused to make a greater impact. This was the case for Karen Banker, as she stated in a 1996 interview:

> I had been doing a lot of volunteer work in the community over a long period of time and became involved in such a wide variety of issues and causes that I was feeling scattered. I wanted to refocus. I decided that I wanted to work with homeless women and that is what brought me to Maryhouse, a Loaves & Fishes program that provides hospitality and shelter to homeless women and children. That was in the Spring of 1988.

Karen, whose husband, Franklin ("Bud") Banker, was a physician, had also worked as a special education teacher. While volunteering at Maryhouse, she noticed that the "children of the homeless women at Maryhouse were not in school." In effect, she continued,

> [T]hey were already elementary school dropouts. I had not realized that if you were a homeless child in Sacramento, you were not in school. I felt it was fundamentally wrong that homelessness—not having an address—meant that you could not go to school. These children had fallen through the cracks and no one seemed to be doing anything about it. The school districts didn't know about these children and even if they did, they did not know what to do with these children who seemed to be coming out of nowhere, from everywhere.

The founding of Mustard Seed School, Karen noted, had a two-fold purpose: first, to provide for the children's emergency needs in a structured and caring learning environment, and second, to get them enrolled in the public school:

---

21 Karen Banker, interview by Susan Herman, February 15, 2023.

> With all the necessary paperwork completed we literally take them by the hand to their new school. We give them a backpack filled with school supplies and even new shoes, underwear or other clothing. We meet their principal and their teacher. We love and care about these kids. We try to be here for them.[22]

Early press coverage about Mustard Seed School added fuel to an ongoing controversy in Sacramento about the actual number of unhoused individuals living there and how best to represent those numbers. "Point in Time" counts were not federally mandated until 2003. Even then, the surveys only counted unsheltered people, often leaving children out of the count, as they would be living out of sight in cars or motels. In her work as founder and first director of Mustard Seed School, Karen was able to raise awareness within her own Carmichael congregation, and elsewhere, that homelessness is a much bigger issue than we can detect through its most visible signs; e.g., people camping on the riverbanks and under bridges—and that children in this situation need safe, stable places where they can learn and study.

For a time, as Karen noted, Mustard Seed even had a satellite center dedicated to outreach. It operated out of motel rooms the school rented on Auburn Boulevard. While talking with families who were living in the "welfare motels," Karen explained, she and her colleague, Patty Zannetti, learned which documents the schools needed and helped the parents locate those documents. They would help families make dental appointments, for example, as these records were needed for re-enrollment. Oftentimes "women lost their paperwork due to family violence," Karen said, so they needed help navigating vital records offices.[23]

Patty Zannetti headed up the motel outreach program until the outreach center moved in 1993 to its current North C Street location. Mustard Seed then acquired a minivan, which allowed Patty to continue connecting with families staying in motels on Auburn Boulevard and 16th Street, bringing children to Mustard Seed each day.[24]

---

22 Karen Banker, interview by Sacramento Loaves & Fishes, February 1996.
23 Karen Banker, interview by Susan Herman, Febraury 15, 2023.
24 Sacramento Loaves & Fishes, "Did you know that Mustard Seed School used to operate an outreach center...?," Facebook, February 20, 2023.

With a spotlight now shining on homelessness as a source of daily stress pervading family life, Mustard Seed School in the mid-1990s became a regular part of CPC's annual Alternative Gift Market. Marie Segur took an educational catalog Karen had provided her, called *Developmental Learning Materials*, and recruited members of the Pinafores Marinership to make dozens of the items pictured, such as lacing cards, for the children. Dave Segur and Art Tookey contributed their carpentry skills, Karen said. "Dave would always ask me: What does Mustard Seed School need?" Speaking of Dave Segur, Karen remembered,

> He converted a shower stall into a storage closet with shelving units; he built a lot of the bookshelves that are still used at the school today. He built sidewalks connecting the school cottages to the playground.

In addition, the church periodically held drives to collect new underwear and socks for Mustard Seed students.

Karen brought the story of Mustard Seed to national attention in 1995 when the school received a visit from Tipper Gore, wife of then-Vice President Al Gore. Mrs. Gore visited the school after speaking at a luncheon on the importance of funding for mental health services. The *Sacramento Bee* reported:

> Gore, who also serves as an adviser to the Interagency Council on the Homeless, watched the younger children make animals out of Play-Doh. She watched them make a weaving and helped one girl on a computer. The older children sang a song they had written that afternoon.
>
> Karen Banker, director of the school at 1300 North C St., sat on the floor with Gore and about 20 children. Ranging in ages from 5 to 15, the children presented Gore with their wishes written out and attached to red roses.
>
> "I wish there were more houses so people wouldn't be homeless," wrote one child.
>
> "I wish to get a home soon," wrote one 11-year-old boy, who explained that his family can afford a hotel room only the first couple weeks out of the month."[25]

---

25 Nancy Weaver, "Tipper Gore Visits Capital; VP's Wife Urges More Care for

Karen was honored in 1999 with a Civic Contribution Award presented by the League of Women Voters of Sacramento.[26] The school's current program director, Lucia Vega, once received services at Loaves & Fishes herself and eventually graduated from the Family Promise of Sacramento (see Chapter 6).[27]

Reaching Out to Teens

In 1997, the Sacramento County Sheriff's Department began organizing a North Area Teen Center in Carmichael to provide a drug-free and gang-free area for teens to hang out between the time school was over and their parents came home from work. Marie Segur, Bobbi Jones, and Faye White of Carmichael Presbyterian Church were some of the initial advisors.[28] CPC members worked at the Teen Center booth at Carmichael Founder's Day that year, sold tickets for a car raffle, and displayed the car at the Carmichael Post Office for a week. The CPC community, through Presbyterian Women and Mission Division, made a monthly pledge to financially support the center that year.[29]

The Teen Center finally opened in June 1998. Joyce Arredondo, Teen Center director, and the program director Fred Hammer spoke at adult education classes and events at CPC during the year. The center had pool tables, ping pong tables, arcade games, video games, a computer center, board games, and areas for just sitting and talking. Over 350 youths used the center during that initial year with a core of approximately sixty. John Wallace of CPC said he began volunteering that year and kept doing so until the Teen Center's closure in 2010.[30]

As of 1999 about fourteen volunteers from CPC had been trained to become involved in tutoring and other activities at the Teen Center. That year the

---

Mentally Ill, Homeless," *Sacramento Bee*, March 10, 1995, Metro.

26 "Community announcements," *Carmichael Times*, March 30, 1999.

27 Sacramento Loaves & Fishes, ""There is no judgement, no matter what your situation is." Lucia Vega, Program Director," September 10, 2021, https://sacloaves.org/there-is-no-judgement-no-matter-what-your-situation-is-lucia-vega-program-director/.

28 John Wallace, CPC History Notes: Pastors, Mission Trips, Stephen Ministry Leadership, Microassistance Program, June 19, 2020.

29 Carmichael Presbyterian Church, *Annual Report 1997*.

30 John Wallace, CPC History Notes, June 19, 2020.

center received support through the Alternative Christmas Market and, again, from Presbyterian Women.[31] Church support for the Teen Center, in the forms of money and time, is mentioned consistently in Annual Reports until about 2004.

Around 2004 the church began supporting Wind Youth Services through the Alternative Christmas Market. As described on its website:

> Wind was first opened in 1994 by the Sisters of Social Service in a small space located next to Loaves & Fishes...as a daytime safe haven for homeless teenagers to seek refuge and receive survival services. As the awareness of the children's needs grew, so did the services the Center provided. The Center broadened its focus to provide programs that would offer tools and resources to teens and help them develop the necessary skills to break the cycle of homelessness.
>
> In 2001, the Wind Youth Services Shelter opened its doors in Carmichael as a result of grants from the U.S. Department of Health & Human Services, Runaway and Homeless Youth Program and the United Way.

Due to its prior involvement with the Teen Center, supporting Wind seemed a logical next step for CPC's Mission Division to take.

In February of 2004, Jimmi Mishler brought CPC into another community partnership to support teens—Sacramento County's Independent Living Program, which was designed for youth who were transitioning from foster care into independent living as legal adults. Jimmi described the program in an email:

> I saw an article in the *Sacramento Bee* about how the Independent Living Program personnel had been providing "Emancipation Baskets" containing needed personal items. They had decided the project was too big for just the few people and were soliciting community help. It seemed like a good fit for CPC, so that's when I wrote up a proposal and took it to Mission Committee.[32]

---

31 Carmichael Presbyterian Church, *Annual Report 1998*.
32 Jimmi Mishler, interview by Susan Herman, February 20, 2023.

Teens who participate in the Independent Living program go through twelve weeks of classes and counseling. Through the classes they are guided to resources and services that will enable them to successfully transition from foster care to independence.

Every year from 2004 until 2018 (except for one year when Social Services was going through a transition and communication with donors was disrupted), CPC members donated practical household items such as cookware and bedding. Since then, Jimmi noted, her contact at the Social Services office said enough outside organizations were donating household items that the church no longer needed to contribute. Seeking to stay involved, however, Jimmi's Presbyterian Women's group, the Dorcas Circle, began making lap robes—that is, 5' x 7' quilts with the top pieces "tacked on rather than quilted"—for the youth. In 2018, members of Dorcas Circle made fifty lap robes, each lovingly folded and tied with a ribbon. "Many of the recipients said that was the first handmade item they'd ever owned," Jimmi said. In 2022, she reported, the sewing circle made ninety lap robes for the emancipated foster youth, giving some also to Family Promise of Sacramento.[33]

Spiritual, Relational, and Mental Health Care

For just over thirty years, the church housed a counseling center staffed by licensed professionals specializing in marriage and family therapy, as well as clinical social work. Its first location was in what is now the Brides' Room, in the wing connected to the chapel. After the renovations of the late 1990s it moved to the upstairs east corner of the education wing. The new office suite was dubbed the Wholeness Center. The center served couples, families, and individuals with a variety of behavioral and mental health needs.

Filling a niche between individualized counseling and stage-of-life fellowship groups were multiple support groups on the CPC campus for people seeking encouragement from peers in specific areas of need. Some of these were outside groups that used church space for their meetings (see also Chapter 2), while others were initiated and led by CPC members. Many support groups continue meeting at CPC today.

---

33 Mishler, interview.

Counseling Center

In 1977 the church established a pastoral counseling center, and designated an advisory board for the center which would report to the Session's Mission Action Committee. The Rev. Richard G. Pearson, a minister member of the Presbytery of Sacramento, was its first director. In its early years, the center's main function was to handle some of the premarital counseling duties normally undertaken by the pastor. [34] CPC's senior pastor at the time, the Rev. Dr. Bill Johnson, was officiating a lot of weddings. Around three-quarters of the weddings were of non-CPC members.[35]

Directors of the Counseling Center were:

Rev. Richard G. Pearson, 1977–1994

Rev. Gail Cullerton, co-director with Rev. Pearson, ca. 1988-1993

Dorothy (Dee) Simpson, interim director, 1994

Kathryn (Kathy) Cann, LCSW, director, 1995–2007

Over time, the center handled much more than premarital counseling. Counselors worked with clients on all manner of issues related to personal growth and change, relationship care, behavioral health, and family systems. The center was outfitted with toys to support play therapy with children as well. During her time as director in the 1990s, CPC member Kathy Cann said that only around a quarter of their clients were couples planning marriage. With premarital couples she and another counselor, Don Peterson, used the Prepare/Enrich series of six facilitated conversations, for which the clients paid a set fee. Kathy said she enjoyed working with couples on positive topics such as communication styles, talking about one another's strengths, and learning conflict resolution techniques.[36] Prepare/Enrich is based on the Family Adaptability and Cohesion Evaluation Scale (FACES), an empirically grounded psychological assessment tool.[37]

The rest of the clients fell into one of two groups, with some crossover between them: 1) people who needed low-cost care, and 2) people who

34 White, Herman, and Segur, *Heritage of Faith*, 169.
35 White, Herman, and Segur, *Heritage of Faith*, 141.
36 Kathryn Cann, interview by Susan Herman, February 21, 2023.
37 "The most trusted assessment," accessed February 28, 2023, https://www.prepare-enrich.com/.

wanted to integrate their faith as part of the therapeutic process. Kathy explained that the fee structure included a sliding fee based on the client's income and family size, from which a fixed amount went towards the center's operating costs. The remainder went to the therapist and was supplemented by church funds (administered through the Mission Division) to equal a set hourly rate. Church members who wanted to support the Counseling Center over and above its Mission-budgeted funding could do so through direct donations or through their workplace's yearly United Way giving campaign.

The Counseling Center also accepted Medicare and Medi-Cal, which offered reimbursement in amounts that were generally higher than what self-pay clients paid with the sliding-fee calculation. This was significant because accepting more of these clients allowed church funds to stretch farther. It also allowed low-income patients to have better access to care, as the county-provided mental health care was usually insufficient. With county mental health, people wouldn't be able to schedule appointments as frequently as they needed, or they would have to see a different counselor every time. "I worked with a lot of difficult cases because they didn't have any place else to go," Kathy said. Many had chronic, ongoing mental health issues and needed a regular routine and care provider to help them manage their medication and stay out of psychiatric hospitals.

In 1993 Rev. Cullerton accepted a call to serve elsewhere and left the Counseling Center. Rev. Pearson went on sabbatical in 1994 to Homer, Alaska, where he established the Peninsula Pastoral Counseling Service. He chose not to return to Carmichael after sabbatical. Dee Simpson served as interim director of the Counseling Center, later returning to her private practice. In October 1995 Kathy Cann was appointed director of the Counseling Center.[38]

By the 1990s pastors and insurers were well aware of the growth in litigation against clergy, both for sexual misconduct and more broadly for providing counseling services while not meeting the licensure and certification standards of professional psychotherapists. This led to growth in the popularity of church Counseling Centers nationwide.[39] As part of

---

38 White, Herman, and Segur, *Heritage of Faith.*
39 Paul Clegg, "Wise Counsel: Giving advice to people in need isn't simple any-more. Here's how pastors are dealing with changing times," *Sacramento Bee,* February 28, 1998.

this trend, a Sacramento center called Samaritan Counseling Center was launched in 1994 as "a joint project between Trinity Cathedral and Fremont Presbyterian Church to establish and maintain a mental health and pastoral Counseling Center."[40] When it started, the Sacramento location was one of about 400 Samaritan Center locations nationwide. The centers were focused on integrating body, mind, and spirit, and most included a member of the clergy, a psychiatrist, and another medical doctor on staff or as consultants.[41]

It may be helpful to note that the model of counseling being offered by CPC's Counseling Center and Samaritan Counseling Center is distinct from a practice known as Biblical counseling. While there are certifying bodies for providers of Biblical counseling, they do not typically require foundational preparation in the social sciences. A major goal in Biblical counseling is to help clients align their heart and mind with Christ by applying lessons from specific scriptures to their thoughts, emotions, and behaviors. Biblical counseling focuses on the Bible as the source of knowledge and wisdom,[42] whereas professional services by a licensed counselor, clinical social worker, or psychologist are more holistic in focus and are based on scientific research findings about the human brain and behavior. These more holistic services respect clients' spiritual experience and can work in concert with other behavioral health techniques to encourage religious practice, to the extent that this supports the client's overall health. It is this latter type of counseling that was provided at CPC's Counseling Center.

According to the 1998 CPC *Annual Report*, the Counseling Center operated six days a week, Monday through Saturday. About one-third of its clients received care subsidized by church funds. That year 181 hours of counseling were subsidized by mission funds to assist the lowest income clients. In 2002, Kathy Cann reported a 154% increase in hours of service provided over the previous four years since moving into its new facility.

---

40 Very Rev. Donald Brown, dean of the cathedral, quoted in Patricia Nakamura, "A Metropolitan Mission," *The Living Church* 210, no. 26 (1995), https://episcopalarchives.org/cgi-bin/the_living_church/TLCarticle.pl?volume=210&issue=26&article_id=1.

41 Paul Clegg, "Divine Guidance: Secular therapists keep a watchful eye as religious groups open professionally staffed Counseling Centers," *Sacramento Bee*, October 14, 1995.

42 Tim Pasma, "Do We Need More Than the Bible for Biblical Counseling?," (October 27, 2017). https://biblicalcounseling.com/resource-library/articles/do-we-need-more-than-the-bible-for-biblical-counseling/.

Kathy stepped down from directorship of the CPC Counseling Center in 2007 to join a private practice group. She shared her reflections on her time at the Counseling Center:

> It worked out well for me to be where my kids were—all three of them attended Carmichael Presbyterian Preschool while I was employed at the Counseling Center. I would see three clients, then pick up the kids, take them home, and then when my husband came home, I'd go back to see evening clients. I saw about twenty clients a week...[As a church member] I would sometimes have to explain that I kept my volunteer service separate from my work. I didn't provide therapy services to church members because that would be a dual relationship. For a number of years, I chose to be the parent representative on the preschool board rather than, say, leading a support group.

Kathy went on to say it was a "strong value" of the Counseling Center to meet people where they are, and to recognize when they do or do not want a faith-based counseling experience. Some clients may remember having come to a church for counseling, though, so even if they never pursued a faith journey, hopefully the church made an impression as a safe space for healing.

When Kathy left, the Session considered whether to enter a new contract with another Christian counseling services group.[43] In 2008 Samaritan Counseling Center, led by Debra J. Tripp, LMFT[44] began to operate out of CPC's space as a satellite office. Samaritan Counseling hired David Dillman, LMFT, a graduate of Azusa Pacific, to lead the new satellite office in Carmichael. Samaritan Counseling operated on the CPC campus through March 2010 when the Samaritan Center's board decided to close. In a note on her LinkedIn profile, Ms. Tripp wrote:

> I am sad to inform the public that the Samaritan Counseling Center of Greater Sacramento, Inc. was closed by the board in 2010. SCC provided faith-supportive, low fee counseling for 14 years. Unfortunately, a move to a larger space in 2008 coincided with the sharp downturn in the economy. Self-pay

---

43 Carmichael Presbyterian Church, *Annual Report 2007.*
44 Debra Tripp's spouse, the Rev. Tom Tripp, was a minister member of the Presbytery of Sacramento at the time.

clients dropped off, and donations fell. Therapists from SCC are working throughout the community in private settings.

Self-Help Groups

> *Al-Anon had a women's meeting at CPC that included child care. This was a valued rarity in the self-help community.*
>
> *—Jason Swain, LCSW*[45]

As mentioned in Chapter 2, spaces at CPC are well used by all kinds of community groups, from Scout troops to sports clubs. Here I highlight a few groups that provided support for families dealing with stresses particular to stigma and social isolation.

Muriel Stoner Follansbee, a CPC member who was active in the music ministry in her younger years,[46] co-founded the Sacramento chapter of PFLAG—Parents and Friends of Lesbians and Gays—with her husband, the Rev. Merrill Follansbee, and their friend Jean Hansen. The chapter met for the first time in 1982 in the chapel at CPC. It's unknown how many meetings were held there. A 2012 issue of *Outward Magazine*, recognizing the thirtieth anniversary of Sacramento's PFLAG chapter, only mentions that CPC was the first meeting place for the group, and that it had started meeting at St. Mark's United Methodist in nearby Arden-Arcade, where it continues to meet as of this writing in 2023. The *Outward* article notes:

> The Follansbees were inspired to start the group by their own journey. When their own gay son and lesbian daughter came out, there were no local support networks in place to help them navigate the challenging process. Little did they know the impact their actions would have.[47]

---

45 Jason Swain, personal communication, March 26, 2023. Jason was a counselor who worked at the Samaritan Counseling Center's satellite office on the CPC campus.

46 Muriel Stoner Follansbee, interview by Wayne MacRostie, August 28, 1996.

47 Bonnie Osborn, "PFLAG Sacramento Celebrates 30 Years of Showing the Love," *Outward Magazine*, March 22-April 12, 2012.

While both Muriel and Merrill Follansbee are now gone, their legacy lives on, not only through the support group, but also through a scholarship created by Sacramento PFLAG in the names of its founders, the Follansbee-Hansen Memorial Scholarship. Eligible students are awarded $2000, or more, and must self-identify as members of the LGBTQ+ community, and demonstrate interest in service to that community.[48]

At least as early as 1973, and probably before that, the church also provided space for Alcoholics Anonymous group meetings. An obituary in the church archives tells of James (Jim) Masterson, husband of CPC member Doris Masterson, who was a leader in the organization. Sober since 1951, he attended meetings with his AA "family" frequently, and served on the Board of Trustees of AA representing the Pacific region from 1963-1967.[49] It is unclear whether Masterson started the chapter at CPC or invited them to use the church. As of the 1990s even though construction disrupted meetings of outside groups on the CPC campus, AA and many others came back soon after the dust settled. A glance at a 2023 weekly calendar shows AA and Al-Anon meetings (for family members of alcoholics) as well as other 12-step groups and "anonymous" fellowships for people with addictions to sex and pornography, gambling, or narcotics. Regarding the sex addicts group, therapist Jason Swain commented,

> There are not a lot of meetings like this in the Sacramento area and [when I worked at Samaritan Counseling] I thought it was awesome that a church did not perceive themselves too squeaky clean to provide a meeting place...I remember thinking this was the sort of thing Christ would be all about—providing healing and a sanctuary for those who have suffered from such a shame-based, stigmatizing, isolating, and lonely struggle.[50]

---

48 Several side notes may be appropriate here. Muriel Stoner's family came to Carmichael around 1939. Her father served as CPC's Clerk of Session from May 1942–August 1946, and her mother taught second grade Sunday school. When the new sanctuary was going up, Muriel and her older brother gave money for the rose window in the north wall of the church in honor of their parents.
49 Steve Gibson, "James Masterson, 83, leader in AA," *Sacramento Bee*, September 7, 2000.
50 Jason Swain, personal communication, March 26, 2023.

Other self-help groups such as Friends for Survival—for people who have lost a loved one to suicide—also meet regularly at CPC, as does an Alzheimer's Association-sponsored caregiver support group for those caring for a loved one with dementia.

As described in Chapter 3, Cancer and Faith Experience (CAFÉ) and another caregiver support group (not specific to dementia), both initiated by CPC members, were open to the broader community and provided space for church members and nonmembers alike to speak openly about the strange, painful, and sometimes humorous aspects of the health journey.

Refugee Outreach

In 2016 Carmichael Times ran a local history piece on the "first refugee" to arrive in Carmichael: Rudy Noll, from Dutch Indonesia. After Indonesian independence, the article notes, many Dutch Indonesians struggled for acceptance in Holland. Noll served the Royal Dutch Army but spent much of World War II imprisoned in Japanese-occupied Indonesia, on the island of Celebes. The article continues:

> Carmichael Presbyterian Church sponsored his immigration. With his first wife Sonja, he crossed the Atlantic to New York in 1956. The newcomers then caught a train to Sacramento. Presbyterian parishioners Warren and Mary MacMillan drove them to a cozy home where they met their landlady, Effie Yeaw. "She was strict," he recalls of the community matriarch. "But she was fair. The Presbyterians didn't care that we were Catholics. On Christmas Eve, they drove us to Mass. Everyone in Carmichael knew all about us. We were the first refugees they'd seen. I'd always lived in cities and we had to get used to village life." [51]

The arrival of the Nolls set the tone for CPC's long-standing commitment to refugees and immigrants.

---

51 Susan Maxwell Skinner, "Citizen Rudy Celebrates 60 U.S. Years," *Carmichael Times*, December 30, 2016.

Microenterprise Assistance Program

CPC's deacons, Presbyterian Women, and others had for some time supported refugees through English language tutoring, Christmas Baskets (see Chapter 6), and donations to Sacramento Refugee Ministry. CPC member Dr. Maurine Huang launched the Microenterprise Assistance Program (MAP) in 1994 as a service providing business development assistance for low-income refugee and immigrant families. At the time she was working at the local affiliate of Church World Service. One of her coworkers there, a Ukrainian translator named Roman Romaso, told her that "People want to start a business and they don't know how. *We have to help them.*" Maurine began developing training for would-be business owners and received donations from CPC's Presbyterian Women and Mariners groups to support the classes. At the time of its founding, MAP served primarily refugees and immigrants from the former Soviet Union and from Southeast Asia, offering business literacy education, technical support, and assistance with developing financing streams to open a business.

The loans themselves came from California Capitol Small Business Development Corporation, which specialized in microloans for starting an enterprise too small to fit into the traditional category of "small business." From this start, the Sacramento Microenterprise Assistance Program became a mission outreach of CPC, as well as five other Presbyterian churches in the area, plus two Disciples of Christ churches, and was endorsed by four large Slavic churches. Sacramento Lao Family Community joined with MAP to apply for a grant from the Sacramento Employment and Training Agency. With the grant money, MAP was able to hire bilingual aides and additional staff to develop the curriculum and ensure it was appropriate in terms of both age and culture.[52]

MAP spun off from CPC's sponsorship in 1997, in favor of an arrangement that would allow them to serve more people—a partnership with the Interfaith Service Bureau. In a letter to the church, the MAP board of directors noted that:

---

52 Faye Gentry White, "'MAP' To Success," *Presbyterians Today*, September 2000.

CPC is to be commended for its forward thinking almost four years ago in sponsoring MAP. During that time, over 200 students have participated in the educational programs and approximately 35 businesses have been started. [53]

After this transition CPC's Mission Division maintained its connection with MAP by soliciting volunteers from the church membership to serve in various roles.[54] In 1998, division chair Katharine DeYoung reported with joy that MAP had awarded a business loan to a Hmong silversmith to support his jewelry business.[55] MAP later became Prosperity Project, part of the wraparound refugee services organization Opening Doors, where Maurine Huang served as CEO from 2003–2009.[56] It receives support from local financial institutions as well as the U.S. Small Business Administration.[57] CPC supported Opening Doors financially through budgeted Mission giving every year until 2019.

In 2004, during a period when over 6000 Hmong refugees were resettled in California, split between Fresno, Stockton, and Sacramento[58], CPC's Mission Division made connections with the resettlement agency and delivered household supplies to five of these families.[59] As noted in Chapter 4, members of CPC's youth group have also made connections with immigrant and refugee communities across the state.

---

53 Sacramento Microenterprise Assistance Program (MAP), Letter to CPC Session requesting dissolution of umbrella relationship between MAP and CPC, April 29, 1997.

54 Carmichael Presbyterian Church, *Annual Report 1997.*

55 Carmichael Presbyterian Church, *Annual Report 1998.*

56 Anne Gonzales, "Microloan gives macro boost to immigrants," *Sacramento Business Journal*, February 3, 2002, https://www.bizjournals.com/sacramento/stories/2002/02/04/smallb1.html.

57 Opening Doors, "Boost for Opening Doors' Prosperity Project brings business microloans to Sacramento region," *CAMEO: California Association for Micro Enterprise Opportunity*, June 28, 2012, https://cameonetwork.org/news/opening-doors-prosperity-project/.

58 *Hmong Refugee Resettlement in California*, Senate Committee on Health & Human Services and Asian Pacific Islander Legislative Caucus, November 16, 2004.

59 Carmichael Presbyterian Church, *Annual Report 2004.*

World Relief Partnership to Support Afghan Refugees

In 2018 CPC began a partnership with an agency called World Relief Sacramento (part of a nationwide refugee services agency) to provide classroom space for ESL classes serving Afghan immigrant women and for child care for their children while they attended classes. Husbands and fathers in this group generally spoke English already, as most had entered the country under Special Immigrant Visas (SIV), which had been granted for their work with the US military during the multi-front conflict initiated after 9/11. Instructors for the women were provided through the agency. Child care volunteers, after passing a background check, came from the church membership and from elsewhere in the community. Under the World Relief partnership, which continues at the time of this writing in 2023, the church also provided space and time for Afghan girls and boys (separately) to play soccer in McMillen Hall.

Space for the ESL classes and child care was created from the newly vacant Carmichael Presbyterian Preschool office and two of its classrooms. Classes moved online during the COVID-19 pandemic, and during this time, volunteers led by Glenda Perrou prepared online lessons for preschool children with accompanying crafts and delivered them to participating families. The following year, volunteers visited families with preschool children on their doorsteps and outdoor walkways of their apartment buildings, teaching lessons and dropping off books and educational materials. As of 2023 CPC volunteers continue to act as online teaching assistants, and help prepare and deliver learning packets to Afghan women enrolled in World Relief's online classes.

A story reported by Presbyterian News Service (PNS) noted that one out of nine Afghan refugees in the United States had settled in the Sacramento area. In describing the partnership with World Relief to PNS, CPC member Kathy Lewis said, "The model is, if there is a refugee resettlement agency in your area, work with them. They know best what the needs are."[60]

---

60 Rich Copley, "Welcoming Afghan refugees is nothing new to this California church," October 5, 2021, https://www.presbyterianmission.org/story/welcoming-afghan-refugees-is-nothing-new-to-this-california-church/.

One of those needs, as World Relief agency staff explained to CPC volunteers, was the importance of offering gender-separate times for play for the older children, as mentioned above. This was important because, as Pastor Ivan noted for the PNS article, the Afghan teen girls needed a safe space where they could "gather with one another and not be responsible for younger children, younger siblings, and not have to spend that hour translating or interpreting for their parents." When the US military withdrew from Afghanistan in August 2021 during the Taliban takeover, the church hosted a prayer service for the entire community. CPC also dedicated its portion of the 2021 Peace and Global Witness Offering to supporting Afghan refugees in the community (denominational special offerings are described in Chapter 8).

In his article for PNS, Rich Copley observed that "Working with the Afghan community has helped Carmichael learn to be a church that does things with its neighbors as opposed to doing things for people." The power of doing *with* others was evident in the words of Afghan women themselves reflecting on what they learned after attending World Relief's online English and cultural integration classes. One woman said, "I went to the doctor, and I could tell him what was going on with me and my level of pain." Another commented, "When I used to go to the store, I would just put all the money on the counter and have the worker take the correct amount; now I can count the money and give it myself without help." Another student said, "I learned how to do the car seat. Before I didn't care if it was twisted or put in wrong but after class, I make sure it is put in right. I even taught my neighbor," and finally: "I had some guests coming over and they needed the address. My son went fast to call my husband to ask for the address, but I told him no, don't call. I know the address. My son said, 'Really mom, you know?' and I said yes, I know. I felt really proud of myself."[61]

---

61 Kathy Lewis, "An Amazing Transformation. Feedback from Afghan Women in World Relief ESL & Health Classes," in *Mission Bell* (October 2022).

Chapter 6
Connecting With and Serving
Our Community:
Food and Hospitality

Responding to God's love through Jesus Christ,
We connect with and serve our community

"**H**ere, take this...just in case." The security guard handed over his Taser to Karen Gray, secretary to Carmichael Presbyterian Church's pastors, and then went to his car to call for backup. One of the guests taking part in the weekday shower program had snuck into the bathroom before others who had signed up for time slots and were waiting their turn. Diane (not her real name) seemed to have suffered a mental break. When asked to come out and let others go first, she began yelling, cursing, and throwing things, refusing to leave the shower area. When the security guard arrived, he quickly determined that the situation was beyond what he could handle and went to his car to call the sheriff.

What in the world am I going to do with this Taser? thought Karen. *If anyone's in need of protecting right now, it's the naked, ranting woman in the shower, not me!* Nevertheless, Karen stayed put, holding the device horizontally in two hands, as far from her own body as possible and keeping her fingers together so as not to accidentally trigger it. Her arms trembled slightly, both from the sheer weight of the Taser and from competing feelings of fear, holy anger, and the urge to burst out laughing at the absurdity of it all.

The sheriff then arrived with a deputy who was also a mental health counselor. After more of Diane's yelling and cursing, the deputy/counselor and other officers were able to escort her, wearing only a towel and carrying her clothes in a bundle, out of the shower and off the church property. *Shoot, that's one of our towels—oh well, Diane can have it*, Karen thought, finally exhaling and carefully returning the Taser to its owner.

Reflecting on this experience in the context of her lifelong involvement at the church, both as a member of staff and as a member of the congregation, Karen Gray wrote:

> I have always been proud to be part of a church that values loving and caring for each other. Even when we've been broken as a congregation and divided on how to move forward, loving and caring for people has been a primary goal. [Working in the church office], I have seen that more than most, as we have provided many services for people experiencing homelessness. Showers, food, help with a tank of gas. Over the months and years, we get to know these folks and some of their stories.

> After he came to speak at CPC, I read in Fr. Greg Boyle's book *Tattoos on the Heart*[1] about the importance of "naming" people—knowing their names. That resonated with me, and I have tried since then to greet people I know by name when they come into the church office and to ask the names of the people I don't know, especially people who come to the office looking for help. Whether they are looking for assistance with rent or utilities, a shower, food, prayers with a pastor, or just a glass of water, almost all of them appreciate being recognized. In a world that often dehumanizes those who are seen as "less than," I hope that the people who come to our doors feel a bit more human, a bit more recognized, a bit more like a precious child of God when they are called by name.[2]

---

1 Father Gregory Boyle of Homeboy Ministries spoke at CPC on September 29, 2012 as part of the Connecting With Our World speaker series. More details on this series can be found in Chapter 4.
2 Karen Tozier Gray, interview by Sharon MacLean, March 15, 2021.

Karen's story illustrates one way in which CPC members have served the community and served alongside others, even when the systems for providing care are imperfect. Carmichael Presbyterian has learned through long experience that helping others meet basic needs for food and shelter will almost always involve frustration, boundary conflicts, and messiness of all kinds. Yet, of all the congregation's traditions, its zeal to connect with and serve the community may prove the most enduring over the next 100 years.

Over the decades CPC's community outreach has had a broad focus—so much so that at least one visioning team has warned against overextending and "spread[ing] ourselves too thin."[3] Another feature of the church's mission, as illustrated in Chapter 5 and extensively in *Heritage of Faith*, is that members of CPC have often been instigators, starting up entirely new programs of community service where none existed before. When not actually starting up something new, they still tended to assume leadership roles, serving on advisory boards and the like. However, with age and membership decline in the congregation occurring in tandem with increased economic distress in Carmichael and Sacramento County, the church has adopted a pattern in recent years of proactively seeking out partnerships with other community organizations. The upshot of Karen's dicey moment, for example, is that the church began administering its shower and bathroom ministry through another organization—Carmichael HART—greatly lessening the chances that church staff or volunteers would be asked to handle a Taser again.

One might speculate that challenges in boundary setting around appropriate use of staff and volunteer time and church resources will continue to test CPC as the church enters its second hundred years. It may help, then, to look back at the origin stories of CPC's food and hospitality ministries for a reminder of how they came about, how the church has adapted them to fit changing needs and resources, and why many CPC members and friends believe the journey of compassion and learning is still worth pursuing.

This chapter traces the history of the church's benevolence fund, also known as Deacons' Fund, and its Christmas Gift Ministry (established in 1966 and 1972 respectively); then delves into food and anti-hunger efforts

---

3 CPC PneuMatrix Task Force, *Matrix for Assessing Mission Division Responsibilities against Mission Statement* (July 17, 2019).

with a history of the Carmichael Food Closet (started in 1973), hunger relief advocacy (1993), and Supper on Saturday (2005). Finally, we explore the church's partnerships with housing organizations such as Project Home (1985–1990), a program of the Interfaith Service Bureau;[4] Habitat for Humanity (1994–1997); Family Promise of Sacramento (2006–present); Sacramento County's Winter Sanctuary program (2016–2019); and Carmichael HART (2016–present).

Christmas Gift Ministry and Deacons' Fund

Heritage of Faith notes that a benevolence fund established by the Board of Deacons in 1966 provided help to four church families in 1969—a time when Aerojet Corporation, a major local employer, had begun a series of layoffs that put hundreds out of work. (The benevolence fund was established separately from annual pledges to the church's operating budget.)

> The Deacons' Fund got a boost in 1972 when the Session voted to participate in the Heifer Project, which provides livestock to people in need throughout the world. A Christmas Tree Fund was established to receive gifts from church members in lieu of monies they would expend on greeting cards to send to church members and friends. Half of the proceeds would go to the Heifer Project and half to the Deacons' Fund to assist families in need in the Carmichael area.

> In 1971 the deacons undertook to provide a complete traditional turkey Christmas dinner and gifts to six families in need...This appears to be the beginning of what has become a tradition of the distribution of Christmas baskets by the deacons.[5]

That first year, six families received the dinner baskets. The tradition seems to have taken off from there. By 1992, Carmichael Elementary School, the

---

4 Now the Interfaith Council of Greater Sacramento, https://sacramentointer-faith.org/

5 Faye White, Margaret Herman, and Marie Segur, *Heritage of Faith: A 75-Year History of Carmichael Presbyterian Church* (Carmichael Presbyterian Church, 1998), 101-102.

Salvation Army, Church World Service (a refugee agency), and several members of CPC referred families to take part in the program, as church secretary Julie Ueltzen wrote in article for the October 2022 issue of *Mission Bell*:

> [B]oxes upon boxes of both food and gifts would be laid out across the floor, with family boxes numbered and prepared for delivery. Once gifts arrived at CPC, custodial staff and young adults from the church would sleep in McMillen Hall to keep the plethora of gifts safe. Gifts for as many as 90 families, totaling 496 people one year, covered the hall and were later delivered to grateful families.
>
> Following the construction of the Mission Building [in 2002], the Gift Ministry relocated their preparations into the warehouse portion of the Food Closet. Tables lined the floors, and boxes covered tabletops, with overflow below. As the Food Closet demand increased, the setup moved yet again into the Howard Crowley Room.

Julie's article indicates the number of families served fell gradually from its peak of ninety in 1989 to thirty-eight in 2021. By 2015 the deacons, seeking both to simplify their task and exercise more sensitivity to families' diverse needs and traditions around food, began purchasing grocery gift cards instead of providing a pre-made food box.[6] In 2019 the deacons reported they "felt forced to decrease the number of families served by about 10 to 15% due to decreased participation by an aging congregation."[7] And in 2020 due to the COVID-19 pandemic, which curtailed much in-person shopping, families received gift cards for groceries and gifts. The gift card-only model stuck for 2021 and 2022—again, for reasons both practical and philosophical. Gift cards would enable recipients to purchase what they wanted for their families and perhaps feel more joy and dignity at being able to provide for their families.

---

6 Julie Ueltzen, "Christmas Gift Ministry a Gift to Many," in *Mission Bell* (October 2022).
7 CPC PneuMatrix Task Force, *Matrix for Assessing Deacon Responsibilities Against Mission Statement*.

The Deacon's Fund was, and is today, available to community members regardless of their connection with the church and is administered without any expectation of payback or church participation. *Heritage of Faith* indicates that at least one family that received Deacon's Fund money in its earliest days paid back the amount in full, and since that time there have been numerous examples of how recipients of benevolences turn their thanksgiving into actions that further the church's mission.

A portion of each year's Deacon's Fund is spent on immediate needs of neighbors in Carmichael. In decades past this included a mix of gasoline assistance, bus passes, rent assistance, emergency motel housing, and utility bills; as of 2021 gas cards for the local fueling stations in the amount of $50 have proven the most practical and impactful.

For families that are well known to the church, CPC pastors have been able to use their discretion in spending Deacons' funds to offer more focused assistance. In California's notoriously high-priced housing market, some families—even those with full-time employment and aid from the government social safety net—still face barriers to staying in market-rate housing, getting into low-income housing, or qualifying for services through nongovernment programs like Family Promise of Sacramento (described below). One such family, facing imminent eviction in August 2022 and having just been scammed out of a large rental deposit by someone posing as a property owner, received rehousing assistance from the church valued in excess of $10,000. Rev. Ivan Herman arranged for move-out and move-in services, storage unit rental, a five-week motel stay, and provided numerous rides to work and the grocery store. No money was given directly to the family. Once the family successfully found new housing, they had to be told the church would not provide them further assistance.[8]

Deacons' funds have also been used for items that increase access to spiritual care. For example, in 2005, a portion of Deacons' Funds went to the purchase of six new hearing aids and a reclining wheelchair for use during worship services, communion sets for in-home communion, and copies of

---

8 Rev. Ivan Herman, Report to the Board of Deacons on January 5, 2023.

the publications *Upper Room* and *Care Notes* for church members desiring devotional study aids. Donations that year also went to the Counseling Center and the preschool tuition assistance fund—and $2000 in seed money was given to start Supper on Saturday.[9]

As mentioned above, CPC members themselves have received help through the Deacons' Fund and individual church members' generosity. Laura Janik told of her family's experience:

> Our family moved to Carmichael from the Bay Area and joined CPC in 2001. I was active in the church and serving as a deacon during those first years here and then our lives were turned upside down the summer of 2004 [when I] separated from my husband and became the sole provider for my two girls.... The church provided food, and they also helped us pay for our monthly expenses. Pastor Keith [DeVries] hired me part time to work with the children of the church, which provided a steady income for a few months....
>
> I had a very hard time justifying the purchase of Christmas gifts when there were so many bills to pay, but that was taken care of by the nearly daily delivery of gifts to our doorstep by our church family. Christmas gifts for the girls and for me [arrived] already wrapped and ready to place under the tree to open on Christmas morning. Let me tell you, it was always an experience to open the front door during that time to see what God had provided for us that day.
>
> Now I don't want to solely focus on the monetary items that the church provided because the sharing of spiritual gifts was tremendous. At a time of great loss, as some if not most of you might know, it is difficult to muster within yourself the strength that is needed to move through a typical day. Whether the loss is a death, an illness, a separation or divorce, many times it is the faithfulness of God's family that provides the peace that is needed to calm your mind so you can make the decisions required to live day to day.[10]

9 Carmichael Presbyterian Church, *Annual Report 2005.*
10 Laura Janik, Faith Story, Story told at Carmichael Presbyterian Church November 16, 2014.

Food Ministries

The year-round food ministry at Carmichael Presbyterian Church is made up of three interrelated programs. The Carmichael Food Closet has since 1973 provided its neighbor families with a three-day supply of emergency groceries, operating most weekdays. Hunger relief advocacy, in the form of letter writing and other policy-related actions, was a regular feature of CPC's public witness in the 1990s and early 2000s. In 2005, Supper on Saturday (SOS) launched, providing a free, monthly hot meal and a welcoming, relaxed indoor environment for human connection.

Carmichael Food Closet

In some ways CPC was on the ground floor of the larger nationwide movement of organized food banks and food pantries beginning in the 1960s.[11] Since that time food banks and food pantries like the Carmichael Food Closet have seen multiple shifts not only in where the food comes from, but also what items are given out, and how food is shipped, stored, and distributed. These changes parallel broader trends in the US food system overall, notably corporate concentration in the food supply chain since 1960.[12] As of 2023 the Sacramento Food Bank (formerly Sacramento Food Bank and Family Services) is the "only game in town" in terms of receiving and distributing food from federal programs, whereas operations were much more diffuse in earlier decades.

While CPC members began collecting food for donation in 1969, the official opening of the Food Closet as its own entity was in 1973. (Thus, the church's 100th anniversary is also the 50th anniversary of the Carmichael Food Closet.) Originally, congregation members brought canned food to donate on communion Sundays, which in 1969 were quarterly, rather than monthly. The senior high Sunday school class collected and kept inventory of the cans and stored them in Room 45. Then the deacons

---

11 "History of Food Banks," Feeding America, accessed October 27, 2021, https://www.feedingamerica.org/about-us/our-history.
12 Institue of Medicine and National Research Council, "Overview of the US Food System," in *A Framework for Assessing Effects of the Food System*, ed. Maria Oria Malden C. Nesheim, Peggy Tsai Yih (Washington, DC: National Academies Press, 2015).

distributed the food to the Sacramento County Department of Social Welfare and other agencies. Money for the purchase of additional food went through the Deacons' Fund.[13]

In May 1972 the frequency of food collection changed from quarterly to monthly due to higher demand. About that time,CPC member Mary Nelle MacRostie, a nutritionist, developed a menu and general plans for the church's new project, which was patterned after an existing program, the South Sacramento Ecumenical Parish Food Closet. Soon after CPC's Food Closet was formally organized the following year, its leaders converted a classroom behind the office, added a Dutch door, and cleared out rows of books to make more room for the food. As more food closets mushroomed in the area, volunteers from CPC and other organizations would have a "bean and rice swap," or a trade of excess food in the parking lot of the Interfaith Service Bureau. In 1974, the service bureau founded the Greater Sacramento Food Closet Coalition, with CPC as a charter member.[14,15]

People who needed food would connect first through the Sacramento County Department of Social Welfare, which would direct them to various resources including the Carmichael Food Closet. With the county department as a referral source, demand for food increased quickly. The need for more space pushed the project to an enclosed section of the back porch. The church looked to other community agencies that might help by supplying both perishable and non-perishable food on a regular basis.[16]

Supplying the Food Closet

One of those other agencies was Senior Gleaners—one of the first in the area to receive surplus or gleaned foods from farms. In the 1980s, through Senior Gleaners, the CPC Food Closet was able to get cheese, milk, butter, honey, and flour supplied by the U.S. Department of Agriculture's Commodity Supplemental Food Program (CSFP). Over time various other agencies

---

13 Marie Segur, An Outline of the Food Closet Ministry at CPC, 2019.
14 Marie Segur, An Outline of the Food Closet Ministry at CPC. 2019.
15 Thuy-Doan Le, "Food closet celebrates 30 years - Carmichael Presbyterian Church has been feeding needy families since 1973," *Sacramento Bee*, February 5, 2004.
16 Brenda Mock and Tiffany Mock-Goeman, Food Closet short history, September 20, 2021

sponsored food closets in the Sacramento area. In 1994 California Emergency FoodLink took over sponsorship. CPC's partnership with Senior Gleaners continued until late 2014, when the agency was subsumed into Sacramento Food Bank and Family Services.[17]

In an interview, CPC member Jack Roach spoke of the stress of coordinating this ever-changing patchwork of food sources. During Jack's time as Food Closet manager in the 2010s, food was being received from Senior Gleaners, FoodLink, and school food drives. Lots of driving was required to pick up food from all these sources every week: from Robla, Rancho Cordova, Citrus Heights, and to schools in the Carmichael area.[18] Volunteer Ernie Chard echoed this concern: "I enjoyed the Food Closet but it became tiring for me; after an hour and a half [of driving each day] I was done. I did enjoy going to the Food Bank [by McClellan Park]." With the streamlining mentioned above, the process of obtaining food simplified somewhat; however, other changes within the system rippled outwards. Ernie noted that at one point,

> Sacramento Food Bank and Family Services took us off their website as a location where people could get food because we had restrictions of zip codes and certain number of times per year a person could be served; we had to drop those requirements in order to be a part of the Food Bank's web outreach.[19]

Terryl Summers, who co-directed the Food Closet from 2015–2020, also spoke of the stress of being part of a large network. "As partner agencies mandated that all ordering and communications be completed online, my responsibilities grew exponentially."[20]

In 1986 CPC member Marie Segur was executive director of the Sacramento Food Closet Coalition. She and others in the organization worked with the *Sacramento Bee* on a series of articles on hunger in Sacramento and private food closets statewide feeling the pinch of cutbacks in federal food

---

17 Cathie Anderson, "Senior Gleaners, Sacramento Food Bank Merge Operations," *Sacramento Bee*, January 9, 2015, https://www.sacbee.com/article5764425.html.
18 Jack Roach and Carolee Roach, interview by Lisa Benadom, September 11, 2020.
19 Ernie Chard, interview by Kathy Lewin, July 29, 2020.
20 Terryl Summers, interview by Karen Orlando, August 16, 2021.

aid.[21] The series was published in nine installments from February through April of 1987. In response to the articles, Marie was contacted by Joyce Raley-Teel of the grocery chain Raley's, and became an advisor to the store as it developed what became the Raley's Food For Families program.

Raley's Food for Families began in 1986 as a holiday food drive, but thanks to early input from the Food Closet leaders, it now raises "millions of dollars and pounds of food annually through food drives, store donation boxes, online giving, support from vendors as well as Raley's team members, and cash and product donations."[22] This supplies hundreds of food banks across the Northern California region. Through the fundraising arm of Raley's Food for Families, money donations were held on an account for each partner agency, reported Food Closet manager Terryl Summers in 2018. Her report further explained:

> Each agency could then order what they needed from a very generous catalogue of products based on donations credited to their account. We used approximately $14,500 this year. This partnership has enhanced the purchasing strength of the Food Closet.[23]

Terryl noted that, effective July 1, 2018, the Food for Families program was subsumed into Sacramento Food Bank and Family Services. Since that time the Food Bank has made many changes, among them an ordering system that requires participating pantries to order entire pallets of a single item. In view of this requirement, CPC members Tim and Barbara Farley suggested adding shelving to the Food Closet. They arranged for the purchase and installation of seventeen new sets of sturdy metal shelves.[24]

Growing the Food Closet

In 1989 Sacramento County cut twenty-two of their twenty-four welfare counselors and established the Community Information Center, with one

---

21 "Soaring Demand Overwhelms Food Banks (3rd in a series of 9 articles)," *Sacramento Bee*, February 24, 1987.
22 "Food For Families History: A True Community Partnership," accessed October 27, 2021, https://www.raleys.com/giving/food-for-families/history/
23 Carmichael Presbyterian Church, *Annual Report 2018*.
24 Brenda Beers Mock, "Food Closet Updates," in *Mission Bell* (February 2021).

phone line to take requests for food. Since this greatly lengthened wait times, CPC established its own dedicated phone line so that calls could be made directly to the Carmichael Food Closet. As the volume of calls increased, a request went out to other local churches for assistance. Beginning in 1989, Celtic Cross Presbyterian, Grace Presbyterian, and Northminster Presbyterian Churches joined in CPC's ministry by providing funds and volunteers.[25] Other churches that sent volunteers over the years included Cypress Avenue Baptist, First Baptist Church of Carmichael (renamed American River Community Church) and Foothill Farms Baptist.[26]

In the late 1990s San Juan Unified School District (SJUSD) began supporting the Food Closet with Peanut Butter Patrols and Tuna Times—designated days during the school year when students would bring their food donations to school. Local TV station Channel 3 (KCRA) soon initiated the Kids Can program. CPC's Food Closet team helped develop the concept with school and television station officials. The Carmichael Food Closet was the recipient of the first food drive from participating schools in SJUSD.

In 2002 the Mission Building was built onto the Robertson Avenue side of the church property. It provided more room for shelving food supplies and, for the first time, cold storage as well, with two refrigerators and four freezers. Between 1998 and the move to the new building in 2002, the number of individuals served by the Food Closet increased over sixty percent, from 10,274 to 16,479, a reflection both of the increased capacity and increased need in the community for emergency food. In 2006 CPC's Session approved a policy statement on medicine products, as the Food Closet needed guidance on handing out over-the-counter pain medicines that had been donated and were frequently requested.[27]

In 2009 the Food Closet began to see significant increased demand due to the global financial crisis and resulting recession nationwide. In May of that year, it received a windfall—a $50,000 donation from an individual. The story goes that CPC member Gene Chaney was taking his dog, Houdi, for a walk in Gibbons Park one day when they met a stranger.

25 Segur, An Outline of the Food Closet Ministry at CPC.
26 Carmichael Presbyterian Church, *Annual Report 2002*.
27 Brenda Mock and Tiffany Mock-Goeman, CPC Food Closet: A Short History, September 20, 2021.

> Three times they met the same man with his dogs. The dogs
> formed a friendship of sorts, as did Gene and the other man,
> speaking of many things including the CPC Food Closet. Out of
> the blue the man asked, "Would $50,000 help your food closet?"
> And that is how the $50,000 grant came to our food closet. [28]

Gene said he never saw the man or his dogs since that day. The Food Closet committee decided to put $5,000 into the Food Closet Dedicated Fund and the remainder into the CD account the church held with the Synod of the Pacific, to be used as the need arose.

Leadership and volunteer numbers grew and their roles differentiated as capacity to serve community members increased. These roles included recruiting and scheduling volunteers, completing intake forms, taking telephone orders, driving to pick up food, operating the warehouse, entering data, reporting to outside agencies, and writing thank-you notes to donors. By 2015 the Food Closet served over 200,000 meals a year.

Serving Food Closet Guests

With the purchase of a commercial grade freezer and refrigerator in 2015, the transformation from "closet" to something much more sophisticated became apparent. Regular leadership meetings were established to review policies and procedures, with the Rev. Ivan Herman as the staff resource person.

The 2016 CPC *Annual Report* listed twenty-three neighboring churches that provided support to the Carmichael Food Closet through various means. The Food Closet, in turn, also provided surplus items from its shelves to Mustard Seed School, Loaves & Fishes, and the Women's Crisis Center.[29]

Carmichael and Arden-Arcade's refugee and immigrant communities have also received help from the Food Closet. Many immigrants and refugees find themselves in situations similar to other "working poor" families, who make up the core of those served. Some are ineligible for government benefits or are reluctant to use such benefits even if eligible, for fear of exposure to any kind of legal authority. In a letter to its 224 partner agencies, dated

28 Carmichael Presbyterian Church, *Annual Report 2009.*
29 Mock and Mock-Goeman, CPC Food Closet: A Short History.

April 12, 2017, Blake Young, President and CEO of Sacramento Food Bank and Family Services, reminded service providers that, "Unfortunately, the current political climate has caused confusion and fear for the people we serve, especially in immigrant communities." Referring to anti-immigrant rhetoric and policies in place at the time, the letter went on to remind leaders that

> [A]s a private, nonprofit organization, SFBFS is not obligated to report the legal status of anyone we serve and will not share personal information with immigration authorities. We track the number of people we serve so we can inform the community about hunger, but we will never share the names of the people who receive food from our organization.[30]

Protecting the privacy of Food Closet users was the tip of the iceberg when it came to the increasingly complex task of providing emergency food. Along with ending the practice of serving only certain zip codes, many other administrative changes were made and discussed during the second half of the 2010s. Food recipients' names were still tracked as a way to avoid abuse of the free resource, though the "do-not-serve" list was abolished, the requirement to present legal identification dropped, and the number of allowed visits increased from six times in a rolling twelve-month period to once a month. Greatly overshadowing these concerns was the fact that the Food Closet came under the jurisdiction of the Sacramento County Environmental Management Department as a food facility subject to permitting requirements and periodic inspection.

During 2019 and early 2020 the Food Closet leadership team also entertained discussion about allowing clients to "shop" for their food needs by entering the warehouse, which would be set up in a marketplace style. The idea was that this would help people retain a sense of dignity by giving them choices, and that it would eliminate the physical barrier presented by the service window where people had previously queued to receive their pre-packed grocery bags. Many volunteers disagreed with this direction, despite its underlying motivations, on grounds of preserving physical boundaries for

---

30 Blake Young, "Letter to SFBFS Partner Agencies re: Legal status of families seeking food," https://static1.squarespace.com/static/5d80f105ec17907c33f4c-c2b/t/5deee4cc99d5d037ef4de925/1575937228968/PA_letter_re_legal_status.pdf.

safety reasons, and because allowing clients to select their own food might invite conflict or misunderstanding (e.g., when volunteers would have to enforce limits on food items or negotiate language differences). With COVID-19 the operation was forced to pivot, quickly tabling discussion about allowing clients inside. Instead the Food Closet leaders implemented a curbside pickup model whereby volunteers would bring bags of food out and load them into clients' vehicles.[31] As of 2023 curbside pickup continues, with the addition of a rolling cart "corner store" stocked with condiments, snack foods, and non-food items such as feminine products and diapers for guests to take if they wish.

While the Carmichael Food Closet was originally envisioned as a source of emergency food for people experiencing temporary need, its leadership also recognized the special needs of unhoused users who did not have cooking and refrigeration facilities. In 2020 Food Closet volunteers customized the selection to include canned goods with flip-top lids and ready-to-eat contents, as well as peanut butter, bread, fresh fruit and vegetables that did not require chopping, protein bars, hard-boiled eggs, nonperishable milk, bottled drinks, and pastries. Supplies for these guests, packed in a heavy-duty plastic bag, also included a roll of toilet paper, toiletries, plastic utensils, and a garbage bag.[32]

During the COVID-19 pandemic Food Closet volunteers were considered front-line workers. Protocols were quickly established to keep both volunteers and guests safe and healthy. In addition to curbside loading, mask wearing was required of all volunteers, and all surfaces (tables, door handles, and phone) were sanitized twice a day after every work shift. Three air scrubbers were purchased to run 24/7 in the two rooms where most volunteers worked.[33] When vaccines became available in early 2021, Food Closet workers of all ages were given Phase 1B priority along with educators, police officers, and grocery workers.[34]

As of April 2023, the Carmichael Food Closet had commercial-grade refrigeration and 3,000 square feet of processing space for the intake of pallets of canned goods from Sacramento Food Bank. Baked goods were

---

31 Rev. Ivan Herman, personal communication, March 27, 2022.
32 Mock and Mock-Goeman, CPC Food Closet: A Short History.
33 Brenda Beers Mock, interview by Karen Orlando, September 20, 2021.
34 Rev. Ivan Herman, personal communication, March 27, 2022.

being picked up weekly at Safeway, fresh meat and assorted groceries from Wal-Mart, and assorted items from Grocery Outlet-Bargain Market. Before COVID-19, the Sacramento Food Bank sold food to Carmichael Food Closet at a discounted price, then waived the fee during the pandemic and continued waiving it well into 2023. The food from Safeway and Wal-Mart was being provided free under the nonprofit Feeding America. All other food was provided thanks to in-kind and monetary donations. Eggs and milk were rarely available from grocery or individual donors, for instance, so the Food Closet Committee voted to purchase them. In 2022 the Food Closet's annual budget was $30,000. At the time of this writing it still operates solely with just over 130 volunteers; over half of them are from the community, not church members.[35]

Food Closet Leadership

Since the beginning of the Carmichael Food Closet, all its managers have been volunteers. Their names are listed below along with the year they started as volunteer manager.

Mary Nelle MacRostie, 1973

Lisa Levering, 1967

Anita Koch, 1978

Marie Segur, 1981

Don Wever, 1992

Leon Hodge, 2007

Jack Roach and Pat Chaney, 2010

Terryl Summers and Gary Lee, 2015

Brenda Beers Mock and Tiffany Mock-Goeman, 2020

A common narrative among volunteers in many of CPC's ministries, including the Food Closet, is that a friend or family member invited the individual into service and their involvement grew little by little. Lisa Levering spoke of her then mother-in-law, Cathy Levering, inviting her to volunteer in the 1970s.[36] Pat Chaney said, "Don and Thelma Wever went

---

35 Carmichael Presbyterian Church, *Annual Report 2022*.
36 Lisa Levering, interview by Susan Herman, February 3, 2021.

to the same dances [my husband Gene and I] did and during that period Don talked me into serving in the Food Closet." She continued:

> I'm not sure, but I think I started taking orders on the phone which eventually included compiling the do-not-serve list, tracking those who received food beyond the FC's limit. Gene joined the FC making runs to Gleaners, FoodLink and any place else that was giving us food. Eventually I got sucked into helping him as his pickup partner moved on. Jack Roach and I were co-directors for a few years, dividing the work between us. In a nut shell, I worked every facet of the FC during my service.[37]

Likewise, Terryl Summers said she began serving in 2000 at Bonnie Hartman's invitation and served one afternoon shift per month. For Brenda Beers Mock, the Food Closet has been a multi-generational endeavor.

> My mom, June Beers, a longtime member of CPC, worked in the Closet in the late 80s and early 90s. When I moved back to Carmichael in 2007, she said, "You take my place, I'm too old." So, I started working in 2008. My daughter and son-in-law, Tiffany Mock-Goeman and Bob Goeman, now work in the Closet almost every weekday. She co-manages with me. My grandson, their son, also works once in a while.

Due to increasing sophistication of the manager's duties, and the need for ongoing planning and visioning, a Food Closet Task Force was formed in 2020. Task force members represented volunteer leaders covering a dizzying array of functions, including volunteer recruitment and scheduling, Sacramento Food Bank liaison and ordering, food purchasing, warehouse management, equipment maintenance, driving, policies and procedures training, food handling, nutrition advising, and coordinating the phone bank. Rev. Ivan Herman fulfilled the role of "inspiration."[38] Different models of management have been piloted, such as having day managers who serve on a set day of the week; developing the manager position into a paid role has also been considered.

---

37 Pat Chaney, interview by Karen Orlando, August 16, 2021.
38 Carmichael Presbyterian Church, *Annual Report 2022.*

Speaking of the many changes at the Food Closet she has seen since 2008, Brenda Mock shared:

> We provide more fresh food, vegetables, and fruit specifically, than we did in the past. It is cheaper and nutritionally better to buy fresh than it is to buy canned from the Food Bank.
>
> The Closet now serves anyone in Sacramento County. We see case workers calling and picking up for multiple families who can't get to the Closet or can't call in for an appointment. More refugee families come and ask for specific food that they prefer.
>
> The biggest change is our volunteer staff. Since the pandemic, many senior volunteers and generally CPC members have not been able to work. After reaching out to the community on social media, Facebook and Next Door Carmichael, a majority of volunteers are not affiliated with CPC. It does bring diversity and has embraced a couple of new members.
>
> The Closet now gives food to people using the shower ministry on Saturday and supplies some items to Carmichael HART to make forty bagged lunches every Thursday that they deliver to the homeless up and down Fair Oaks Blvd. Crossroads Church picks up surplus snacks and drinks once a week to distribute to homeless folks around the different encampments in Carmichael....
>
> The best day for me at the Closet is when all the volunteers show up, all the folks who need groceries come to pick up, and we have a birthday cake to give a family that has requested one for their child.[39]

Hunger Relief Advocacy and Hunger Sunday

Hunger Sundays were first recognized at CPC in 1993. Their purpose was to raise awareness about the root causes of hunger and the magnitude of the issue nationwide and around the world, and to encourage church members to engage in actions that would lead to long-term systemic change in

---

39 Mock, interview.

dealing with hunger. On Hunger Sundays, to be observed quarterly, church members would be invited to gather after worship and write letters to their elected state and federal officials regarding policies related to hunger and hunger relief. The church had enrolled as a member congregation with the nonpartisan organization Bread for the World in the late 1970s. [40] Since its founding in 1974, Bread for the World has supplied educational materials for congregations to assist them in advocacy efforts.[41] CPC member Lisa Levering said that she, Marie Segur, and Wayne MacRostie were part of the team that proposed to Session that the church observe Hunger Sundays. They proposed using Bread for the World's mobilization resources as a guide for determining the specific message or call to action for each Hunger Sunday. The team eventually became known as the Hunger Relief Advocacy Committee.

> It was really easy to get people to do. After church we were all set up with the letters and pens and everything and they just had to copy the letter and sign it. So it was not a hard task.... [At that time] Bread for the World was about [supporting] the WIC program.[42]

In partnering with Bread for the World, CPC was following the lead of the larger denomination. The Presbyterian Hunger Program had identified Bread for the World as an effective nonprofit. Lisa noted that, despite this, some church members were averse to the letter-writing approach, preferring not to mix church and public policy.

As of 1997 three members of CPC's Mission Division served as rotating chairpersons for Hunger Sunday. That year's annual report stated that

> ...passage of the Federal Welfare Reform legislation in August 1996 led to significant innovations in the CPC [hunger relief advocacy] program. Members of the [congregation] attended hearings by legislative committees, participated in parallel activities of the faith community through the Interfaith Service Bureau and attended a Child Resources Event in November. In January, the

---

40 White, Herman, and Segur, *Heritage of Faith*, 213.
41 "Mobilize Your Chuch," https://www.bread.org/about/.
42 Levering, interview. WIC refers to the federal government's Women, Infants, and Children supplemental nutrition program.

congregation was asked to comment on priorities for the State to observe in formulating its response to the federal law. These suggestions were analyzed and made available in February for the congregation to put before state legislators as they designed the California program. In May, the Rev. Leslie Sauer [husband of CPC associate pastor the Rev. Sharon Sauer, speaking on behalf of the California Council of Churches] described the overall recommendations of the faith community....The Legislature passed and the Governor signed the Work Opportunity and Responsibility for Kids Act (CalWORKS) in August.[43]

In 1999 CPC members engaged by writing hundreds of letters over four Hunger Sundays, urging Congress and members of the state legislature to raise food stamp allowances and support school breakfast programs. They also wrote in favor of Jubilee 2000, the campaign to cancel billions of dollars of debt owed by the world's poorest countries. [44]

In 2001 a total of 240 letters or cards were sent on Hunger Sundays. The campaigns varied from advocating for foreign aid to pushing for state and federal legislation allowing people who owned personal vehicles to retain their eligibility for welfare assistance. They also urged the expansion of nutrition benefits for working families and elderly people.[45] A member of Session's Mission Division, Bob Scott, also reported in 2002 that some CPC members participated in a "fast sit-in to let our county officials see and meet the needs of the homeless."[46]

Letter writing continued with regularity until roughly the time the Supper on Saturday ministry started in 2005 (see next section). It picked up again in Spring 2010 and continued sporadically after that. During the Lenten season of 2013, the Rev. Ivan Herman's family observed "forty days of SNAP," during which they set their family's grocery budget to roughly equal what a family of four would receive in Supplemental Nutrition benefits (formerly food stamps) if their income were 130% of the federal poverty level. They wrote a blog about the experience, parts of which were re-published on

---

43 Carmichael Presbyterian Church, *Annual Report 1997*.
44 Carmichael Presbyterian Church, *Annual Report 1999*.
45 Carmichael Presbyterian Church, *Annual Report 2001*.
46 Carmichael Presbyterian Church, *Annual Report 2002*.

Bread for the World's website. Pastor Ivan was also interviewed in an article for the magazine *Presbyterian Outlook*.[47] The Hermans' Forty Days of SNAP blog helped spark conversations around hunger in the church. For example, as part of a Drama Team presentation held during worship, actor Kristen Zeman pushed a grocery cart while remarking to a fellow "shopper," "I'm getting this jar of peanut butter for my church's food closet... but, did you know that SNAP—yes, the government program—provides way more hunger relief than food banks do?"[48]

Pastor Ivan hosted a screening of the documentary film *A Place at the Table* after a Wednesday dinner in early 2013. The film follows the stories of several individuals and families experiencing hunger to illustrate the many dimensions of food insecurity, and to explain proposed solutions. The following Sunday fifty-one letters were sent from CPC to members of Congress urging them to protect SNAP and other anti-poverty programs from funding cuts. (Unfortunately the reductions did take place.)

Over the years church members took a variety of other actions, both practical and symbolic in nature, to learn about and fight hunger. Among these was an adult mission trip to Delano, California, in 2009 to participate in gleaning of vegetables left in the agricultural fields post-harvest and repackaging of that food. The following year a group went to Dinuba, California, with Gleanings for the Hungry, a program of Youth With a Mission (YWAM).[49]

Starting in 2001 and for several years after that, congregation members participated in CROP Walk, which shares funds raised between Church World Service and local food banks.[50] CPC volunteers were active members of the planning committee for the 2010 Sacramento event.[51]

---

47 Eva Stimson, "Pastor's family takes on the 'Food Stamp Challenge'," *Presbyterian Outlook*, June 19, 2013, https://pres-outlook.org/2013/06/pastors-family-takes-on-the-food-stamp-challenge/.
48 As of 2020 the federal government provides approximately nine meals for every one provided through food banks. See Kate Leone, "Feeding America statement on House introduction of HEROES Act," May 12, 2020, https://www.feedingamerica.org/about-us/press-room/heroes-act-1.
49 Carmichael Presbyterian Church, *Annual Report 2009*.
50 CROP was originally an acronym for the Christian Rural Overseas Program. When it started in 1947 its primary mission was to help Midwest farm families to share their grain with hungry neighbors in post-World War II Europe and Asia.
51 Carmichael Presbyterian Church, *Annual Report 2010*.

In 2012 youth leader Jeremy Meehan organized a team of teens and adults to participate in a local Thanksgiving Day event called Run to Feed the Hungry, which raised funds for Sacramento Food Bank and Family Services (and is not associated with religious groups). A CPC team again participated in 2019, running or walking either a 5K or 10K course with over twenty thousand others through East Sacramento and midtown. In 2020, race team organizers Anne and Steve Parker urged church members to donate and run in their own neighborhoods, as COVID-19 had led to the cancellation of the large event. In 2021 and 2022 the Parkers led participants (about twenty-five each time) on a five-kilometer route from the church through Ancil Hoffman Park and back, with the dual goal of supporting the food closet and strengthening social ties after the isolation of the pandemic.

Supper on Saturday (SOS)

Until the late 1990s the Carmichael Food Closet was CPC's main method of outreach for providing direct food aid to people in the community. Then, in 1997, the Session's Mission Division went on a retreat led by Nancy Eng MacNeill, the Hunger Action Enabler of the Presbytery of Sacramento. There they discerned a call to begin volunteering at Loaves & Fishes and the North Area Teen Center (see Chapter 5). Beginning in 1998 the church sent a team of volunteers monthly to help serve lunch at Loaves & Fishes for the 800–1,200 people who were experiencing homelessness and could get to the C Street location. In the beginning a team of seven or so would serve lunch on the second Monday of the month.[52] The team's numbers increased to a high of about twenty-five, then diminished to ten in 2015, and five in 2021. As of 2022 the congregation no longer participated in serving lunches, though it continued supporting Loaves & Fishes with an annual donation from its regular budget.

During this period Supper on Saturday (SOS) launched at CPC. Associate Pastor K. C. Wahe suggested to Garrett Torgerson, who was a member of Mission Division in 2005, that the church provide a free hot meal once a month for people in the community. As division members discussed the idea, someone suggested that the model might be similar to St. Philomene's Tuesday evening meals. A small team from CPC visited St. Philomene's Catholic Church on El

---

52 Carmichael Presbyterian Church, *Annual Report 1999.*

Camino Avenue to learn how their system worked and to gather insights. Karen Orlando was part of the scouting team and went to work at a few of the dinners "to get the hang of the system." With a gift of $2,000 in startup money from the Deacons' Fund, CPC's first SOS was held on September 24, 2005.[53]

"My notes show that we were going to plan for 300 people the first time. In fact, I had. This is my inventory of the desserts for 312 people," said CPC volunteer Carolyn McGregor, sharing the list she had saved from that time.[54] In fact, only two individuals showed up for the first meal. Pat Chaney, who served as administrative chair for starting the dinners, described the events leading up to the event:

> Karen Orlando wrote a lot of letters around to the community asking for support.... The youth went around and put out little flyers [to advertise the meal]. Then [my husband] Gene and I went out one day and put up the same flyer. We went to laundromats, we went to low-income apartment houses, in the laundry rooms. We put them everywhere. And then got the banner for outside. And came the first day and we were prepared for...a lot of people. We had two people who showed up; a husband and wife. We had a lot of leftovers. The meat we put in the freezer for future use. The kids who were going to help to serve, they sat down and they ate.... We came the next month with less food, but still a lot of food. I think we had three people attend. The same couple, and they brought their son.[55]

Despite the low attendance at the beginning, news about the monthly hot dinner soon spread. Even though the ministry was suspended from May 2006 through June 2007 during construction of the new McMillen Hall, attendees quickly returned, and their numbers remained steady until the start of the pandemic. Preparation crews filled individual plates—always real dishes and flatware, not paper or plastic—and served them to guests, restaurant-style. Volunteers came around with drink and dessert carts to serve guests at their tables. Musicians often provided live piano or guitar

---

53 Pat Chaney, Garrett Torgerson, Karen Orlando, Trina Spivack, Memories of the Supper on Saturday Ministry at CPC, December 9, 2020.
54 Carolyn McGregor and Pat Chaney, interview by Jimmi Mishler, January 31, 2014.
55 McGregor and Chaney, interview.

music. Guests were also offered to-go boxes for leftovers. In its first years, SOS dinners were held on the fourth Saturday of the month, but later, and in coordination with other congregations in the area with similar offerings, moved to third Saturdays.

Trina Spivack started volunteering with SOS in its first days, noting that she felt comfortable bringing her children, David and Sarah, who were then elementary-school age, to help. Teaming up with Marti Wallace, Trina took over administrative leadership of the program from Pat Chaney in 2011. Barbara Farley took over supervision of meal preparation from Marti Wallace in 2013. Trina said, "The ministry has been remarkably consistent throughout the years, despite changes in leadership and volunteers. Overall, once the program was up and running, we have had an average of 75–80 guests per month, with the largest attendance being approximately 110." Trina explained that in March 2020, when SOS volunteers began offering to-go meals due to COVID-19 restrictions, participation decreased significantly and averaged twenty to twenty-five meals per month. "I believe it is because a significant number of our guests were coming not only for the food, but for the fellowship, as well," she said.

Volunteers at SOS range in age from teenagers to senior citizens.[56] Some of the Scouts who participated, observed Carolyn MacGregor, were very young as she recalled when serving with them:

> These two boys were going to help me with the desserts. I had made apple crisp, it was still warm. I put it in the bowls and was going to squirt it with the whipped cream. Well, these two little boys wanted to help me. Can you imagine, seven- or eight-year-olds. One was just about to squirt it in his mouth and I grabbed it.

When the boys wanted to help at the dessert table again, Carolyn gave them another job to do.[57]

Over the years, SOS volunteers have offered additional types of aid, including toiletry items and towels for those who wished to take showers.

---

56 Terry Kaufman, "Soup for Supper: A local congregation runs a unique program that feeds the hungry," *Inside Arden*, December 2008.
57 McGregor and Chaney, interview.

CPC staff member Lisa Torgerson organized donations of coats and other warm clothes to give away each winter. Garrett Sellers, a local insurance agent, came on a monthly basis for several years, and continues to do so as of 2023, to provide information on free health plans available for those who qualify for Medicare and Medi-Cal. One year, flu shots were provided. CPC member Viki Tozier provided flower arrangements from Safeway and Brothers Papadopoulos, a local florist, for the tables each month, "creating an atmosphere of welcome and respect for our guests."[58]

Recalling the first Christmas of SOS, Pat Chaney reported that 125 people came:

> We had music, we had Trina's husband and his brother come to play their musical instruments and everything was hustling, bustling. We gave away underwear, socks, and warm clothing. Dottie Bjur organized that. It was a great affair. The chef [Ed LaFranchi] had cooked four or five big hams. Otherwise, if it hadn't been for him, we couldn't have fed 125 people. We began to run out of other things so we just began pulling stuff off of the shelves really quick and we fed them all. It was really God working because it was, "Oh my gosh, we're running out of vegetables." Any time really large cans came into the Food Closet, I would grab them and take them to SOS. Those large cans can't be given to families. So that's how we managed to feed everybody on the first Christmas.[59]

Within the church a food-sharing ecosystem of sorts did develop, as Pat noted. As the next SOS dinner approached, large donations of bread and cakes from Safeway would be diverted from the Food Closet for the occasion. Occasionally SOS leftovers were even donated to Loaves & Fishes.

Help doesn't always flow in one direction, and those who intend to provide help and care sometimes see it take shape in unexpected ways, as Trina Spivack observed:

> It has been wonderful to see the support that our guests offer to each other. Many of our guests know a number of other guests, and they share with and care for each other. The guests

---

58 Chaney et al., Memories of the Supper on Saturday Ministry at CPC.
59 McGregor and Chaney, interview.

frequently let us know when someone is ill/injured or has died. They inquire about others when the others are not there. They enjoy sitting together, and even "making the circuit" of tables just to chat. There have been multiple times when a person arrives after the meal is finished, but one of the guests who has received a "to go" meal through the lottery has given up their meal.... The thing I have appreciated the most about SOS is the opportunity I have had to get to have a long-term relationship (relationship may be too strong a word...but the long-term nature of the connection is great) with some of our guests. Some of the memorable guests for me:

Jimmy rides his bike or takes the bus from Watt/Auburn to eat with us. He is extremely affable and knows many (if not most) of the other guests. He is an extremely picky eater (some months, he only wants a roll), he always tells me the exact date of the next SOS meal. He continues to come during this COVID time, and usually stays for at least forty-five minutes just to chat.

Whenever Gary is there, he always has to come to me and tell me three to four jokes, which I am then required to pass on to [my daughter] Sarah.

Lynn is a caretaker. She originally came with her mother, but her mother has since passed. She always takes the leftover milk to provide to others (families with children) in her apartment complex.[60]

Reflecting on the people at SOS, Trina's brother Garrett Torgerson shared this story:

I learned a little compassion from the least likely person. I'll refer to him as Bill. He was one of the most angry people I have ever met: hair trigger, potentially violent, always looking to take offense with someone, and always on the edge of lashing out.... The funny thing, though, was that Bill wasn't a bad person. He had just been cursed with a demon of sorts, an incredibly angry disposition. He wanted to do the right thing, but had, in the words of TV's *Dexter*, a dark passenger. Toward the end of Bill's

---

60 Chaney et al., Memories of the Supper on Saturday Ministry at CPC.

life, Bill would park his car in the back lot and angrily guard the church. He loved the church. Bill slowed down some, but as far as I know, he stayed somewhat pissed off until the end. And God loved Bill. And a part of me did, too.[61]

Housing and Shelter Ministries

In 1964 California's statewide ballot included Proposition 14, which would create a state constitutional right for persons to refuse to sell, lease, or rent residential properties to other persons. Its passage that November, with sixty-five percent voting yes, had the effect of voiding a state statute called the California Fair Housing Act of 1963, which prohibited discrimination based on race, color, religion, natural origin, or ancestry in the sale or rental of residential dwellings containing more than four units. In 1966, the California Supreme Court ruled that Proposition 14 violated the equal protection clause of the U.S. Constitution's Fourteenth Amendment; the U.S. Supreme Court upheld the state court's ruling the following year. Before the ruling Justice Byron White wrote that "[Proposition 14] was intended to authorize, and does authorize, racial discrimination in the housing market. The right to discriminate is now one of the basic policies of the State."[62]

Rev. Dr. Pyron McMillen, then pastor of Carmichael Presbyterian, denounced Proposition 14 in a letter to the editor of the *Sacramento Bee*:

> The courts of the church have denounced as a moral evil the current ballot issue on housing known as Proposition 14, which denies fair housing to all men. They are convinced that the long dream which began with Paul's insights of the equality of all men in the sight of God [from the biblical book of Ephesians], reiterated in the Declaration of Independence, fought for in the war to eradicate slavery, must not now be allowing self interest to write into the constitution of our state an initiative which would make discrimination not only legal but respectable.[63]

61 Chaney et al., Memories of the Supper on Saturday Ministry at CPC.
62 "California Proposition 14, Right to Decline Selling or Renting Residential Properties to Persons Initiative (1964)," https://ballotpedia.org/.
63 Rev. Pyron McMillen, "Liberty and Justice for All? Liberty and Justice for None?," Letter to the editor adapted from a sermon, *Sacramento Bee*, October

This story of Dr. McMillen's act of public theology against racism resurfaced at CPC when his letter was reprinted in the September 2020 issue of *The Mission Bell.* At that time the church's Session was discerning whether to sign on to the denomination's Matthew 25 initiative to eradicate systemic poverty and racism (which is described in more detail in Chapter 1). Among the many points brought up in those discussions was that CPC had entered a time when people in the congregation were ready to go deeper on issues of systemic poverty, which in California included affordable housing shortages and policies still undergoing incremental change after decades of redlining and actions like Prop 14.

As early as 1985 the congregation had been involved with housing assistance of various kinds. That year saw the launch of a transitional housing program called Project Home by the Interfaith Service Bureau. The church participated during all five years of Project Home's existence, after which they joined in Habitat for Humanity's work in the Sacramento area.[64] Then in 2006, shortly after the newly formed national organization Family Promise of Sacramento started its Sacramento affiliate, CPC signed on to be a host congregation.

Family Promise

Billie Seekins brought the Family Promise program to the attention of CPC's Mission Division. In 2005 a chapter of the organization was forming in Sacramento.[65] Family Promise works with families that are at risk of eviction or at other points in their struggle to find or keep housing. As of 2023 the Family Promise website reports that eighty-one percent of the families they serve nationwide find permanent housing.[66] The Sacramento Family Promise affiliate program started out using a "rotational shelter" model and continued doing so until disrupted by COVID-19 in 2020. With congregations providing space and volunteers, each evening the participating families would have dinner, fellowship time, nursery play

---

25, 1964.

64 White, Herman, and Segur, *Heritage of Faith*, 172-73.

65 John Wallace, CPC History Notes: Pastors, Mission Trips, Stephen Ministry Leadership, Microassistance Program, June 19, 2020.

66 "FAQs," accessed March 20, 2023, https://familypromise.org/frequent-ly-asked-questions/.

time for children, showers, and private rooms with bedding to sleep in. Children would spend the day at their regular schools or at the Mustard Seed School downtown; adults, if not employed, would be transported to the day center to learn skills needed to search for jobs and permanent housing. Partner congregations would host four families for one week, three or four times a year.

The program includes intensive case management. Family Promise case managers help clients navigate supportive services such as mental health services, substance abuse counseling, medical exams, and life skills training. The program banks seventy percent of what the parents earn, so that when the family "graduates" they have jobs, a savings account, and their first and last month's rent for permanent or transitional housing—some clients even acquire a car.[67]

Once CPC's Session voted in favor of church involvement, Billie Seekins began serving as the congregation's liaison, or host coordinator, to Family Promise of Sacramento. The church hosted the first families during the week of January 19–25, 2006. During its first six years of partnership with the organization, CPC hosted families three times a year for one week each, increasing the commitment to four weeks in 2013 as a larger group of volunteers filled out a core team.[68] As of 2017 CPC was one of fifteen participating congregations in the Sacramento area.

CPC has had five Family Promise volunteer host coordinators since becoming involved with the program: Billie Seekins, Barbara Farley, Carol Jones, Mary MacDonald, and Bob Curtis. Since Family Promise of Sacramento brought in their first families, 319 families have been placed in either transitional or permanent housing. In addition, 128 families have received rental assistance, preventing them from losing their housing and ending up in the vicious cycle of homelessness. In part because of the help of congregations like CPC,twenty-six program participants have been able to earn their GED, four high school students have received full scholarships for higher education in the in the California State University system, sixteen participants have received their college degrees, and nineteen have purchased their own homes.[69]

---

67 "Family Promise," accessed March 20, 2023, https://www.familypromisesac-ramentoca.org/.
68 Carmichael Presbyterian Church, *Annual Report 2006*.
69 Mary MacDonald, personal communication, March 31, 2023.

Mary MacDonald began serving on Family Promise of Sacramento's Board of Directors in early 2023, following six years of involvement as host coordinator and in other volunteer roles with the organization.[70]

As part of its commitment to Family Promise, CPC offered McMillen Hall as a space for it's annual dinner fundraiser when hotel venues became too expensive. Because of the pandemic, in 2020 and 2021 the format was to-go. People could order boxed dinners for $60 per person or $300 for a "table" of six. The dinner, which consisted of tri-tip, garlic potatoes, crisp-tender roasted vegetables, salad, and rolls, was donated by CPC member Branden Rodgers' business, Jackson Catering.

In 2021 Family Promise of Sacramento adopted a fixed-site model, after COVID-related restrictions in 2020 posed challenges and led the program to temporarily house families in hotels. The fixed site, called Safe Harbor, was established in North Sacramento and comprised a small cluster of tiny homes with outdoor gardens and a shaded common area. Beginning in 2022 Family Promise collaborated with the Salvation Army to provide rent subsidies for families who needed help staying in their homes. Carmichael Presbyterian continued to support the organization financially, and, in 2023, also began volunteering for periodic clean-up days at the site.

Winter Sanctuary, HART, and Homeless Ministry

Winter Sanctuary was a program jointly funded by Sacramento County and area nonprofits that began in 2010 and ended in 2019. Sacramento County congregations hosted up to 125 people in need of shelter overnight in their facilities on a rotating basis, from November through March. Small groups from CPC volunteered in 2014 and 2015 at the overnight site at St. Mark's United Methodist Church. On February 25–27, 2016, CPC hosted the program in McMillen Hall for the first time, for eighty-one men and women. During each of the three nights after dinner, guests were able to take showers, play cards, and watch a movie. Members of CPC's youth group put together survival care packages for the guests to take with them when they left after their three-night stay.

---

70 "Family Promise Highlights Mary MacDonald," in *Mission Bell* (April 2023).

In addition to hosting Sacramento Winter Sanctuary in 2016, CPC's Mission Division took several steps that year to deepen its commitment to sheltering unhoused people. Among these were agreements on behalf of the church to:

- Operate as a satellite intake center for Sacramento Winter Sanctuary.

- Join with other faith communities in the area to form Carmichael Homeless Assistance Resource Team (HART). Other HART groups were also organized in Elk Grove, Rancho Cordova, and Citrus Heights as coalitions of community members, faith-based organizations, businesses, and local nonprofits. As of 2023 there were ten HART groups serving various communities in Sacramento County.

- Appoint a task force to coordinate CPC's homeless ministry.[71]

The task force began its work in 2017 and included representatives from the church's Session, deacons, office staff, preschool staff, and at-large members of the congregation. The group met eight times in 2017 and began developing systems, such as online signups for laundering towels used in the shower ministry, as well as policies regarding when the church's the church's unhoused neighbors would be allowed on the campus.

The church continued as a host site for Winter Sanctuary for four nights in 2017, then lowered its commitment to two nights per season for 2018 and 2019, after which the county discontinued its funding and the rotating shelter program ended. During that time, Carmichael HART developed its own winter shelter program, and the church began hosting in partnership with that organization. For ten nights in 2018 the church hosted fifteen to thirty men and women from the Carmichael area, and in 2019 hosted seven nights. Winter overnight shelter ended during COVID-19. In its place, Carmichael HART began offering Winter Respite three days a week from 9:00 a.m. until 1:00 p.m. in January and February. Outside of the winter months, HART offered a Saturday morning respite in McMillen Hall with breakfast and showers available.

---

71 Carmichael Presbyterian Church, *Annual Report 2016*.

In 2018 the church also hosted an event called the Homeless Outreach Partnership Event (HOPE), in conjunction with the Sacramento County Sheriff's Department and twenty other participating organizations. In 2021 the church again hosted the event, which included a COVID-19 vaccination clinic, veterinary service providers offering free care for pets, haircuts, and other resource connections through the county's Department of Human Assistance, Loaves & Fishes, Sacramento Self-Help Housing, and Volunteers of America.

Due to the outsize burden the church's bathroom and shower ministry placed on its office staff, the ministry shifted from weekdays to Saturdays during 2020, and was thereafter administered jointly by community volunteers, including church members, and Carmichael HART. In 2020 CPC's Mission Division also worked on details with HART for the organization to lease a small private home on the Robertson Avenue side of the property (Robertson House; see Chapter 1), rehabilitate it, and turn it into transitional housing for four men, with a house manager living on site. During 2021, HART completed the remodel of Robertson House, and in early 2022, the first clients moved in. Sacramento Self-Help Housing provided the house manager.

Pastors, staff, volunteers, and Session leaders execute a daily dance of push and pull between setting boundaries and exercising compassion when it comes to carrying out CPC's homeless ministries. Lighting bollards at the parking lot entrance are broken from time to time by people wanting to charge their devices overnight using the electrical outlet, while also having adequate darkness for sleeping. Before the installation of a large security fence blocking off the alley next to the church office, drug users would occasionally find privacy there. The large fountain on the Marconi Avenue side of the property served as a nighttime toilet for people sleeping on the lawn until the church's Buildings & Grounds Committee made the decision to shut off the water

With every kind of person calling or entering the church office, said Lisa Levering, office administrators Julie Ueltzen and Karen Gray must handle situations with great care:

> Julie always says, "if I answer the phone and someone's on the phone and they just want to talk to you forever—you just listen."

> ...I'm really proud of our homeless ministry as well, Winter Sanctuary, Family Promise and all. It's a struggle with drugs and when [people] break stuff. But that ministry is really important.[72]

Researchers in 2008 studied a national sample of over 500,000 US churchgoers and found that while involvement in a religious community often parallels high rates of individual involvement in voting, charitable giving, advocacy, and other forms of civic or political participation, the collective action of churches more often addresses the *symptoms* of larger systemic problems. Churches are more likely to be involved collectively in providing emergency food, clothing, or shelter and providing counseling services and support groups, rather than in advocacy or capacity-building activities in their community such as job training, financial literacy, microloans, or community organizing.[73] In doing so many of these activities over the years, CPC has been somewhat unusual. Certainly, the congregation's energy for community outreach has been focused on symptoms; however, some of it has also been directed towards structural change and capacity-building.

CPC members and friends have learned that mission outreach of all kinds is hard to do in a coordinated way that maximizes impact. Whether the goal is to influence policy or provide a direct service to someone in need so they can get through another day, there are always challenges.

Marsha Cook, a CPC member, offered some insight on staying grounded when serving others. Speaking of challenging situations in her work with children, Marsha said it helps to remember, "I know who I am. A child of God."[74]

Like Marsha, all who are part of the CPC family get periodic reminders of their identity as children of God—those who work or volunteer with struggling people perhaps get more reminders than others. As children of

---

72 Levering, interview.
73 Woolever and Bruce, *A Field Guide to U.S. Congregations: Who's Going Where and Why, Second edition*, 73.
74 Marsha Cook, personal communication, January 25, 2023

God, we are meant to ask *why*, like all children do. Why do people get stuck in cycles of poverty? Why does working with the Sacramento Food Bank involve such a maze of administrative work? Why do people we're trying to help damage our property? Why is it so hard to replace volunteers? As long as people at CPC continue to explore these questions with a spirit of openness," God will keep leading the way.

Chapter 7
Connecting With
and Serving Our World:
Youth Mission Trips

Responding to God's love through Jesus Christ,
We connect with and serve our world

Maundy Thursday fell on April 1—April Fool's Day—in 1999. As gray clouds blotted the sky, something must have seemed "off" to the thirty-plus volunteers who had traveled from Carmichael to the Mexicali Valley desert village of Chorizo. Most days it was a challenge to keep from breathing too much dust, as it rose in billowing clouds around the construction site and playing field where the volunteers spent most of their time. But when they gathered that night with their hosts in the village for a festive dinner of barbecued meats and a round of piñata smashing, the rain started falling.

"There were no lingering good-byes,"[1] as the Carmichael delegation returned to the multi-acre tent city, where they spent the nights during their week of service with around a thousand other youth organized by Azusa Pacific University's Mexico Outreach Program. Work boots squelched in the deepening mud while everyone retrieved their sleeping bags and clothes. Faye White reported about the rainy night in an article for the neighborhood newspaper *Carmichael Times*:

---

1 Faye White, "Youths Have Mexican Adventure," *Carmichael Times*, May 4, 1999.

Back in the cars and vans, the drivers raced to reach the paved highway which led across the border to Yuma, Arizona. Unable to travel the short-cut to cross the border at Algodones, the vehicles drove into Sonora, the next Mexican state to the east where the rained-out volunteers had to wait an hour and a half in a traffic jam at the San Luis border crossing.

Eventually the group made it to Yuma, ate at Burger King, and slept at Motel 6. They returned to their tent city next morning and found a quagmire. All the vehicles used for transporting building materials and tents were stuck in the mud. Someone would have to stay behind with them while the ground dried.

Just as that decision was being made, however, "a young Mexican man appeared out of nowhere driving a Caterpillar tractor that quickly pulled all the vehicles out of the mud." Reflecting on the trip afterward, youth leader Ken DeYoung mused that maybe "God drives a tractor."[2]

Building Relationships and Homes in Mexico

Many Carmichael Presbyterian youth who came of age in the 1980s through early 2000s say that the seeds of their faith were planted during their Holy Week service mission to Mexico. Beginning in 1985 with a scouting trip by youth leader Paul Verduin, alongside a group from Christ Community Church, and continuing with CPC youth from 1986 through 2008, these adventures to the Mexico borderlands gave teenagers and adults alike powerful opportunities for personal encounters with Mexican agricultural workers and their children in the hardscrabble *colonias* where they lived.

For about the first decade of these mission trips, the van driver was Laurie Mixell, also known to the youth as Roller Coaster Mama. In some years, the group from CPC was joined by others from Peace Presbyterian, Celtic Cross, and St. Stephen's Presbyterian.[3] Members of the Korean church that met at Carmichael also were included. And there were times when friends of youth group members who were not regular churchgoers would join the group, though all participants were generally expected

2 White, "Youths Have Mexican Adventure."
3 St. Stephen's Presbyterian Church closed in 2014.

to take part in the months-long effort of preparation and fundraising. Partnering with Azusa Pacific University, and later with a group called Amor Ministries, teens and adults from CPC were able to understand, on a visceral level, the precarious living situation of Mexicans who lived in improvised communities along the border—that is, communities built from materials its residents had at hand, without formal zoning, development, utility service, or government representation.

Some participants were also conscious of the larger forces that were making Mexicans' lives more uncertain during that era. Severe devaluation of the peso, trade liberalization policies such as the General Agreement on Tariffs and Trade (GATT) and the North American Free Trade Agreement (NAFTA), along with domestic reforms by the Mexican government, ushered in numerous changes. Among those was a rapid shift in agricultural areas away from cotton and sunflower seed farming to crops mainly grown for export, such as cantaloupes and onions. Mexican producers who had previously benefitted from government price supports saw these subsidies diminish over time.[4]

Ultimately, agricultural companies such as Driscoll's, as well as the multinational corporations that brought assembly plants (known as *maquiladoras*) to the area, offered many more job opportunities for Mexicans than they'd had before. However, neither private industry nor government could fill the important gaps, such as housing and childcare, for workers who left their communities to come to the border.

Azusa Pacific Mexico Outreach

Accounts of CPC delegations' mission trips, in partnership with Azusa Pacific University, show that their main activities were centered around supporting a pastor, Antonio Montoya, who had felt God's call to provide spiritual leadership for his farmworker community. Pastor Montoya's village, Chorizo, was about twenty-five miles southwest of Yuma, Arizona. As Ken DeYoung described it, supporting Pastor Montoya's ministry took various forms and evolved over the years:

---

4 Antonio Yunez-Naude, *Lessons from NAFTA: The Case of Mexico's Agricultural Sector* (2002), http://web.worldbank.org/archive/website00894A/ WEB/PDF/YUNEZ_TE.PDF.

> The [Azusa Pacific Outreach Ministries] program was very exciting for the youth because we were involved in Vacation Bible School and recreation and we learned early on that there was desperate need for building. As the years [went by] we became involved in a building program which included building a church in Chorizo. And subsequently, we built three houses in that village for families that were basically living in cardboard and thatched roof shacks and dirt floors. And we drilled a well in the village so that there would be a reliable source of water...
>
> Pastor Antonio Montoya...is kind of the welfare department in that particular region. It is very rural and it is an agricultural farmland region. The people that end up being destitute can always come to him for help. We helped him out by building him a new home that had facilities that at least offer a place of rest for people and some food.[5]

On a few of the trips in the late 1990s, CPC member Dr. David Fair set up a dental clinic and provided dental care to community members in Chorizo. One year, he and a small team "jury-rigged an air compressor and shop vacuum to power a dental drill" for use in filling cavities.[6]

The teenagers in the Carmichael delegation were in charge of Vacation Bible School for the children of the village, whose school break also aligned with the Easter holidays. Regarding preparing the youth group for the trip, former youth leader Mark Studer said:

> We worked on the skits in Spanish. The kids actually all wrote out their testimony, which is kind of funny with sixteen of them. It's kind of like you do for confirmation, but they wrote their own faith story, and then translated it into Spanish and practiced it in Spanish, so they could read it down there. The pastor of the church in Chorizo was Pentecostal. So, testimony was the big thing.

---

5 Ken DeYoung, interview by Wayne MacRostie, March 24, 2003.
6 Faye White, "Carmichael Youth to Visit Mexican Mission in Chorizo," *Carmichael Times*, March 30, 1999.

> We talked about what you can wear—you had to wear pants or a long dress/skirt—and so really that was the training to get ready for the trip to go down there. [Some of the training was cultural but] a lot of it was preparing, because if you're going to put VBS on every day for a week, it was really getting the kids ready to do that. So we did it every Sunday morning. I even made a policy at one point that you had to either come to Sunday school or youth group on a regular basis to go to Mexico.... So, part of the training was making sure for safety reasons that they understood what needed to happen.[7]

Several interviewees who went on the trips said that the Mexico missions helped them develop leadership skills. Jennifer Boyd, for example, said:

> I was a youth leader for the mission trips when I was a high school senior and that was really meaningful, mostly because, you know, it feels good to have people that you respect put you in that kind of a position.[8]

The Azusa Pacific Mexico Outreach program would bring roughly one thousand youth from throughout California and the rest of the country to the Mexicali area each year during the Holy Week school break. Each group was assigned a village, where the main task was to support its spiritual life. Within those general guidelines there weren't too many specific expectations. Before and after going out to the villages for the day, the large group would have worship and community building activities at the tent city, led by Azusa Pacific volunteers.

While sharing highlights from their experiences in the villages, someone from another group would often say something along the lines of, "We saved forty-five kindergarteners today." Jen Boyd remembered that in meetings with her home group from CPC, leaders would respond to this kind of declaration by reminding the youth that in our faith tradition, "[we] don't save anybody—Jesus does." In other words, the mission wasn't to bring Jesus to Mexico; it was to recognize the many ways in which Jesus was already manifest there and to provide validation for a local pastor's ministry.

---

7 Rev. Mark Studer, interview by Susan Herman, October 26, 2022.
8 Jennifer Boyd, interview by Susan Herman, October 27, 2022.

Garrett Torgerson, who went on several of the trips as a volunteer youth leader, said:

> Worship experiences in Mexico were very different from ours at home. The music was moving and fun, and the speakers had great stories; however, the theology was far more conservative than we were used to. Gary [Califf, associate pastor at CPC] and Mark Studer, who was the youth group leader at the time, would often have to take time with the youth group after each worship experience to break down the theology and provide a counter interpretation of the scripture. Those post-mortems were interesting, and our discussions [as leaders] would extend long after the rehash with the youth was over.[9]

Leaders of CPC's Mexico missions maintained ties with the Chorizo community throughout the year, independently of the Azusa Pacific Mexico Outreach organization. Ken DeYoung explained:

> During [1986-2000] in addition to taking the youth group during the Easter spring break, my wife and I, knowing what the needs were of some of those people in the local area, would continue to solicit donations from the members of the congregation and we would make two or three extra trips a year into the region to provide food and clothing for the people who lived there. During the first fifteen-year period I am not sure how many trips I made, probably fifty trips into Mexico.[10]

By doing their own engagement outside of the formal Azusa-based outreach program, Ken and his wife Katharine were able to share up-to-date information that helped Carmichael folks stay connected and enthusiastic about the mission all year long.

Fundraising for the Mexico ventures included touring dramas and musical performances by the youth. The adults participated as well, notably in 1993 by organizing a multi-stage bicycle ride. John Wallace described it this way:

---

9 Garrett Torgerson, CPC History Notes, December 11, 2020.
10 DeYoung, interview.

Scott Merner recruited me to ride my bike to Mexico with him to raise money for a building project in Chorizo. CPC members pledged money per mile ridden. November 4 – 15, 1993 we bicycled from Carmichael to Chorizo, 730 miles, spending nights in Modesto, Fresno, Bakersfield, Barstow, 29 Palms, Salton Sea, and Brawley. Laurie Mixell drove the SAG [supplies and gear] vehicle. Chris Pro and Harry Jones also rode most of the trip. Several members of the church joined us for portions of the trip including Gary Califf and Carol Honnold. The majority of the work party led by Ken DeYoung and Glen Cagley met us in Brawley, CA; many of the younger members rode the final 40 miles to Chorizo going across the border on bicycle. The work party built the concrete foundation for a home in Chorizo that was completed on the next spring mission trip.[11]

Despite the relationship-building efforts, creative fundraising, and enthusiastic buy-in across generational segments of the church membership, the Chorizo mission eventually ran its course. Over time, Mark Studer noted, there was a decline in the number of Chorizo village children who were present to take part in the Holy Week VBS. In 2000, he said, only four children attended VBS, while eighteen youth had traveled from Carmichael to share their carefully rehearsed songs, games, and crafts with them. After much research and a somewhat dicey process of persuasion with other leaders, Mark presented a new option for doing mission service in Mexico: Amor Ministries.

Amor Ministries

Amor Ministries, a nonprofit organization based in San Diego, describes its mission as "keeping families together." Its main activity now, as it was when it began operations in 1980, is building homes for families to live in together.[12]

Because of widespread poverty and because foster care is virtually nonexistent in Mexico, many children whose parents cannot afford to care for them grow up in orphanages. The children are not technically orphans, but

---

11 John Wallace, CPC History Notes: Mission Trips, January 4, 2023.
12 "Our Story," https://amor.org/about/.

their parents may be working far away from the support of extended family who would otherwise help with child care. Some sources even describe situations where "baby-finders" are hired by the orphanages' sponsoring agency to approach financially-strapped families with the offer of secure housing and food for their children. The orphanages themselves can even realize a profit by charging outsiders to visit on mission trips.[13]

Families who receive homes through Amor Ministries, and who in most cases also help with the building of them, live in border communities near Tijuana with no services or self-supporting economic center, similar to the communities that partner with Azusa Pacific. The adults commute long hours to work in agricultural fields or *maquiladoras*.

John Wallace noted that in 2001 "there was a lot of soul-searching in the decision" to change over to Amor, "but in the end, this was the best move for our youth." During their trips to Chorizo, the youth had not been allowed to participate in construction, though they did help build some retaining walls out of tires. The year when only four Chorizo children came for sports and VBS, CPC youth were permitted to help build the church addition. That project, according to John, instilled a desire in them to do more "meaty" building projects on mission trips. He describes the first trip with Amor Ministries:

> CPC completed two Amor single houses. A single house is two rooms built on an 11 x 22-foot concrete slab with a one-foot sloping roof.
>
> Thirty-two adults and youth went on this trip giving us two work parties of sixteen. These houses had identical floor plans. The five-day project entails leveling the site, pouring the foundation, building wall/roof supports, tar-papering and stuccoing the walls, tar-papering the roof and putting in two windows and one door; a lot of work that required great teamwork.
>
> We also experienced rain during four of our five days at the work-site, something foreign in Chorizo. Amor does not

---

13 Tina Rosenberg, "The Lasting Pain of Children Sent to Orphanages, Rather than Families," Opinion, *New York Times*, October 16, 2018, https://www.ny-times.com/2018/10/16/opinion/orphanages-children-latin-america.html.

provide a ministerial program or food, as Azusa did, so this was another new challenge and bonding experience had by all, led by Carol Honnold.[14]

In her interview, Carol recalled being the cook for several successive years with Amor Ministries trips. She said she purchased and prepared all the food in Carmichael—simple meals like spaghetti or rice and beans—freezing it, and thawing it on arrival in Mexico. "I didn't poison anyone," she joked, "so they kept asking me back."[15]

In 2002, John reported, the trip went similarly, with the team building two more homes in the same neighborhood of Tijuana:

> Unlike last year, these two houses were right next to each other, so our group could work cooperatively rather than in two separate work groups. We did not see the rain that we saw last year, but the whole week was much cooler, and overcast most of the time. The best part of the trip for me, being the van driver, was that I got to drive an almost brand new, recently purchased 15-passenger van. Carmichael Presbyterian purchased this 2001 van with about 30,000 miles on it from a donation by Christi Black.[16]

CPC continued to partner with Amor for three more years, then returned to Mexicali with Azusa Pacific in 2006 and 2007. In 2008, they returned to Tijuana with Amor.

Stories of Faith From the Mexico Missions

In contrast to the somewhat flexible relational ministry that CPC group leaders had established through the Azusa Pacific partnership, Amor Ministries held groups to a tighter set of expectations. According to Mark Studer, a few of the volunteer builders once chuckled that they had added certain "custom" features to the Amor homes they had worked on. They

---

14 John Wallace, CPC History Notes: Pastors, Mission Trips, Stephen Ministry Leadership, Microassistance Program, June 19, 2020.
15 Carol Honnold and Caron Treon, interview by Susan Herman, March 1, 2020.
16 Wallace, CPC History Notes.

were taken aback when Mark responded that they should add those same features to all the houses in the community. Amor's building specifications were standardized, he said, so as not to introduce inequities or invite comparisons among the families that received them.

After the 2008 trip, several CPC families expressed fear about the safety of traveling to Mexico, in regard to recently reported instances of Americans being caught in the crossfire of the drug cartel wars.[17] As it happened, 2008 was the last year of the Mexico missions. Ken and Katharine DeYoung, who had championed the experience for youth, moved to Redding in 2009, and a new youth director, Abby Fox, was brought in that same year. The Rev. Ivan Herman also came on to CPC's pastoral staff in September of 2009. In addition to the natural turnover among families as their children graduated and aged out of the youth group, the change in leadership brought in new ideas about mission trips.

Though this was by no means a majority opinion, some people interviewed for this book did express doubts about whether the Mexico missions were a good fit for CPC's youth. Did the benefits outweigh the theological misalignments? Was there enough value in what CPC groups offered to the partner communities to justify going year after year? Was the relationship equally nurturing to both the partner communities and the travelers?

Answers to those questions differed, but what is certain is that these experiences touched hundreds of CPC youth over the years, and informed their faith. They learned to question their own limitations and took away valuable lessons about living in community.

"I learned it's important *not* to be the hammer," said Steve Ueltzen in his Youth Sunday reflection after returning from Mexico in 2002.[18] He explained that the hammer is a metaphor for someone who insists on getting their own way all the time. Not listening to others means you may not realize when you're making a mistake. It means you may need to back up and re-do your

---

17 Lizbeth Diaz, "Four Americans Die in Drug-smuggling Mexican Area," *Reuters*, May 19, 2008, https://www.reuters.com/article/us-mexico-drugs-americans/four-americans-die-in-drug-smuggling-mexican-area-idUSN1954747020080519.
18 Steve Ueltzen, *Seeing the Love of God in Mexico* (Youth Sermon at Carmichael Presbyterian Church July 28, 2002), VHS Recording.

work. "Try not to be the nail either," the eighteen-year-old went on. When you're a nail, you let others beat you down, and then you're stuck—better to speak up from time to time.

Above all, "When working on a construction site, wear eye protection!" Steve told of the searing pain he experienced when he got a splinter in his eye while working on an Amor house with his group. But also understand, he concluded, that there's no other way to do God's work than to do it together. Living in Christian community and trying to cooperate makes us vulnerable, he said. Even when wearing work gloves to protect us from splinters, we'll still sometimes get hurt on the jagged pieces. In the same way, Christians get snagged on the splinters in life just like everyone else. The difference is, Christians allow themselves to be vulnerable on purpose. Being vulnerable, Steve said, means we are open to seeing each other's needs and feeling the hurt of those around us.

Learning Alongside Mission Partners in Belize and Honduras

In 2008, the search began for mission agencies that CPC youth could partner with for spring break or summer travel-work trips. In 2009, the high school youth traveled to a Native American reservation in Arizona, and, in 2010, the high school youth group participated in urban ministries in San Diego and the junior high youth group also did urban outreach in Modesto.

Jeremy Meehan, who came on staff as youth director in 2011, posed the idea of rotating among local, regional, and international trips. The idea was to help teens understand how global issues like immigration, homelessness, natural disasters, climate change, and so on play out locally as well as abroad, and to see the interconnections among them. Other reasons included saving money and allowing time to vet different mission agencies alongside options that might be available through the presbytery or another group with denominational ties.

Thirst Missions: Belize

In April 2014 a group of ten high school youth and five adults, all from CPC, traveled to Orange Walk, Belize to spend time in San Luis Village with the Ministerios Casa del Alfarero community, (abbreviated MCA in Spanish, translated to The Potter's House in English). Jeremy Meehan had made the initial contact with Thirst Missions, an organization based in Minnesota, and Pastor Ivan followed up the connection. Despite its name, the organization does not provide clean water systems; rather, it focuses mainly on cultural immersion. In the case of the Carmichael trip, the group's mission was simply to learn from the people in the San Luis village and provide moral support to the MCA church and its leaders by attending services and leading a Vacation Bible School for the children.

Thirst Missions' website[19] describes the benefits for local communities of receiving visiting groups from the US. The basic idea is that short-term mission teams, by their very presence in the community, help local faith leaders build up their churches. Bringing in groups from the US generates excitement in the village; special events are planned to make the visitors feel welcome; locals who aren't regulars at the church attend the festivities and mingle with the foreign guests; and hopefully, some of these locals eventually become members of the congregation.

After landing in Belize, "we got on a shaky old bus and we knew we were going to be safe, because our driver was Jesus," reported Derek Tomlinson in his Youth Sunday sermon after the trip. "His name was *Jesús*," he clarified, providing the Spanish pronunciation.[20]

Pastor Ivan's journal reveals a few more details about the trip. For example, on Sunday, April 13, the team ate a breakfast of fry jacks, beans, eggs and *salchicha* (sausage), fresh bread, and bananas. Lunch was chow mein with shrimp. Supper was a Belizean burrito of chicken, beans, and cheese, with a cabbage salad on the side.

Skipping forward to Tuesday, the meat pies purchased from a vendor in Orange Walk Town were "filled mostly with gravied gelatin and spices—wow! Different!" Thursday featured *salbutes*, a Belizean street food consisting of a fried, puffed corn tortilla filled with shredded chicken and slaw. Fish pancakes were also on the menu. Photos posted by Thirst Missions

---

19 "Thirst Missions: Short-term Missions, Long-term Impact," https://thirst-missions.org/.
20 Derek Tomlinson, Kelly Young, and Maya Roberto, *Mission Trip to Belize* (Youth Sermon at Carmichael Presbyterian Church May 18, 2014), Audio CD.

on Facebook from that day show CPC folks gnawing on freshly-cut sugar cane and drinking coconut milk right from the fruit.

Aside from the food reports, Pastor Ivan's journal includes information on daily activities. On their first evening in San Luis, the group accompanied MCA church pastor Rev. Polin Perez around the village. They visited a store run by a Taiwanese immigrant and learned that the "Chinaman's shops," of which there are several, stay open on Sunday afternoons, whereas the Belizean owners generally close their shops to attend evening church services.

High schooler Derek Tomlinson and CPC volunteer leader Bobby Brow played drums and guitar with the worship band at MCA. Pastor Ivan was invited to share a message on Sunday and to assist with communion serving on Maundy Thursday. The youth offered a Vacation Bible School for the village children for four afternoons. Attendance on Monday was around twenty-five, and grew to forty-five by the end of the week.

During the week, some language translation—of English to Spanish and vice versa—was needed both in church and in the VBS, but as most Belizeans speak some English, often the main work of translation was cultural. For example, one of the lessons introduced children to snow and the building of snowmen. Ivan noted that Perla Fernandez, Thirst Missions' Belize-based guide and translator, easily translated snow (*nieve*) and that the children were a little bit familiar with penguins, but when it came to explaining snowmen (*hombres de nieve*), the concept didn't quite land as expected. How can snow be a building material? What do you do with a snowman once you build it? He wrote:

> The [Carmichael] youth are continuing to realize how distant this culture is from our own. I perhaps put too much weight on the language as a moderator of culture. Not all English speakers are versed in American culture and geography, particularly if they live in the villages (or even the towns) of Belize.

Shortly after the group returned from their trip they reported on it during the sermon time on Youth Sunday. Kelly Young, in her Youth Sunday talk, said that negotiating language differences was a highlight of the trip. "As the week progressed," Kelly said, "the kids started opening up to us. We learned that they actually knew a lot more English than we thought. And they even started teaching us Spanish...they were so interested in showing us their lifestyle and everything they loved."

Derek added that being the butt of the Belizean children's jokes, while humbling, was a good thing. "Laughter is one of the things that brought us together," he said, the other thing being *fútbol* (soccer). These shared experiences transcended all language blunders.

The CPC team also visited the Mayan temple ruins at Lamanai and went swimming in the nearby New River Lagoon. (Maya Roberto, another member of the youth group, said she had acquired the nickname "Maya Temple" from the children who attended VBS). On another day, they went snorkeling in Caye Caulker. Back in the village, they played a lot of soccer, one evening getting soaked to the bone in a rainstorm. The snack that evening "was another round of *alborotos*, a caramel-flavored puffed corn," Pastor Ivan wrote.

Mornings were occupied with walking around the village or in Orange Walk Town with guides. While visiting people's simple thatched-roof homes, the CPC group met multi-generation households where men and teenaged boys worked in the cane fields. Other villagers were shop owners; one did custodial work at the saw mill.

Pastor Ivan's notes hint that something felt amiss with Pastor Polin's church, and in fact, Pastor Polin himself alluded to a falling out that had happened. After one conversation with MCA church members, Carol Honnold reported that someone in the village apparently "stole the pastor's house and lives in it now." Pastor Ivan speculated that this may have been in reference to another evangelical community that had claimed "turf" included the pastor's manse. But he felt it was best not to ask too many questions.

As with the Mexico trips, differences of theology bubbled up during the week—for example, a "prosperity gospel" message was prominent in church leaders' preaching, according to Pastor Ivan. In addition, only those who had been baptized by immersion were invited to partake in communion (the CPC contingent, most of whom had been baptized via the "sprinkling" method, included themselves anyway). Leaders from CPC shared these ideas in a few of their group meetings, inviting adults and youth alike to reflect on diverse practices and expressions of Christianity. Even within our home country, they said, Christianity can look different and emphasize different things from place to place; these variations can seem even more foreign when they intersect with unfamiliar cultural features in another country.

Overall, the team from CPC practiced the art of receiving hospitality. "Unlike previous trips I've taken with youth group, this time we didn't build anything," said Maya Roberto. The teens brought craft supplies and well-rehearsed VBS lessons, but quickly learned to roll with Belizeans' relaxed time structure and the children's preference for soccer over all else. During the week they did go into town and purchase shower heads for a few church members' homes. They also bought sixty pounds of rice and forty pounds of pinto and red beans to contribute to the communal meals. On their return, they were treated to Pastor Polin's special chicken dish, a recipe that Pastor Ivan recorded in his journal:

> A little oil, lots of boneless chicken, onions, garlic, sweet red pepper, a little tomato, salt, pepper, and a good amount of paprika. Cook in liquid over fire for 5-7 hours.

Students Helping Honduras

A special opportunity for high school and college students at CPC arose in 2016, when another pastor in the presbytery, the Rev. Bob Azzarito, publicized and recruited participants for Students Helping Honduras. This nonprofit organization aims to help Honduran children stay in school by supporting local community leaders who are engaged in addressing the education crisis in their own country. Students Helping Honduras focuses mainly on building schools. If the facility is there, the Honduran government commits to providing a teacher.[21] Shin Fujiyama, a graduate of the University of Mary Washington in Virginia, where Rev. Azzarito had previously worked, founded Students Helping Honduras as a secular organization with his sister, Cosmo, in 2006, and had maintained ties with his former campus minister. Rev. Azzarito invited Fujiyama to Sacramento, where he spoke at University Presbyterian Church (UPC)[22], where Rev.

---

21 "Students Helping Honduras," https://shhkids.org/.
22 University Presbyterian Church formed in 2014 and was nested at Fremont Presbyterian in East Sacramento, as some Fremont members wished to retain

Azzarito was then serving, as well as at CPC and other churches in the presbytery.

John Wallace reported that in August 2016 a twenty-member delegation from the Presbytery of Sacramento traveled to El Progreso, Honduras. The group included Rev. Azzarito and UPC member Edrine Ddungu, plus four college students and two other adults from CPC. He wrote:

> It was a one-week trip that included the hottest days in Honduras for the year. The school needed the concrete floor (about 1875 square feet) and sidewalk (400 square feet) completed with hand-mixed concrete and a coat of paint inside and out. Our group was also able to haul fill-dirt and dig a 75 x 3-foot trench at a preschool in Villa Soleada Village, El Progreso.... Students Helping Honduras' goal is to build 1000 schools in Honduras; this school was number 32.

Delegations including Carmichael folks returned to Honduras in 2017 and 2018 and continued work on the same school each time. After their return in 2018, Riley Chabino and Ethan Dahlke shared their experiences at Youth Sunday service. Riley reported learning from Honduran hired masons how to use the pickaxes and shovels to dig the new building's foundation and how to mix all the ingredients needed for the concrete. "The country was grief-stricken," she said, due to years of gang warfare and corruption, "but the country and the people we interacted with were beautiful."

Ethan spoke with admiration about the self-sufficient operation of the girls' and boys' home next to the school, where they raised chickens and rabbits, as well as their own bananas, pineapples, and mangoes. He alluded also to environmental alterations of the land to serve the food industry, noting that the Villa Soleada Bilingual School is "next to a palm oil plantation on land that used to be a swamp." In addition to their work digging holes and mixing concrete, he said, the teens got to spend one hour per day with students tutoring them in English—and joking around afterwards and playing soccer. "Being able to connect with them made all the work worthwhile."

---

their affiliation with the Presbyterian Church (USA) when their leadership chose to join with the Evangelical Presbyterian Church (EPC). University Presbyterian closed in 2022.

The biggest takeaway for Ethan was learning that the Honduran government funds education for children only up to fifth grade, and that forty percent of the country's children do not attend school at all because of the need to work or the displacement of their family due to gang violence. Being able to make school accessible to children, Ethan said, "is part of God's work."

In March 2020, John Wallace reported:

> [F]ifteen adults from Northern California (mostly Sacramento Presbytery members) went to Villa Soleada, Honduras, to do the final touchups on the high school, named the Ken and Lynn Hall[23] High School, and dedicate it with the students.... Because of the worldwide COVID-19 pandemic, all schools in Honduras were closed the third day the team was there and the team had to leave before the airport closed. We accomplished most of the painting we were to do but none of the concrete work.[24]

Shin Fujiyama, who had lived nearly full time in Honduras since founding Students Helping Honduras, remained there during the pandemic lockdown phase and received prayers from CPC members that its grassroots organizing efforts would be able to continue—which indeed, they did. With around fifty chapters of Students Helping Honduras established nationwide and a mix of religious and secular supporters, the organization was able to secure a more predictable stream of monthly giving.[25] Fujiyama returned to Sacramento in March of 2022 for an event to raise funds for college scholarships for the first graduating class from Villa Soleada Bilingual School.

---

23 Ken and Lynn Hall are members of Sierra Vista Community Church in Arden-Arcade. Beginning in the mid-2000s, they hosted CPC's Easter sunrise services at their home overlooking the American River, continuing the tradition of their former neighbors who were longtime CPC members.
24 Wallace, CPC History Notes.
25 Jill Laiacona, "Alumnus Shelters in Honduras to Save UMW-Born Nonprofit," *UMW Voice*, April 20, 2020, https://www.umw.edu/news/2020/04/20/alumnus-shelters-in-honduras-to-save-umw-born-nonprofit/.

Chapter 8
Connecting With and Serving
Our World: Mission Partnerships

Responding to God's love through Jesus Christ,
We connect with and serve our world

Adult mission trips at CPC have varied widely in format and have often involved just one or two members of the church traveling on behalf of the congregation, with the mission to learn and bring back lessons or partnership contacts to develop over time. Sometimes, the traveler stays inside the US—say, to attend a conference or training that touches on international issues—and sometimes they go abroad.

For example, in 2012, CPC member Karen Banker traveled to Washington, DC, for an event called Ecumenical Advocacy Days, in which people from across the country were invited to meet with their representatives in the U.S. Congress to advocate for peace and justice issues in which faith communities are actively involved. Before the day of office meetings (known as Lobby Day), participants attend trainings on how to do advocacy engagement with their elected officials on specific issues of concern. Karen attended sessions on Israel and Palestine, workshops on how faith-based leaders can influence policymaking budgets, and how to use "new social media tools for educating and communicating."[1]

---

1 CPC Mission Division, Meeting Minutes from April 10, 2012.

When CPC sends its members abroad, they typically travel with others from the presbytery or a multi-denominational mission network. It was in this spirit that, in October of 1994, the Rev. Dr. Gary Califf and John Wallace, along with Laurie Mixell, participated in an adult mission trip to Mérida, Mexico. John noted that:

> We partnered with Emmanuel Presbyterian Church in Mérida on their mission project to build a church in the suburbs of Mérida. Our work included building security walls and a church foundation. The trip was advertised throughout the Sacramento Presbytery and a member of Davis Community Church, Susie Boyd, joined us. She was mayor of Davis at the time.[2]

As with the youth trips described in Chapter 7, the 1994 trip described above and others involving CPC adults generally revolved around connecting with Christians who were already at work "being the church" in their home country. They were never about converting non-Christians to the faith. The Mérida, Mexico, church extended an invitation to partnership with US Presbyterians for the building project. In other cases, the Christian communities CPC adults visited did not ask for any labor or material goods from their US partners. Rather, they sought validation, moral support, and empowerment.

Supporting Christian Communities Around the World

The Rev. Leslie Sauer, husband of CPC associate pastor Rev. Sherry Sauer, shared in a 1998 guest sermon how the larger concept of supporting indigenous Christian leaders, communities, and movements has sometimes been hard for US Christians to understand. As a child of missionary parents in India during the early 1950s, Rev. Sauer said, his upbringing was a happy one. His parents served at a vocational training high school for boys and girls, the first school of its kind. All the other missionary adults—mostly Presbyterians and Methodists—were his "aunts" and "uncles," and his mother took the children to stay on a houseboat in Kashmir during the hot Punjab summers.

---

2 John Wallace, CPC History Notes: Mission Trips, January 4, 2023.

Then from about 1954 to 1960, he noted, mission work underwent a big transition. Instead of "mission to" people in foreign lands, the philosophy changed to become "mission with" Christians worldwide. Missionaries became known as fraternal workers. The school where Les's parents worked was turned over to Indian nationals. Sadly, mission support from the US dropped precipitously once US Christian leaders were no longer in charge. He said:

> I'd become a bit cynical about all of this until Marie Segur and I had the opportunity a few weeks ago to visit with some of our present-day church colleagues in the Philippines. We were sent as representatives of Sacramento Presbytery to join the General Assembly of the United Church of Christ in the Philippines in celebration of their 50th anniversary. What we discovered was that even though mission support from churches in other parts of the world has declined in recent years, the life and witness of these indigenous churches has become more vital than ever. We visited with churches outside of Manila that were starting other churches—small churches throughout that region of Luzon provinces—and it was just incredible, the kind of enthusiasm and dedication that the young pastors in these congregations were demonstrating.
>
> We also met some short-term Presbyterian mission coworkers [from the US] who are assigned there. But now [their presence] is at the invitation of the United Church of Christ in the Philippines, and it's in support of the evangelism and mission outreach programs designed and directed by that indigenous denomination, made up of former American mission churches, who are now working together in Christian partnership.[3]

Joining Hands Against Hunger in India

In researching this chapter, it became clear that partnering with Christian communities in other countries usually means a lot of coordinating work back home in the US, and a lot of education. Actual travel to the partner

---

3 Rev. Les Sauer, *Where Are the Missionaries?* (Sermon at Carmichael Presbyterian Church June 7, 1998), VHS Recording.

country is only the tip of the iceberg. Lots of preparation is involved, but the follow-up is also key, because it encourages church folks to stay engaged and to keep asking questions.

One example of CPC's involvement in such efforts during the last twenty-five years was their participation in the Joining Hands Against Hunger in India network. In the early 2000s, the Presbytery of Sacramento established a Joining Hands network locally for partnership with India, with guidance from the Rev. Leslie Sauer. Joining Hands is a denomination-wide initiative of the Presbyterian Hunger Program whereby presbyteries in the US "work with national networks of churches and grassroots organizations overseas to address hunger through comprehensive and coordinated activities."[4] Leading up to that, the Rev. Sherry Sauer, during her pastorate at CPC, had championed the Mission Action Committee's advocacy on anti-hunger issues.

In September 1999, after Pastor Sherry had resigned from CPC to pursue spiritual direction, the newsletter of the Sierra Mission Partnership reported that she and Les had been appointed as short-term Presbyterian mission coworkers in India:

> Following a three-week orientation period at the end of January, Les will begin serving as Partnership Consultant under the Worldwide Ministries Division of our denomination to facilitate communication and program coordination between our PC(USA) offices in Louisville and the church organizations to which we relate throughout India.[5]

Pastor Sherry was subsequently called to be chaplain at Woodstock School, an international boarding school in Mussoorie, India, in the foothills of the Himalayan mountains.

On the Sauers' return to Sacramento, which fell shortly after the September 11, 2001, terror attacks in the US, Pastor Sherry preached at CPC. During her sermon she lit a small candle and placed it on the wide ledge of the pulpit. Having just visited Ground Zero in New York a week after her return from India, she lit the candle in dedication "for all who died on 9/11

---

4 "Give to Joining Hands Against Hunger," https://www.presbyterianmission.org/donate/E051608/.
5 "SMP Missionaries to India," in *Sierra Scroll* (September 1999).

and for the thousands who die in India because of poverty…a holy fire to burn all the hatred and darkness." She continued, "I felt in a palpable way your prayers for me when I was in India," saying it shone a light in the darkness she saw there. Moreover, she noted, "Your dollars in the offering plate for mission—unified giving from the PC(USA)—are able to give so much light in darkness."[6]

She spoke about having an Indian woman in her personal service every day, stating that providing employment in this way was seen in India not as something only the ultrarich do, but as merely the proper thing for any foreigner to do. Pastor Sherry discovered she needed help with everyday tasks; interdependence was the key to daily survival. "I needed to allow Rajeshwari to do her work, for me." As a school chaplain she discovered deep lines of cultural and religious division among the staff and students, and she tried to serve as the bridge that others could walk across. She started a voluntary student worship service in the dorms, based on the Godly Play Sunday school model and always leading with the signature Godly Play question: "I wonder…?"

In this spirit of partnership, bridging, and wondering, the congregation in 2003 welcomed to its pulpit the Rev. Thomas John, an Indian pastor based in the South Indian state of Kerala. He was the main coordinator in India of the Joining Hands mission network, managing its relationship with the grassroots coalition Chethana in India. Chethana helps "Dalits [the Untouchable caste], women, artisans, small and marginal farmers, and minorities take control of their own communities and livelihoods so they can freely choose to resist the influence and control of outside companies."[7]

Rev. John's sermon highlighted the story of how a man "lame from birth" entered the temple in Jerusalem, where the apostles Peter and John healed him and lifted him to his feet (Acts 3:1–10). He noted that entrance through the Beautiful Gate has a special meaning for Indians, who live in a social system where entry to certain places is denied to those of lower castes. In addition, he related the importance of looking at one another as Peter and

---

6 Rev. Sharon Sauer, *Wait On Me* (Sermon at Carmichael Presbyterian Church October 7, 2001), VHS Recording.

7 Rick Jones, "India's Food Soverignty at a Crossroads," May 15, 2015, https://www.pcusa.org/news/2015/5/14/indias-food-sovereignty-crossroad-spart-two/.

John looked at the man in the story—really seeing them, without making prior judgment about what they lack or need. This, Rev. John said, is the essence of mission partnership.

Poverty dehumanizes people and makes them powerless, he continued. True mission is economic development that empowers others, rather than "what people with money do for the poor that makes the poor their beneficiaries." He reminded the congregation that when writing a donation check, our commitment does not end there. Like Peter and John, he said, "You have to bear witness to the power of the resurrection by extending the right hand of fellowship"—that is, by investing the time needed for learning and for making personal connections.[8]

Following on Rev. John's visit, the congregation in 2004 received a delegation from India for lunch and conversation at CPC. The delegation had just come from the Joining Hands and Presbyterian Peacemaking Program conferences in Tacoma, Washington.

In 2007, with help from the Presbytery of Sacramento's Mel Angell[9] Scholarship, John Wallace was able to participate in a nineteen-day trip with Chethana in southern India. John wrote:

> Rev. Garry Cox, pastor at Westminster and chair of the Presbytery's partnership, was the leader. The trip was a real eye-opener into the "caste" system and the subsequent poverty that comes with it. The group met 13 of the 18 organizations under the Chethana umbrella, escorted by Rev. Thomas John of Kerela, India. Land ownership and accompanying water rights were the two biggest [things] the Dalits and marginalized farmers need to prevent their hunger. Other needs include basic human rights and dignity. Globalization is ruining the economy of India's marginalized communities. Examples include: (1) Monsanto's infertile seed that keep farmers from growing crops that produce seed for future crops, (2) Coca-Cola removing so much water from the aquifer for bottling purposes that villages

---

8 Rev. Thomas John, *The Power that Makes People Stand Up and Walk* (Sermon at Carmichael Presbyterian Church June 1, 2003), VHS Recording.
9 Mel Angell and Hazel Angell were longtime CPC members. Mel was committed to denominationally-connected peace and justice movements.

cannot reach potable water with their drills (too salty & fluoride contamination), and (3) Wal-Mart driving down tariffs to the point that handloom weavers cannot make a profit on their wares. India's government has passed a "seed law" that mandates that farmers only use Monsanto seed, and has created 160 special economic zones where foreign investors get complete tax relief to operate in India.

John Wallace became chair of the presbytery's Joining Hands Against Hunger in India project in 2008.[10]

In recent years the Presbytery of Sacramento (now Presbytery of North Central California) ended its sponsoring relationship with Joining Hands in India, though it did host Rev. Thomas John on at least one other occasion after 2008. While the partnership lasted, a portion of CPC's One Great Hour of Sharing Offering went to Chethana. At the time of this writing, the Presbyterian Hunger Program lists Joining Hands partnerships in Sri Lanka, Democratic Republic of Congo, Cameroon, Peru, Haiti, and El Salvador, but no longer in India.[11]

Romania and Project Centipede

"Did y'all know they're serving Bailey's on this flight?" Pastor Carol asked the three twenty-somethings Darci Drawbert, Tara Studer, and Aimee Gillette, who were part of the CPC adult mission team en route to Vienna, Austria. "You should get some," she recommended, turning to go back to her seat.

In May of 2004, the Rev. Carol Pagelsen led a group of fourteen CPC adults to Europe. Despite her mention of the Irish liqueur, the mission trip was not a bar-crawl affair. Rather, Tara (Studer) Calderon shared this outtake moment from the airplane flight to illustrate how much she enjoyed getting to know Pastor Carol, as well as the others on the trip, outside of their usual interactions in church life. When asked via email in January 2023, Pastor Carol herself didn't remember the comment about Bailey's but gave permission to

10 John Wallace, CPC History Notes: Mission Trips, January 4, 2023.
11 Presbyterian Mission Agency, "Joining Hands," https://www.presbyterian-mission.org/ministries/compassion-peace-justice/hunger/internationalde-velopment/joininghands/.

share the story, as "everyone knows I'm not a teetotaler." Of the 2004 Eastern European mission trip she recalled, "It wasn't an easy, luxury trip."

> I required the participants to pack in a carry-on and be able to walk three miles a day. Sometimes we slept in cots. In Budapest there were five to six women in one room. We always took mass transit, and once had to get out of the bus, in the dark, to go over a dam. At the end, I'm sure many were exhausted but blessed.[12]

The Eastern European mission was to support partner relationships between schools and Reformed churches in Romania, Hungary, and the Czech Republic.[13] "It was a mission study trip," said participant Len Tozier, with emphasis on learning what it was like to be a Christian in Europe in the post-communist era.[14] The group first met up with Pastor Carol's son Marc in Vienna, Austria, along with two other members of the Vienna Community Church, Heinz and Louise Pickart. Together they traveled as volunteers for an organization called Project Centipede.[15]

During the early 2000s, Project Centipede served children in orphanages, though now the country has more of a foster care system, explained Len Tozier. Participants would deliver "colorful boxes" to the orphans, full of coloring and puzzle books, along with personal hygiene items like toothbrushes. Heinz Pickart had started the organization, inspired by care boxes that he had received as a child during World War II.

One of the stops in Romania was at a school for children with developmental and intellectual disabilities. Len remembered:

> My wife, Viki, suggested buying toys for them. We bought crazy sunglasses and balloons—turns out we bought exactly the right number: ten. There were ten kids in the class. We went to the school and talked to the kids. They arranged for us to meet one-on-one. Viki and I met with a little girl, and when Viki brought out the sunglasses and balloons, she was all smiles and

---

12 Carol Pagelsen, Notes on the Project Centipede trip, January 7, 2023.
13 Carmichael Presbyterian Church, *Annual Report 2004*.
14 Len Tozier, interview by Susan Herman, November 21, 2022.
15 Vienna Community Church, "Project Centipede," *American and Foreign Christian Union* (2016). https://afcubridge.org/vcc-news/.

giggling. Viki wrote in her journal that the girl we met gave her a sticker in return. "I was smitten for sure," she wrote.

Len continued:

> We also went to a technical high school in Romania where we dropped off the defunct laptops that people from Carmichael had donated, and we had brought in our luggage. At the high school the students learned to refurbish laptops. We didn't get to interact with the students; school was out when we arrived. It was meaningful, though, because they were preparing these high school students for careers.

After returning to Vienna and saying goodbye to the Pickarts and Marc, the study-travel group went by bus to Prague, where they visited with PC(USA) mission coworkers and representatives from the Evangelical Church of Czech Brethren, which had an active ministry with Roma (gypsy) people.

They met with a group of Roma adults who were trying to exit their very closed community so they could become literate in the local language and receive vocational education. The church supported their basic living expenses and the activities of the school that served them. Len reported that the school had "received 110 applications the year we were there, and were able to accept forty people."

There were many moments during the trip, Len said, when no giving of donations or receiving of gifts took place, and some in the group may have felt the odd sense of not knowing if an action was called for or what the "right" action may be. In those moments, they learned to simply observe, and to pray. Of one instance, Len said:

> While on the bus as we were traveling through the Carpathian Mountains, traffic stopped for two hours. We got word there had been a very bad accident up ahead where two people had died. Pastor Carol had us all get off the bus and pray.

Pastor Carol added that on exiting the bus, "little Roma children just appeared out of the woods, begging for money." Unprepared for this and unable to communicate with the children, the group again "circled up, sang songs, and prayed."

Accompaniment Mission to Colombia

In April 2018, following an intensive four-day training course in Chicago held the previous October, the Rev. Ivan Herman and John Wallace traveled to Barranquilla, Colombia, on a "mission of accompaniment" organized by the Presbyterian Peace Fellowship and Presbyterian World Mission. They were aided on the ground by Presbyterian mission coworker Sarah Henken, along with Germán Zárate, who represented the denomination in Colombia, known as la Iglesia Presbiteriana de Colombia (IPC). The accompaniment model of mission is largely about bearing witness to the problems and solutions that local Christians are working through, and offering them encouragement and support through their presence. Accompaniment does not involve proselytizing or physical labor, nor do accompaniers bring money or material gifts.[16]

John and Pastor Ivan traveled to Colombia to learn about conditions there following the 2016 signing of peace accords between the Colombian government and the Revolutionary Armed Forces of Colombia (FARC), and to witness how the IPC was participating in the peace process. John's notes summarized the main points from their training:

> Colombia has lived through over fifty years of conflict between many armed groups: guerrilla forces, paramilitary troops, police, soldiers, foreign armies, and in more recent years, gangs and narcotic-trafficking bands joined the mix. The 2016 peace accords between the Colombian government and the FARC signaled the beginning of the possibility of peace in a portion of the conflict. Oil extraction and mining complicated the fragile political situation, drawing the interest of multinational companies. The U.S. government and its tax dollars also have a long history of exacerbating the violence and further arming an already volatile situation. Since the signing of the 2016 Peace Accords, violence, intimidation, threats and murder of human rights defenders has not stopped.[17]

---

16 Katie Bernabei, "Walking With Others: Case Studies of the Accompaniment Model," *Bridge/Work* 2, no. 1 (2016), https://scholar.valpo.edu/ilasbw/vol2/iss1/3/.
17 John Wallace, CPC History Notes: Mission Trips, January 4, 2023.

With this background information in mind, John and Pastor Ivan considered the following questions during their travels: What does the work of building peace look like after hostilities are formally ended? And what can Christians in the US learn from the efforts of Christians in Colombia who have actively participated in these peace efforts? During their month-long April trip to Colombia, they shared several stories on the Presbyterian Peace Fellowship blog. On April 9, they wrote:

> We set off on foot up the slope into the community of Tierra Grata. An ex-combatant in his mid-20s greeted us as we reached the shade of a large tree. We were accompanying four Colombians and another American who were visiting this community. There is still a United Nations presence, we were told, but the UN now remains in the background. We sat all morning in the wall-free community building with a couple of FARC ex-combatants and heard their stories and their hopes for the future.[18]

After visiting communities of ex-combatants trying to rebuild their lives around something other than war, John and Pastor Ivan also spent time at the Colegio Americano (a K-12 school) and Universidad Reformada, both run by the IPC. They later met with farming families who, displaced by violence from their original homes in the countryside, were able to obtain seven and a half hectares each of overgrown land to develop it for planting. This community was working to form an association of farmers that would empower and protect each other, with the goal of producing crops or value-added products to support themselves economically.

On their last day, they worshiped with the Sixth Presbyterian Church of Barranquilla. Their blog dated April 23 reflected:

> The Presbyterian Church of Colombia continues to model what it means to extend hope and hospitality in the name of Jesus Christ. We have seen it at work in the lives of those who are displaced, those who are immigrants, and we have experienced it ourselves. Colombian Presbyterians are combating fear and xenophobia by sharing the generous love

---

18 Rev. Ivan Herman and John Wallace, "Colombia Accompaniment Report: Tierra Grata (Pleasant Land)," *Presbyterian Peace Fellowship*, April 9, 2018, https://www.presbypeacefellowship.org/accompanier-reports/.

of Christ. In extending hospitality to us and others our eyes have been opened to the risen Christ in them.[19]

Supporting Mission and Global Partnerships

Whether connecting with and serving our world through travel or by other means, CPC members are able to engage because of the church's strong foundation of giving and its members' commitment to learning about our world. After personnel, mission giving makes up the largest portion of CPC's general fund to which its members pledge annually. Most of these funds may be considered "connectional mission giving," as they support humanitarian work through the Presbytery of North Central California, Synod of the Pacific, and PC(USA) nationwide.

As mentioned in Chapter 1, outside of regular pledges, many CPC members and friends participate in one or more methods of "second-mile" mission giving, such as the PC(USA) quarterly Special Offerings, Alternative Gift Market, Presbyterian Women, and the Planting Seeds of Faith auctions. To raise funds for their international trips, youth members and their families have put on musical dramas, pancake breakfasts, and other one-time events.

Special Offerings and
Alternative Gift Market (AGM)

The four PC(USA) Special Offerings recognized today were initiated at different times in the life of the denomination—the Christmas Joy Offering started in the 1930s, One Great Hour of Sharing in 1947, Peace and Global Witness in the early 1980s, and Pentecost Offering in 1998. Carmichael Presbyterian participated in the Peace and Global Witness Offering early on and is now recognized as a "Four for Four" congregation. As of 2019 only about half of PC(USA) congregations participated in all four special offerings.

---

19 Rev. Ivan Herman and John Wallace, "Colombia Accompaniment Report: Being Venezuelan in Colombia," *Presbyterian Peace Fellowship*, May 18, 2018, https://www.presbypeacefellowship.org/accompanier-reports/.

Each offering has its own focus, summarized below. The Peace and Global Witness Offering sends the most dollars abroad, but all of them make possible various kinds of connections with our world.

The **One Great Hour of Sharing** offering funds Presbyterian Disaster Assistance, Presbyterian Hunger Program, and Self-Development of People. Self-development takes multiple forms but has included training people in areas of land rights, farming, social development, and addressing gender-based violence.

The **Pentecost Offering** is dedicated to youth and children. Forty percent of the Pentecost Offering can be retained by individual congregations wanting to make an impact in the lives of young people within their own community. For example, following Hurricane Sandy in 2012, CPC member Lillian Janik received Pentecost Offering funds from the church and presbytery to join Habitat for Humanity's rebuilding effort in New Jersey. The remaining sixty percent is used to support children at risk, youth, and young adults through ministries of the Presbyterian Mission Agency.

The **Peace and Global Witness Offering** funds peacemaking ministries that address systems of conflict and injustice across the world. Individual congregations are encouraged to utilize up to twenty-five percent of this offering to connect with the global witness of Christ's peace. Presbyteries and synods retain an additional twenty-five percent for ministries of peace and reconciliation. The remaining fifty percent is used by the Presbyterian Mission Agency to advocate for peace and justice in cultures of violence, including our own, through collaborative projects of education and Christian witness.

The **Christmas Joy Offering** provides support for current and retired church leaders, and for future leaders. The offering distributes gifts equally to the Assistance Program of the Board of Pensions and to Presbyterian-related schools and colleges equipping communities of color.[20]

---

20 "Special Offerings," accessed May 13, 2022, https://specialofferings.pcusa. org/.

Beginning in 1991 another, more interactive, option for supporting worldwide missions started at CPC. Deborah Young, through the Session's Mission Division, brought the Alternative Christmas Market, later called Alternative Gift Market, to CPC. For several hours on a Sunday morning and afternoon, individuals representing local area ministries, alongside Mission Division members representing Heifer International and other organizations, chatted with church and community members in a festively decorated McMillen Hall where they sold handmade, fair-trade gift items as well as "shares" of livestock animals to be gifted to families across the world. (Shares refers to the cost of a single animal, such as a water buffalo, being shared across multiple donors.)[21]

The Alternative Gift Market (AGM) tradition has continued each year since 1991. In 2021 it expanded to two days—the first Saturday and Sunday in November—to give more options for members of the church and the broader Carmichael community to shop and make donations. During construction of the new McMillen Hall, the event was held in the Gathering Place and Parlor.

In 2000 the Tracy family set up a livestock pen and animals on the church campus to underline the goal set by Mission Division to raise $5,000 for Heifer International's Build an Ark initiative. Build an Ark encouraged churches to raise enough money to buy several commonly used animal pairs (two by two, as on Noah's Ark) for self-development of people worldwide. That year the gift market raised $7,000 for Heifer alone.

Amounts raised from the AGM have generally increased over time, though it is important to note that the receiving organizations varied over the years and always represented both international and domestic missions.

For example, vendors of fair-trade items in 2021 included:

- United Women's Alliance
- Friends of San Juan de Oriente
- African Team Ministries
- Heavenly Treasures
- One World Fair Trade

21 Carmichael Presbyterian Church, *Annual Report 1997.*

Organizations receiving donations included:

- Mustard Seed School
- Family Promise of Sacramento
- Carmichael HART
- CPC Food Closet
- Coalition of Concerned Medical Professionals
- World Relief
- Heifer International
- Habitat for Humanity
- Children's Health in Haiti

In 1997, AGM receipts totaled $9,830. In 2007, AGM raised approximately $13,000. And in 2021 the total came to $19,455.

Staying Open to the Stories and Witness of Others

To boost the congregation's energy for connectional giving, CPC's mission and worship leaders often invite guest speakers to tell their stories. For example, in September 1998, the Mission Division sponsored an evening program featuring Dr. Julia Duany, a mediator and peace facilitator in Southern Sudan and Nairobi, Kenya, whose talk focused on equal access and participation in education for women, children, and refugees.

In 1999 Marie Segur and the Rev. Leslie Sauer gave a dialog sermon on the presbytery's international partnership with the Philippines as a follow-up to their trip there. This international partnership received Mission funds and the Two Cents a Meal funds raised at Wednesday Works dinners during 2000.

The Rev. Ivan Herman and a high schooler, Ambrosia Holland, presented another dialog-style sermon in 2018 during which they drew parallels between the rejection of Jesus at Nazareth (Mark 6:1–6) and the plight of Venezuelans displaced to Colombia and the US by violence and economic chaos.

In the 2010s, as a way to more systematically dedicate attention to areas of concern worldwide, CPC's Education Division launched a speaker series called "Connecting with Our World" (described in Chapter 4). Speakers and guest preachers have also included former PC(USA) moderators, including the Rev. Dr. Fahed Abu-Akel in 2005 and Rick Ufford-Chase in 2011. Rick Ufford-Chase had led Presbyterian Border Ministries before serving as moderator and afterwards became director of Presbyterian Peace Fellowship.

Many people who were interviewed for this book mentioned that they appreciated the global mission orientation of CPC. The Rev. Christa Brewer said:

> I really appreciate how CPC is open to different kinds of ministry and mission work. I admire how they let Pastor Ivan and John Wallace go on the Colombia accompaniment mission with Presbyterian Peace Fellowship. CPC members see that kind of mission as part of who they are and they supported them on that one-month trip. Elsewhere there would probably have been a conversation with [the personnel committee] like, "You're going to be away for a whole month?! How much of this is vacation and how much is study leave?" From an outside pastoral perspective, I love what I see about the support pastors and staff get at CPC. They are open and flexible about where the spirit leads.[22]

That openness and flexibility has led to challenges, too. As Steve Ueltzen pointed out in his youth sermon cited in Chapter 7, being open to human relationships means being vulnerable. It means being open to recognizing potentially damaging patterns in relationships and finding ways to move forward together.

Another pastor in the presbytery, the Rev. Dr. Pamela Anderson, made a connection with a Ugandan couple in ministry, Pastors Joseph and Florence Kaweesa, and introduced them to CPC. Together the Kaweesas led Harvest Time Ministries, a worshipping community with various projects to support children orphaned by AIDS in the country. CPC had the pleasure of hosting Pastor Joseph Kaweesa for two weeks in 2018 and Pastor Florence about a year later. John Wallace made the trip to Uganda with a group from

---

22 Rev. Christa Brewer, interview by Susan Herman, June 7, 2022.

the presbytery in 2019. During this time the congregation responded to a presbytery-wide invitation to support a goat farm the Kaweesas operated as part of their ministry.

The Kaweesas shared videos and email greetings from time to time, showing the goat farm, and showing their community in worship. CPC responded with prayers and a "goat stick" fundraiser, where the children would collect quarters in a tall, clear plastic cylinder during worship at Children's Time to help with the goat farm. As with other mission relationships, CPC members caught the excitement of the personal connection. However, lacking a formal agreement or memorandum of understanding between the parties, certain aspects of the relationship grew murky. What amount, beyond symbolic giving, should the congregation commit to the Ugandan ministry, and what would be the process for increasing donations when solicited? Who would be the designated person to receive incoming calls to action, whether for prayer or money or other resources? With the COVID-19 pandemic throwing Harvest Time Ministries into crisis, urgent requests for help started coming in frequently.

In response, CPC's Mission Division agreed on set donation amounts to be sent to Uganda during 2021. The division also took the time to draft an agreement called The Gift of Partnership, to be used as a template for all groups within the church to guide them proactively in planning their financial or personnel activities.[23] The memo lays out a framework for defining each party's obligations to each other and a method for reporting the outcome of the project. It reaffirms the church's commitment to open, honest, and equal partnership. Here are some excerpts from the document:

> We will be guided by this quote attributed to an Australian Aboriginal woman: "If you have come to help me, you are wasting your time. But if you have come because your liberation is bound up in mine, then let us work together."
>
> As we develop relationships with different people and mission projects, we will probably be asked for financial support. These requests may be either direct or implied. They may come from an

---

23 Carmichael Presbyterian Church, *The Gift of Partnership: A Guide for Giving and Receiving* (2020).

individual or from a partner institution. We may receive letters, emails, or notes through social media asking it if is possible to help with travel expenses, provide for expensive medical treatment, or assist with education costs.

In considering such requests, we must be mindful that providing financial support may in some situations create unintended burdens in the long term or prop up inequalities (e.g., structural racism or cultural colonialism) in the ministry context. Money is a commodity and a symbol that can often give those who have it power and control over those who do not have it. When a partnership is established both parties will attempt to be sensitive to the role that money can play in a relationship.

The document lays out several specific guidelines; among them are having a regular evaluation of the partnership's activities in light of its stated purpose, and designating a partnership liaison who brings all needs and requests to the Mission Division for discussion before any funds are disbursed.

The Rev. Leslie Sauer's sermon cited earlier in the chapter speaks to the change in mindset that took place among Presbyterians in mission in the middle of the twentieth century. In the early 1980s, successive rounds of mission discernment at the national level led to increased recognition of the "political and economic power in [US Christians'] hands due to access to wealth, and...the barriers which exist between ourselves and some other Christians as a result of this power." Another big concept to emerge at that time was the idea that evangelism is inseparable from social justice.[24] In other words, wherever God's people are experiencing oppression, Christians are called to break those bonds and set people free.

Often, it's the Christians in Nicaragua or Uganda or the Philippines who can best describe the sources of oppression and who can best imagine how the process of liberation will work. Therefore, for Presbyterians in mission, whether long-term or short-term, the first task is to listen to the locals.

---

24 Daniel J. Adams, "From Colonialism to World Citizen: Changing Patterns of Presbyterian Mission," *American Presbyterians* 65, no. 2 (1987), https://www. jstor.org/stable/23330436.

Carrying out partnerships with national churches is hard work, and is not always popular. As Presbyterians began joining with other Christians in ecumenical groups such as the World Council of Churches and National Council of Churches, they largely opposed the "dirty wars" in Latin America and apartheid in South Africa. They also instigated the sanctuary movement and antinuclear campaigning at the close of the Cold War, earning criticism both from the outside and from the pews of many Presbyterian churches.[25] Why are Christians meddling in "politics" when they should be focusing on worship and study of scripture?, some asked.

If you polled people in Carmichael Presbyterian's pews, odds are good that most would say social justice is important, even though their working definitions of the term may vary. For some, it looks like learning how other Christians "do" Christianity—in the *colonia*, in the sugarcane fields, in post-communist Eastern Europe, and in FARC re-education camps in Colombia. For others, it looks like swinging a hammer (alongside those for whom the structure is being built), playing soccer, or attending an advocacy training and bringing its lessons back to the congregation. Our expressions of service and connection with our world are continually evolving, as we become more sensitive to power dynamics, and as we learn more about intersections: how care of the Earth intersects with caring for people, for instance. The one constant is that CPC people are open, generous, teachable, and intentionally vulnerable.

---

25 Theodore A. Gill Jr., "Historial Context for Mission, 1944-2007," in *A History of Presbyterian Missions 1944-2007*, ed. Scott W. Sunquist and Caroline N. Becker (Louisville, KY: Geneva Press, 2008).

Appendix: Calendar of Centennial Celebrations, 2023

Date	Event
January 22	Centennial Kickoff Brunch with scrapbook and memorabilia viewing
January 22	Guest preacher: Ryan MacLean, CPC member and M.Div student at Princeton Theological Seminary Letter from the Rev. Jim Clark read in worship
January 29	Meet the Artist event with photographer Clair Daugherty, whose photos of McMillen Hall's construction are displayed in the Gathering Place through June
February 19	Guest preacher: the Rev. Jeri Viera Dahlke, Stated Clerk of the Presbytery of North Central California
March 19	Presentation of First Bibles to 3rd graders; all attending worship invited to share their first Bibles with the children
March 26	Letter from the Rev. Sharon Sauer read in worship
April 16	Letter from the Rev. Dr. Gary Califf read in worship
April 22	Earth Day Nature Walk in Effie Yeaw Nature Center with Bep Van Der Mik and Whitney MacLean
May 7	Guest preacher: Maggie Harmon, Presbyterian Foundation Leaving Your Legacy workshop lead by Harmon and sponsored by CPC Gifts and Bequests Advisory Council
May 7	Celebration Concert with Hannah Ludwig, mezzo-soprano and John Cozza, piano
May 20	Plein Air art day on the CPC campus
May 21	Heritage Sunday recognition Guest preacher: the Rev. Dr. Gary Califf, former CPC associate pastor

May 21	Unearthing the 2001 Time Capsule Dedication of courtyard bench given by Skipjack Mariners Potluck lunch and vintage cookbook swap
June 11	Celebrate Love: Photos from CPC weddings on display in the Gathering Place
June 18	Guest preacher: Nancy Martin Vincent, Synod Executive for Synod of the Pacific Letter from the Rev. Carol Pagelsen read in worship
June 24	Artists' Reception for plein air artists, whose works are displayed in the Gathering Place through December
June 25	Guest preacher: Garrett Torgerson, member of CPC
July 4	"Celebrating 100" float in the Carmichael Fourth of July parade
September 16	50th Anniversary of Carmichael Food Closet BBQ and recognition by local dignitaries
September 17	Guest preacher: the Rev. Christa Brewer, Myrtle Beach First Presbyterian Church
September 30	Membership & Outreach represents CPC at Carmichael Founders' Harvest Festival
October 8	Guest preacher: the Rev. Aart van Beek, former interim CPC associate pastor
October 15	Guest preacher: the Rev. Ok-kee Kim, former pastor of Holy Mountain Korean Fellowship
October 22	Letters from the Rev. Dr. Bill Johnson and the Rev. Larry Jung read in worship
October 29	Q & A with Scott Young of Carmichael HART
November 12	Presentation of Centennial Quilt by the Liturgical Arts Committee
November 19	Guest preacher: the Rev. Jack McNary, former interim CPC associate pastor
December 1	Centennial Gala Welcome Reception and Book Signing with music by Chris Studer
December 2	Centennial Concert

| December 3 | Centennial Worship service
Burying the 2023 Time Capsule, Campus Tours
Gala Luncheon |
| December 31 | Guest Preacher: the Rev. Mark Lyndaker-Studer, Neshaminy-Warwick Presbyterian Church, Warminster, PA |

Index

www.ingramcontent.com/pod-product-compliance
Lightning Source LLC
Chambersburg PA
CBHW071449140726
47997CB00005B/1655